D0442031

DISCARD

THE
POKER BRIDE

ALSO BY CHRISTOPHER CORBETT

Orphans Preferred

Vacationland

THE
POKER BRIDE

The First
Chinese
in the
Wild West

CHRISTOPHER
CORBETT

Atlantic Monthly Press
New York

Grateful acknowledgment is made to the University of California Press for
permission to reprint excerpts from *Songs of Gold Mountain: Cantonese
Rhymes from San Francisco Chinatown* by Marlon K. Hom.

Published simultaneously in Canada
Printed in the United States of America

FIRST EDITION

ISBN-13: 978-0-8021-1909-4

Atlantic Monthly Press
an imprint of Grove/Atlantic, Inc.
841 Broadway
New York, NY 10003

Distributed by Publishers Group West

www.groveatlantic.com

10 11 12 13   10 9 8 7 6 5 4 3 2 1

FOR REBECCA AND MOLLY

Contents

The cautious reader will detect a lack of authenticity in the following pages. I am not a cautious reader myself, yet I confess with some concern to the absence of much documentary evidence in support of the singular incident I am about to relate. Disjointed memoranda, the proceedings of ayuntamientos and early departmental juntas, with other records of a primitive and superstitious people, have been my inadequate authorities. It is but just to state, however, that . . . I have met with many more surprising and incredible stories, attested and supported to a degree that would have placed this legend beyond a cavil or doubt. I have, also, never lost faith in the legend myself, and in so doing have profited much from the examples of divers grant-claimants, who have often jostled me in their more practical researches, and who have my sincere sympathy at the skepticism of a modern hard-headed and practical world.

—BRET HARTE, *THE LEGEND OF MONTE DEL DIABLO*
OCTOBER 1863

I will not say that this story is true: because, as you will soon see, it is all truth and no story. It has no explanation and no conclusion; it is, like most of the other things we encounter in life, a fragment of something else which would be intensely exciting if it were not too large to be seen. For the perplexity of life arises from there being too many interesting things in it for us to be interested properly in any of them. What we call its triviality is really the tag-ends of numberless tales; ordinary and unmeaning existence is like ten thousand thrilling detective stories mixed up with a spoon. My experience was a fragment of this nature, and it is, at any rate, not fictitious. Not only am I not making up the incidents (what there were of them), but I am not making up the atmosphere or the landscape, which were the whole horror of the thing. I remember them vividly, and they were truly as I shall now describe.

—G. K. Chesterton, *The Secret of a Train*

Polly Bemis in her wedding dress, 1894.
Idaho State Historical Society – 75-228.43/H.

Preface

◆

The stakes in a game of cards . . .

The old woman came down out of the mountains in central Idaho the same way she had gone in more than half a century earlier: on the back of a saddle horse, across some of the most rugged and remote country in the American West. The two prospectors who brought her out in the summer of 1923 took her first by horseback along the steep banks of the nearly inaccessible Salmon River—known as the "River of No Return"—to the end-of-the-road mining camp of Warrens. From there, she went by car along largely unpaved roads, nearly 100 miles to Grangeville, the Idaho County seat. Not only had she never ridden in an automobile; she had never seen one. She had never heard a radio or seen a train, an airplane, a motion picture, or electric lights.

The old woman's arrival in the county seat was the major news story of the week in the *Idaho County Free Press,* which gave it a headline in a large font across the front page, above the banner. The newspaper's editor, J. F. Safley, who interviewed her at length, later likened her arrival in Grangeville to Washington Irving's short story "Rip Van Winkle." In the *Free Press,* her trip out of the Salmon River country eclipsed tributes to the late president Warren G. Harding, who had died suddenly two weeks earlier, as well as news about the release of 90,000 tiny trout into four creeks, the arrest of a notorious bank swindler, and a statewide decline in property valuations.

The old woman's name was Polly Bemis, and her trip out of the remote Salmon River mountain country reversed a journey she had made in the summer of 1872. Polly Bemis was a Chinese concubine who had been won in a poker game by a feckless Connecticut Yankee gambler named Charlie Bemis and had lived with him for decades at a remote ranch deep in a canyon of the Salmon River. That was the story—or one story.

Her life in the American West was straight out of a dime novel. As a teenager, the girl had been sold by her parents in a village in China during a famine, so that her starving family might survive. It was a common enough practice in rural China, where women had few or no rights and were often traded or sold like livestock. This girl was pretty, and the men who bought her—she said they were bandits—sold her in turn to procurers, who scoured the countryside in those days for girls and young women to supply the sex slave trade. In the middle to late nineteenth century, many of them would be shipped to California to live in a mining camp brothel or in the labyrinth of San Francisco's crowded Chinatown, where everything was for sale, especially flesh. It was a hard life and for many it was a short life, too.

But Polly Bemis, as she would be known, was bought by a Chinese merchant—sight unseen—for what was then a fabulous sum and smuggled into the United States on a ship that sailed from China. From San Francisco, the great port of entry from the Far East, she was taken by an old Chinese woman on a steamer up the Pacific coast to Portland, Oregon, and from there upriver to the boomtown of Lewiston in the Territory of Idaho. She was then packed overland on the back of a horse to the remote mining camp of Warrens, where the merchant who had purchased her lived. The "Chinaman"—the term used in those days—eventually lost her in a poker game to Charlie Bemis, a local saloonkeeper, cardsharp, and idler. That was another part of the story.

Bemis would later survive a shooting by a disgruntled gambler and would be nursed back to health by this Chinese woman. He then did something almost unheard of in the American West: he married her when she would have been likely to be deported, at the height of the anti-Chinese campaign that inflamed the country in the late nineteenth century.

The couple then retreated deep into the Salmon River canyon country to a secluded homestead under a mountain called the Buffalo Hump. Here, ringed by towering mountains and a countryside that was snowbound six months or more of the year, they were seldom seen, glimpsed only by the reckless and daring few who risked the passage down the "River of No Return" in rough wooden boats. The wildest river in America, which had turned back Lewis and Clark and the Corps of

Discovery, the Salmon was not successfully navigated until the end of the nineteenth century. Few places in the continental United States were less accessible. As nearly as could be figured when Polly Bemis arrived in Grangeville that summer, she had not been off the ranch since the mid-1890s and then only to hardscrabble Warrens, now called Warren, a cluster of unpainted shacks and log cabins literally at the end of the road.

For many years Charlie and Polly Bemis lived deep in the Salmon River canyon country in a log ranch house on a small parcel of fertile bottomland, surrounded by a lush orchard of fruit trees and vegetable gardens. The mining town of Warrens was a day's ride away. They were entirely self-sufficient. Bemis operated a ferry on the Salmon River when he felt like it but declined payment on the rare occasion when he had a customer who wished to cross the water. He did, however, like to play cards with travelers passing through. Poker was the game that made him, but as an old man he had settled for cribbage. Charlie and Polly kept as a pet a live cougar that ate at the table with them from a metal plate, which had been nailed down. Rare visitors, when asked to dinner, found the half-wild animal an unsettling tablemate.

When Polly Bemis arrived in Grangeville the summer after her husband had died, she was a celebrated curiosity, a living reminder of the Gold Rush that was fast becoming a legend in the Pacific Northwest. She was, in the words of one writer, "Idaho's Most Romantic Character."

The old woman weighed less than 100 pounds. One observer said later that she was "no taller than a broom," about four and a half feet. She smoked a pipe. Unaccustomed to so much attention and so many people, she was extremely shy. She giggled almost continuously when she talked or was asked questions. The *Idaho County Free Press* described her attempts at English as "gibberish." She had more or less forgotten how to speak Chinese, too. The newspaper noted that she could neither read nor write. She wore a simple cotton dress ordered by mail from Montgomery Ward. Her gray hair was tied up in a tidy, tight bun and bound with a kerchief. She held a handkerchief to her deeply tanned, weathered face. At the home of Mrs. Anson Holmes, where Polly stayed for a week, visitors besieged her. Old-timers, prospectors from the great gold strikes of the nineteenth century who remembered the wild boomtown days and had known her when she lived in rough-and-tumble Warrens, where she kept a boardinghouse for many years, turned out to see her. Some people even brought their children. Polly was especially delighted to hold babies.

The world astonished her. She had been living outside it for a very, very long time. She had gone up into the mountains of central Idaho a mere seven years after the American Civil War was over, when the Indian wars were still raging and there was still an emperor on the throne in Peking. Everything was different now. She became so excited by the wonders of the modern world that she wept with joy and fear, according to the newspaper. But such novelty also made her tired, she told interviewers at the time.

On her feet were shoes that had been made for a boy—size four— and the newspaper explained that apparently, during her long-ago childhood in a China that had ceased to exist, her feet had been bound. Foot binding was a practice normally reserved for the upper classes in China, so this detail added yet more mystery to her already mysterious life.

But it was not merely her romantic story, whether she had been won in the poker game or not, that explained her appeal. Polly Bemis was part of a nearly forgotten history. The Chinese had once flocked here— thousands of "Chinamen," thousands of "coolies" who first worked on the transcontinental railroad and later, looking for gold, trudged into the Idaho high country with everything they owned balanced on the ends of long bamboo poles on their shoulders. In their heyday, they had far outnumbered whites in some mining camps. They played a largely overlooked and incalculable role in the development of the Idaho Territory. But in the summer of 1923, with the "roaring twenties" in full swing, the "Chinamen" of the old days were a nearly vanished species— long dead or gone back to China—a fragment of an era that, like so much of the old West, was rapidly becoming myth.

The life of Polly Bemis in the Idaho backcountry covered the arc of the Chinese experience in the American West. When she rode into the Territory of Idaho on a saddle horse in the summer of 1872, the mining boom was at a height and millions of dollars' worth of gold was being drawn out of the ground. Before the Gold Rush, the Chinese in America had been so rare that some were exhibited in freak shows. By the time Polly Bemis came off a ship from China there were tens of thousands of her countrymen here. She lived through many a boom and many a bust, and the newspaper reporting her death in 1933 noted on the same page—the front page—that speculators were planning once again to mine the ground in remote Warrens. Dreams of gold die hard.

The life of Polly Bemis encompassed most of Idaho's early history. Polly was in Idaho at a time when being a "Chinaman" in the American West was not always a healthy situation. She knew the West of the proverbial "Chinaman's chance": no chance at all. She was living in Idaho when vigilantes there lynched five Chinese in the mining camp of Pierce City, and when bandits killed dozens of Chinese miners on the Snake River at Hell's Canyon. And she was in the American West when one of the worst acts of vigilantism in the nation's history—the massacre of more than forty Chinese coal miners—took place at Rock Springs in the Wyoming Territory. No one was ever punished for any of those crimes. She came up the river to Portland, Oregon, the same summer that Mark Twain's *Roughing It* reached the Pacific Northwest. Anyone who had been looking would have read in it the first largely sympathetic view of the Chinese in the West, a view shared by very few of Twain's countrymen at the time.

Polly Bemis came into the United States during the "Chinese Must Go" movement, which started in San Francisco and spread quickly across the Pacific Slope. Chinese workers, at first welcomed in California in the early days of the Gold Rush, were now too numerous, the argument ran. The "yellow peril," as it was then referred to, must be stopped.

Politicians, conservative newspaper editors, and labor agitators were howling for the Chinese to be deported and for immigration from China to be halted. Chinese immigrants were blamed for everything from disease—they were thought to carry illnesses terrifying to Americans, such as leprosy—to stealing jobs from white workers. Polly Bemis survived the Chinese Exclusion Act of 1882—one of the very few instances in American history when the federal government enacted laws aimed at a specific ethnic group; this act essentially barred or severely restricted the immigration of most Chinese into the United States until World War II.

Polly Bemis came into a country where Chinese immigrants coming off ships in San Francisco were welcomed with a gauntlet of abuse and catcalls and were pelted with rocks as they walked up from the docks to Chinatown, the only safe place for them in the booming port. Polly Bemis also knew a West where the Chinese—especially in the early days—were often not allowed to vote. When the Chinese were allowed to own land, or file a mining claim, it was frequently only after white miners had worked over that mining claim and abandoned the site. The Chinese were not as a general rule allowed to testify in court against whites or become American citizens but were nevertheless subjected to petty poll taxes, miners' taxes, and other official annoyances. Casual physical assaults on the Chinese were routine and were often treated comically by newspapers of the period. No immigrant group in the American West of the nineteenth century was so mistreated, so marginalized.

When Polly Bemis rode down from under the Buffalo Hump in the summer of 1923, the *Idaho County Free Press* headlined the news of her arrival: "Polly Awakes after Half Century Slumber in Mountains."

After a week or so in Grangeville, which included a brief ride on a train, Polly went back up into the mountains the way she had come down. She had traveled to the county seat to get eyeglasses; her vision was poor. She went to a dentist, too. And then she went back up to her ranch on the Salmon River, hard by Polly Creek, which surveyors had named for her. She came down again the following year to travel to the state capital, Boise, to see other amazing sights and then returned to her ranch until the end of her life. Visitors who stopped to see the fabled "poker bride" found her spry and welcoming.

Her last years were spent alone on the banks of the "River of No Return," tending her garden and orchard. She liked to fish, too. Her only neighbors were the prospectors Peter Klinkhammer and Charles Shepp, who had settled on a homestead on the other side of the river in the early 1900s. She left them her ranch with the understanding that they would care for her in her old age, and they did. When the prospectors brought her down to the county seat again late in the summer of 1933, Polly Bemis was dying.

An old friend from the pioneer days, Mrs. Bertha Long, later recalled visiting Polly in the last weeks of her life. "You'll soon get well," Bertha told her. But Polly knew this was not to be. "No, me too old to get well, me have to go to other world to get well."

She was eighty-one when she went to the other world, dying at the county hospital in Grangeville on November 6, 1933. For a time, she was buried at the Prairie View Cemetery there, but later her remains were reburied on the ranch on the banks of the "River of No Return." At the end of her life, she had asked Shepp and Klinkhammer only to see that she be buried where she could hear the river roar.

Charles Shepp died in 1936, but Peter Klinkhammer lived on in the Salmon River country until his death in 1970. He left behind Polly's personal effects—her marriage license, her residency papers, some jewelry, silverware, a wedding dress, and some gold scales that had belonged to Charlie Bemis. The recipients of these items, the personal effects of an old Chinese concubine, were an order of Benedictine nuns at the Convent of Saint Gertrude on a hillside in Cottonwood, Idaho. One of those nuns, Sister M. Alfreda Elsensohn, who had spent a lifetime teaching children at the convent school, settled down in her retirement to chronicle the history of Idaho County and the Chinese who played such a significant and largely overlooked role in its pioneer days. Along the way, she immortalized the legacy of Polly Bemis and saved, too, the memory of "the poker bride."

THE
POKER BRIDE

HARPER'S WEEKLY.

JOURNAL OF CIVILIZATION

VOL. XXI.—No. 1049.]　　　NEW YORK, SATURDAY, FEBRUARY 3, 1877.　　　[WITH A SUPPLEMENT.
PRICE TEN CENTS.

Entered according to Act of Congress, in the Year 1877, by Harper & Brothers, in the Office of the Librarian of Congress, at Washington.

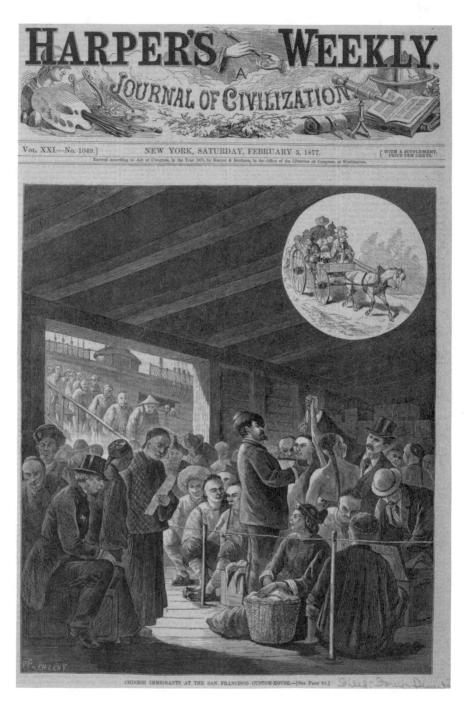

CHINESE IMMIGRANTS AT THE SAN FRANCISCO CUSTOM-HOUSE.—[SEE PAGE 91.]

Chinese immigrants at the San Francisco Customs House being inspected on arrival in California.
Denver Public Library; Western History Collection, *Harper's Weekly,* February 3, 1877, Z-3810.

One

◆

CELESTIALS AND SOJOURNERS

Although some one hundred thousand coolies sailed to the California coast in the three decades following the Gold Rush of 1849, most were illiterates whose horizons and American experiences were limited, and they left little in the way of writings published in China.
—*LAND WITHOUT GHOSTS*
(EDITED BY R. DAVID ARKUSH AND LEO O. LEE)

Swallows and magpies, flying in glee:
  Greetings for New Year.
Daddy has gone to Gold Mountain
  To earn money.
He will earn gold and silver,
  Ten thousand taels.
When he returns.
  We will buy a lot of land.
—NINETEENTH-CENTURY CANTONESE RHYME
(TRANSLATED BY MARLON K. HOM IN *SONGS OF GOLD MOUNTAIN*)

The story of Polly Bemis in the American West is a story about gold. Gold was the reason she left China. If there had not been a Gold Rush in California in the mid-nineteenth century, thousands of Chinese peasants would have had no reason to brave the Pacific crossing, and girls like Polly Bemis in poor villages in China might have never been sold by their starving families to supply the burgeoning sex slave trade in the

American West. Polly Bemis was eventually sold for gold, too. But first her story was the story of the Gold Rush and the "Chinamen," who left their villages and families and everything that was important to them with the dream of finding wealth on *Gum Sam*, or "Golden Mountain," as they called California.

Before he ate his breakfast on the morning of January 24, 1848, James Wilson Marshall was inspecting the site where he was building a sawmill on the American River in California, about forty-five miles from what is today Sacramento. His partner in this venture was John A. Sutter, a Swiss entrepreneur who had settled there a decade earlier when the area was part of Mexico. Marshall, a millwright from New Jersey, noticed something shiny in the millrace, the channel for conducting water at a mill. He stooped down to pick up a tiny nugget that he said later was about half the size of a pea. And then he picked up another such nugget. He was not sure what these fragments were, but he had his suspicions. Years later, Marshall wrote an account of that day for *Century* magazine. It was a reminiscence of an event that would launch one of the greatest migrations in human history—the California Gold Rush.

"It was a clear, cold morning; I shall never forget that morning," Marshall recalled. "As I was taking my usual walk along the race, after shutting off the water, my eye was caught by a glimpse of something shining in the bottom of the ditch. There was about a foot of water running there. I reached my hand down and picked it up; it made my heart thump for I felt certain it was gold. The piece was about half the size and shape of a pea. Then I saw another piece in the water. After taking it out, I sat down and began to think right hard. I thought it was gold, and yet it did not seem to be of the right color; all the gold coin I had seen was a reddish tinge; this looked more like brass.

"When I returned to our cabin for breakfast, I showed the two pieces to my men. They were all a good deal excited, and had they not thought that the gold only existed in small quantities they would have abandoned everything and left me to finish the job alone. However, to satisfy them, I told them that as soon as we had the mill finished we would devote a week or two to gold hunting and see what we could make of it."

The gold discovered at Sutter's Mill was only the first bit of pay dirt, as it was then called. Gold mining that started in this California riverbed would sweep through Nevada, Utah, Colorado, Montana,

Wyoming, the Dakotas, and the Pacific Northwest, and eventually even to the Klondike in Alaska. From Denver to Deadwood and points in between Americans (and foreigners aplenty) went looking for gold. The total value of the gold produced in California alone in the first decade of the rush was nearly $600 million, according to the mining historian William S. Greever.

Neither Marshall nor Sutter, who had founded an outpost that he called New Helvetia (Helvetia is Latin for Switzerland), would profit from the find. The fame of having begotten the Gold Rush followed Marshall around for the rest of his life, but he would be best known as a public drunkard. Sutter, who one historian noted had lived like a medieval baron on his vast estates before gold was discovered, lost everything. His employees ran off to look for gold and squatters seized his lands. He spent the rest of his life seeking recompense from the federal government and died in a hotel room in Washington, D.C., still waiting for that to happen.

But some others got rich. When news that gold had been discovered in California spread across the country and around the globe, "the world rushed in," as J. S. Holliday, a distinguished historian of the Gold Rush, would say. Men came from Ireland, Australia, Peru, Chile, France, Mexico, and China. They sailed around Cape Horn (a journey that could take half a year from the East Coast). They crossed the Isthmus of Panama on foot (a quicker route but a more dangerous one), and some even walked across America. They risked typhus, cholera, dysentery, scurvy, drowning, and Indian attack to reach the goldfields.

San Francisco, still a mere village, was almost evacuated, the early history *The Annals of San Francisco* reported, noting that the town seemed as if it had been struck by a plague:

> All business and work, except the most urgent, was forced to be stopped. Seamen deserted from their ships in the bay and soldiers from their barracks. Gold was the irresistible magnet that drew human souls to the place where it lay. . . . Avarice and the overwhelming desire to be suddenly rich . . . led to a general migration.

The world had never seen anything quite like the California Gold Rush. Nor had the world seen such men. "It was a driving, vigorous, restless population in those days. It was a *curious* population," recalled

Mark Twain in *Roughing It*. "It was the *only* population of the kind that the world has ever seen gathered together, and it is not likely that the world will ever see its like again." It was also, Twain remembered, a world that was almost entirely made up of young men, "the very pick and choice of the world's glorious ones. No women, no children, no gray and stooping veterans,—none but erect, bright-eyed, quick-moving, strong-handed young giants—the strangest population, the finest population, the most gallant host that ever trooped down the startled solitudes of an unpeopled land."

Most of them did not strike it rich. Many died trying. Others simply died. And many a would-be gold miner in "the days of '49," as the old folk song put it, simply went home defeated. (Word of the gold strike reached the East so slowly in 1848 that the first great wave of miners— the true pioneers by California standards—did not reach the gold fields until 1849.) Greever noted that gold mining was secretive work and miners tended to hold their cards close to their vests. If a miner was doing well, why attract attention to a rich claim? And if he was not, there was always the matter of pride. Twain, who was an eyewitness to the fabled Comstock Lode mining boom in Nevada, took all that into account when he later mused: "And where are they now? Scattered to the ends of the earth—or prematurely aged and decrepit—or shot or stabbed in street affrays—or dead of disappointed hopes and broken hearts—all gone, or nearly all—victims devoted upon the altar of the golden calf— the noblest holocaust that ever wafted its sacrificial incense heavenward. It is pitiful to think upon."

James Wilson Marshall's morning stroll along the millrace would change everything. "The California gold rush made America a more restless nation—changed the people's sense of their future, their expectations and their values," noted Holliday. "Suddenly there was a place to go where everyone could expect to make money, quickly; where life would be freer, where one could escape the constraints and conventions and the plodding sameness of life in the eastern states."

When Marshall made his discovery, there were only a few thousand people living on the Pacific Slope. California was not a state yet; it had only recently been part of Mexico. Within two years there would be 100,000 new arrivals on the West Coast, most of them digging for gold or providing some service that gold seekers needed. By 1860, the population of California—rocketed into statehood in 1850 because of gold—

would approach 400,000. Little more than a decade later, when Polly Bemis was smuggled into the port of San Francisco, probably in a padded crate, the population was nearing 600,000. And San Francisco, which had been a sleepy village at the time of James Wilson Marshall's discovery, was a city—one of the ten largest in the United States.

Word of the discovery of gold in the California hills in the winter of 1848 had the same impact among the peasants of the densely populated Pearl River delta in southern China as it did in Boston's Back Bay or along the rocky coast of Maine or in the rolling Berkshire foothills of western Massachusetts. New England sent some of the first pioneers, but the world did, indeed, rush in, and part of that world was from China. By the end of 1852, an estimated 25,000 Chinese immigrants were living in California. Horace Greeley's star reporter, Bayard Taylor, jostling on the crowded waterfront of early Gold Rush San Francisco, could not help commenting on the mysterious "Chinamen," with their long queues, their mysterious eyes, and the almost immediate popularity of their strange cuisine—much favored by pioneers of all nations, for it was tasty and, at one dollar a plate, a fine bargain in a world where few bargains were to be had. Of all the Argonauts—as the Gold Rush pioneers were called, in reference to the adventurers of Greek mythology who joined Jason in his search for the Golden Fleece—no one was more exotic on the Pacific Slope than the Chinese.

The news of gold on the American River was said to have reached Hong Kong before it reached Boston (the sailing time across the Pacific Ocean was considerably faster than travel to the East Coast, and there were long-established trade routes in those waters). California was a far country in those days, and there was no telegraph line linking it with the East. The transcontinental railroad was twenty years in the future. Even the swift couriers of the Pony Express had not yet crossed the country. Word drifted back East slowly. Major newspapers did not begin noting the gold strike until late summer, and even then many accounts were based on letters that residents of California had sent home.

But the first word of gold in California reached Hong Kong as early as the spring of 1848, according to the historian S. W. Kung. The Chinese appear to have heard about the gold strike before President James Polk—Polk did not address Congress on the subject of gold in California until December, nearly a year after the discovery—and they wasted no time in responding. First hundreds, soon thousands, and then tens of thousands of Chinese peasants would sail for California. The lure of gold and the hope of riches were enough to send them across the ocean into an unknown world.

"Before long, China sent forward her thousands of thrifty wandering children, feeble, indeed, both in body and mind, but persevering, and from their union into laboring companies, capable of great feats," noted *The Annals of San Francisco* (with no small tinge of racism) in 1855.

The rush to California attracted an enormous number of risk takers. Peasants in the Pearl River delta saw California as a place of wealth and opportunity, Marlon K. Hom, a historian of Chinese immigration and translator of Cantonese poetry written by early immigrants, points out. For a peasant from the Pearl River delta, the trip to "Golden Mountain" was largely a financial undertaking, a risky chance to ensure his family's economic future.

Each ship coming from California to China, especially in the early boom days of the Gold Rush, when lucky strikes were more common, brought the kind of news that sent thousands of Chinese peasants to the Pacific Slope. The early Chinese immigrants were often successful; the historian Corrine Hoexter recalls that in the winter of 1850–1851, the sloop *Race Horse* brought several Chinese miners home to Hong Kong with fortunes of $3,000 and $4,000 each.

"The glamour of gold outweighed the dangers in the first few years. . . . As they showed the gold dust to friends and relatives at homecoming banquets, reports of the fabulous 'Gum Shan,' the "'Mountain of Gold,' across the water spread like flames through dry underbrush," Hoexter notes. Every ship leaving Canton carried more and more peasants headed for the gold fields. The Custom House in San Francisco recorded 2,716 Chinese immigrants in 1851. One year later, that figure leaped to 20,000. By the time Polly Bemis arrived in the country, more than twenty years later, there were more than 100,000 Chinese on the Pacific Slope.

Virtually all these Chinese immigrants to the United States came from the Pearl River delta—Kwangtung (Guangdong) province, near Hong Kong, Canton, and Macau—which had first had relations with foreigners and which boasted open ports. Subtropical Kwangtung province was then the most populous and one of the poorest parts of China, plagued by years of famine, floods, drought, war, and civil unrest. The land was crowded with far more peasants than it could support, so it was natural that Kwangtung would send an army of laborers across the ocean. There was also something of a tradition of immigration in this part of southern, coastal China. Immigrants from the Pearl River delta—the so-called "overseas Chinese"—had for decades traveled to parts of Southeast Asia to work in mines or on plantations. Chroniclers of the period often report that the Chinese officially discouraged immigration, noting that the penalty for leaving China was beheading, but the punishment appears to have been little invoked, for it in no way impeded the rush to Golden Mountain or elsewhere.

With the exception of a small but dominant merchant class, the Chinese who came to the United States were peasants. They were nearly all male. They spoke dialects of Cantonese and rarely any English. They were frequently illiterate. They wore their hair in a queue down the back. This long braid, reaching past the waist of the wearer, was a sign of obeisance to the emperor and would not be discontinued until the early twentieth century. They came from small rural villages and were accustomed to doing backbreaking labor, scratching at the earth in China as they would do as miners in faraway California. They were ideal travelers into the mid-nineteenth-century American West, where there was often a great demand for cheap labor. They were traveling into a world they thought barbaric, remote, and violent. And coming as they did from the warm coastal countryside of southern China, they would arrive in a world—a place of dense forests, mountains, and bleak deserts—that bore no resemblance to the land they left behind.

The trip to Golden Mountain from a village in the Pearl River delta first involved traveling by junk or raft to Hong Kong. From there passage was arranged to California. The travelers, however poor and uneducated, were free men who often were married and were making this journey in hopes of improving their lives at home in China, notes the historian Shih-Shan Henry Tsai. Many were traveling on the "credit ticket" system—travel now, pay later. Mining in California was at first the chief draw, although railroad construction would replace it in the 1860s. Thousands of Chinese would eventually become restaurant workers, laundrymen, and domestic servants, jobs that would not have typically been done by men in China.

Crossing the Pacific was difficult and dangerous. Numerous accounts attested to the hazards of sea travel. Voyages were often made in old, battered hulks pressed into service for the Gold Rush. "Foreign shipmasters and Chinese entrepreneurs who chartered such vessels conspired to pack as many passengers as possible. Passengers in steerage were bundled together shoulder to shoulder and head to toe in poorly ventilated holds. Water was scarce, and the food prepared in ships' galleys was poor. Fatalities were frequent," the historian Jack Chen has pointed out. Under sail, if the weather and the winds did not cooperate, it could take as long as eighty or even 100 days to make the crossing—twice what good sailing time would have been. But with the introduction of the steamship in the 1860s, the passage from China was reduced to a matter of four or five weeks.

Steerage on the China run was damp, dark, poorly ventilated, and filthy. In a typhoon, a tropical cyclone with wind speeds of 100 miles per hour or more, Chinese passengers quartered on the "between deck," below the ship's waterline, occasionally drowned when these sections of the ships flooded. Ships often carried nearly twice the legal number of steerage passengers. Passengers slept on narrow bunks—some little more than a foot wide—with less than two feet of headroom. Some passengers traveled as standees and took turns sleeping in shifts. The notorious bark *Libertad*, which carried 560 passengers (although its legal limit was 297) lost 100 passengers on one run from China to San Francisco. Its passengers died of thirst—they had no water for the last week of the voyage—and the *Libertad* is frequently described by chroniclers of the passage from China as a "floating hell." The year after Polly Bemis arrived, the American government investigated the steamship trade on the Pacific run and found conditions not much changed over the years: "thus the darkness, foul-smelling bilge water, the tainted atmosphere and kindred evils of the early sailing days were repeated."

Government reports noted that "access to the main deck from lower ones was difficult, and when passengers were seasick, 'they were content to remain below rather than exert themselves trying to reach the pure air and light of the main deck,' as much as four to five stairways above. It was not uncommon for distressed passengers to remain below during entire voyages."

Most vessels sailed from Hong Kong to San Francisco without stopping. "Fresh meat and vegetables were rarities and living accommodations dangerously inadequate," the historian Robert J. Schwendinger points out. He adds: "Many steerages were provided with makeshift bunks and primitive kitchen facilities that were inoperable in bad weather, so that passengers went without food for days at a time, unable to cook meat or boil rice. Emigrants paid additional costs in several ways: brokers charged them a twenty-dollar fee for their services, others sold rotten beef or pork to vessels that was dumped overboard during the voyages; and some captains charged passengers for setting up bunks or water tanks in steerage. Risks of shipwreck or epidemic attended all ocean travel in wooden hunks, and hunger and thirst accompanied many."

Still, many ships' captains treated their passengers kindly. When the *Balmoral*, commanded by Captain J. B. Robertson, reached San Francisco, his Chinese passengers presented him with a gold ring and raised a silk flag on the vessel's main mast proclaiming, "Presented to J. B. Robertson by 464 of his Chinese passengers who have experienced much kindness and attention from him during the voyage from Kwangtung to the Golden Mountain." In 1857, the Chinese merchants of San Francisco saluted a Captain Slate, who brought 700 emigrants without a single case of sickness or death.

One week after Polly Bemis arrived in Portland en route from San Francisco to the Idaho Territory mining camp of Warrens, the bark *Garibaldi,* whose captain was A. Noyes, tied up at Moffett and Stephens's wharf to discharge its cargo, after coming upriver in tow of the steam tug *Ben Holladay.* The *Garibaldi* had sailed from Hong Kong on May 13 and took sixty days to reach the mouth of the river—fair time but no record—bucking headwinds throughout the voyage, the *Oregonian* reported. The newspaper commented favorably on this vessel's voyage. "She brings 270 Chinese passengers. During the voyage not a single case of sickness occurred on board, and the passengers arrived in good order." The editor of the *Oregonian* was delighted with these new arrivals, telling readers, "We have not seen a more healthy or robust lot of Chinese than the *Garibaldi* brought. All are well-proportioned, handsome looking fellows."

Between 1867 and 1875 (the time when Polly Bemis would have traveled to the United States from China) at least 168 round-trip voyages were undertaken, transporting some 124,800 Chinese in both directions. Steerage sales alone accounted for $5.8 million during those years. (Ships' manifests, whether for vessels traversing the Pacific or for coastal steamers coming up from San Francisco, listed Chinese passengers only as steerage, a kind of human ballast.)

In the 1850s, the average number of Chinese immigrants making the Pacific crossing was 6,680 annually. At the rate of thirty to fifty dollars per ticket, this traffic would have produced $250,000, and it prompted much competition. Return passage to China was only ten dollars.

The historian Gunther Barth has described the resulting tensions: "During the course of the voyages, the dark, dank depths of the sailing vessels grew increasingly oppressive to men who were present under compulsion and afflicted by superstition, apprehension, and dreams of their destinations. When barrel after barrel of rotten pork had to be thrown overboard, when rough seas prevented travelers from using the badly constructed cooking places, arranged with an eye to maximum economy on the crowded lower decks, when cheaply built bunks continued to break down to the risk of heads and limbs, the strain-charged air could explode at any moment."

San Francisco's district attorney at that time, Henry Byrne, declared that the captains responsible for bringing the Chinese "packed their live freight like herrings in a barrel, get their fare in advance, and care not how many of the unfortunate creatures perish." He took several of the captains of such vessels to court in the 1850s for carrying excess passengers. At worst, however, the captains might have been fined.

But there were also riots and near-mutinies on vessels, and scurvy and fever took their toll, too. Steerage accommodations were tight. The competition for travelers—and the volume of Chinese who wished to immigrate—was so high that the price of the ticket soon dropped as low as $13.

Chinese travelers often fought with the crews of vessels, sometimes because of simple misunderstandings. At other times, mutiny was a last resort. Captain Leslie Bryson, master of the American sailing ship *Robert Browne*, was taking 450 Chinese from Amoy to San Francisco in March 1852 when the travelers mutinied. The ship was overcrowded and the travelers had been duped into thinking they were headed for California, but they were actually going to plantations on the Sandwich Islands (Hawaii) as coolie labor. This would be a cruel fate that many Chinese would meet when they were shipped to the guano mines on the coast of Peru or to sugarcane plantations in Cuba. Bryson had ordered the Chinese scrubbed and their queues cut off, believing they were not clean. The Chinese mutinied, killed the captain and officers, and took command of the ship. The incident, the first case of an actual coolie uprising on an American vessel, was much publicized at the time. The mutineers—or at least some of them—were later arrested when they sailed the ship to a remote island, but the case, though highly controversial, was never resolved because the Americans and the Chinese could never agree on exactly what had happened.

Only a few weeks after Polly Bemis arrived in Portland, the bark *Manila* tied up there. The *Manila* drew much comment in the *Oregonian* after the Chinese passengers mutinied during a quarantine stop in Astoria on the Oregon coast to ensure that the vessel would not bring any diseases into the country. After a few days of being detained, the Chinese—419 men by the best count—attempted to seize the vessel and be allowed ashore. The captain and the ship's officers had to quell the rebellion with force, the *Oregonian* reported:

> Finding gentle means ineffectual, the captain and the first and second mates descended to the cabin and procured their pistols and knives. They returned with the weapons drawn and cocked, and drove the mutineers from the forecastle, threatening instant death to any one who refused to obey orders. This effectually cowed them. They soon went below, and gave no more trouble during the remainder of the voyage up the river. At one time bloodshed appeared imminent and unavoidable. But for the coolness, bravery and resolution of the ship's officers, serious difficulty would without doubt have resulted.

It was unclear whether the Chinese aboard understood why they were being detained, or whether the tension and confinement of being at sea for many weeks had finally triggered the revolt. On many ships there was no translator on board; typically, some of the officers who had been long in the China trade spoke a gibberish of Cantonese they had picked up in Hong Kong and Canton. The water cannon or a marlinspike was the preferred means of communication. On particularly rough passages, the Chinese were kept belowdecks under conditions that commentators compared to the Middle Passage, the voyage of slave ships coming from Africa.

Typical of travelers on the China run was Fatt Hing, a nineteen-year-old fish peddler who heeded the call of the Golden Mountain, which he heard about while buying fish on the South China coast. Fatt Hing's family raised the money for his passage by selling the water buffalo and pawning his mother's jewelry, according to the historian Betty Lee Sung. He was smuggled on board a Spanish ship bound for California. Fatt Hing's passage was brutal and terrifying. With dozens of other young Chinese like himself, he slept, sat, ate, and waited on a straw mat in a ship's hold that was "stifling and foul, putrid from the vomiting of those who had yet to acquire their sea legs," Sung writes. It was too cold for the Chinese to go on deck, as they were wearing thin cotton and flax clothes that were common in the Pearl River delta. Most of the time the Chinese would not have been allowed on deck in any case.

It took ninety-five days for the Spanish vessel to reach San Francisco —more than twice the normal sailing time. The passengers were terrified, believing they had been sold into slavery, but Fatt Hing eventually arrived.

Recollections such as Fatt Hing's are unusual. Even the Library of Congress, in compiling *"California as I Saw It": First-Person Narratives of California's Early Years, 1849–1900,* lamented the absence of Chinese records, noting in 1997 that "no first-person memoirs of the Chinese experience in nineteenth-century California are known to survive."

The explanation for this lack of first-person accounts of the trip to Golden Mountain had much to do with who was making that trip. Peasants did not write books. Most of the Chinese travelers were illiterate, and they left no trace of their voyage. A modern Chinese scholar, Li-hua Yu, believes it is likely that the few existing materials were lost during the anti-Chinese movement. The Chinese collection of the Idaho State Historical Society, she notes, largely contains records and documents belonging to the Boise Chinese organizations after the mid-twentieth century.

"It must be remembered, however, that any possibility for a thorough understanding of the Chinese and their activities has always been over-shadowed by the fact that all the records and writers were external observers of early Chinese communities," Li-hua Yu observes. "There was hardly any bilingual person nor any Chinese who wrote about the

Chinese experience in Idaho." Many older Chinese found the memories of discrimination and abuse in the early days too painful to recall or discuss, she adds.

Most pioneers like Fatt Hing and Huie Kin, another rare Chinese memorist, were typical of the travelers who first sailed to Golden Mountain. They knew almost nothing about America. And America knew almost nothing about them.

Huie Kin remembered how his ship finally reached San Francisco "on a clear, crisp September morning." This sojourner's heart soared as he described his elation:

> To be actually at the "Golden Gate" of the land of our dreams! The feeling that welled up in us was indescribable. I wonder whether the ecstasy before the Pearly Gates of the Celestial City above could surpass what we felt at the moment we realized that we had reached out destination. We rolled up our bedding, packed our baskets, straightened our clothes and waited. In those days there were no immigration laws or tedious examinations; people came and went freely. Somebody had brought to the pier large wagons for us. Out of the general babble someone called out in our local dialect, and like sheep recognizing the voice only, we blindly followed, and soon were piling into one of the waiting wagons. Everything was so strange and so exciting that my memory of the landing is just a big blur. The wagon made its way heavily over the cobblestones, turned some corners, ascended a steep climb, and stopped at a kind of clubhouse, where we spent the night. Later, I learned that the people from various districts had their own benevolent societies, with headquarters in San Francisco's Chinatown. As there were six of them, they were known as the "Six Companies." Newcomers were taken care of until relatives came to claim them and pay the bill. The next day our relatives from Oakland took us across the bay to the little Chinese settlement there, and kept us until we found work.

In those days, the so-called Six Companies, often referred to as the Chinese Consolidated Benevolent Association—mutual-aid societies made up of people from particular districts in China—largely spoke for the Chinese in the American West, acting as protectors, arbitrators, and to some extent labor brokers. Before China formalized its diplomatic relations with the United States in the late 1860s, the Six Companies acted as a virtual government agency. For all practical purposes during the nineteenth century, the government of Chinatown in San Francisco—and by extension the life of the Chinese in the American West—was a combination of the Chinese consulate general and the Six Companies.

The risk that Huie Kin and Fatt Hing undertook was worthwhile, for historians note that a peasant in rural China then might earn between three and five dollars per month, whereas the wages in California for performing even the most menial and brutish tasks would amount to one dollar per day on average. In the 1860s, railway workers—and China provided thousands of these for the construction of the Central Pacific Railroad—earned on average thirty to thirty-five dollars a month, lived on half of that, and could easily send home thirty dollars a year, a fortune in the poverty-stricken Pearl River delta. By living frugally and by pooling their resources, Chinese workers often saved significant amounts of money.

The Chinese would have an almost immediate impact on California, for not only did they immigrate in significant numbers, but they would soon corner the labor market in jobs no one else wished to do, ranging from running laundries and restaurants to gardening and rolling cigars. The Chinese would do any work and they would do it cheaply, too.

Whites traditionally called immigrants from China "sojourners," the literal translation of a term for Chinese who had gone abroad as temporary visitors. They expected to be only briefly in the United States. Whites also frequently referred to the Chinese as "celestials," a reference to the "Celestial Empire," a common Western term for the Manchu dynasty that ruled China at the time and a name that emphasized how exotic the Chinese were.

The intention of nearly all Chinese to return home with a bit of a grubstake may explain why many of them did not assimilate. The Chinese simply saw no point in putting down roots.

"The majority of Chinese came here intending to stay only a few years until they accumulated enough money to return to their homeland and live out the remainder of their lives in comfort. They did not try to assimilate into American life because they did not intend to make a permanent home here, and their efforts to earn as much money as possible left little extra energy or time to devote to learning new ways of life in a strange country," the historian Robert McClellan has pointed out.

In the American West, the notion that the Chinese were not planning to stay was received as good news. However useful they might have seemed at first, the Chinese were largely not wanted as permanent residents. The Chinese themselves were fiercely ethnocentric, too; even the peasants of the Pearl River delta believed that there was no place like home and they would return there as soon as they had acquired a little money in the goldfields of California.

The New England journalist Samuel Bowles, who toured the West at this time, assured his readers that because the Chinese had not come to stay, their expenses were different from those of immigrants who came as extended family groups in which a man might be supporting a wife, several children, and even parents.

"They do not come to stay or become citizens, but simply to make their fortunes and go back home and enjoy them," Bowles told readers of the *Springfield Republican,* a widely read newspaper with a national audience. "Neither their families nor their priests follow them; they show no desire to domesticate themselves here; they dread nothing more than to die and be buried here, and nearly every China-bound steamer or ship carries back home the bodies of 'Chinamen,' overtaken, as death overtakes us all, in the struggles of their labor and ambition."

Regardless of how long the Chinese planned on staying in Golden Mountain, the allure of the place, a dreamland of untold riches, was aggressively marketed in China. A nineteenth-century circular posted in the Pearl River delta by a Hong Kong brokerage office, for example, was aimed at enticing peasants to California:

> Americans are very rich people. They want the "Chinaman" to come and make him very welcome. There you will have great pay, large houses, and food and clothing of the finest description. You can write to your friends or send them money at any time and we will be responsible for the safe delivery. It is a nice country, without mandarins or soldiers. All alike; big man no larger than little man. There are a great many "Chinamen" there now, and it will not be a strange country. China god is there, and the agents of this house. Never fear, and you will be lucky.

But not everything written for the would-be sojourner was so cheerful. Many of the phrases in *An English-Chinese Phrase Book* (1875), quoted by the modern historian Xiao-huang Yin, are frightening to read:

I cannot trust you.

I have made an apology, but still he wants to strike me.

He took it from me by violence.

He assaulted me without provocation.

He claimed my mine.

He tries to extort money from me.

He cheated me out of my wages.

He was murdered by a thief.

He refused to pay the money which he owes me.

The immigration will soon be stopped.

Such phrases indicate the terrors of daily life a Chinese laborer would face in the American West. This was the world of the "Chinaman's chance," a world where the Chinese had little or no standing in the courts and could not depend on what little law enforcement as existed to protect them.

The very language used to speak of Chinese immigrants was problematic. Nineteenth-century Americans (and Europeans) often used the word "coolie" to describe Chinese immigrants, but strictly speaking, the peasant who came to California from the Pearl River delta was never a coolie.

At the time Americans did not understand the meaning of this term or realize that it deeply offended the Chinese in the United States. The word *k'u-li,* which appears to derive from the Tamil (Indian), is often translated as "hard strength" or "bitter strength." It referred to the resolve necessary for a laborer to sell himself into a kind of indentured servitude—called a contract-labor system—which might approach slavery. Unlike the traditional coolie, Chinese immigrants to the United States, however humble, were their own men.

Actual coolie laborers from the southern coast of China were shipped to sugar plantations in Cuba or elsewhere in the West Indies or to the notorious guano mines off the coast of Peru. These unfortunates were literally slaves, and the death rate among them was very high.

As early as 1870, William Speer, a Presbyterian minister who served in China and later ministered to the Chinese in San Francisco, scolded his countrymen for using the word. "The word 'coolie' is wholly inappropriate to the Chinese immigrating to this country," he told his American readers.

But the most common and the most offensive term used by every chronicler of the American West, whether sympathetic or not, to describe the Chinese on the Pacific Slope was "Chinaman." The word pervades popular accounts. Even Mark Twain, Bret Harte, and Ambrose Bierce, writers who were sympathetic to the Chinese, called the new arrivals "Chinamen." Newspapers almost always referred to the Chinese as "Chinamen," to such an extent that in the popular imagination the term did not even seem derogatory, and it was carried into the early twentieth century.

"The ethnic slur usually describes the point of view of its author better than it does its object, and the slang pertaining to the Chinese was no exception. The most characteristic word in use at the turn of the century to describe the Chinese was 'Chinaman,'" McClellan notes. "It carried the meaning of 'one of them,' or someone from 'that place,' and indicated inferiority, foreign origin, and a kind of subservient anonymity. A somewhat comparable example is the use of the word 'boy' in referring to Negroes, the implication being that the individual possesses insufficient worth to be identified beyond the level of his particular racial class."

But however poorly the Chinese immigrant might be regarded, the sojourner of the nineteenth century in the American West was not a slave. He may have faced many unknowns but he was traveling of his own free will and paying his own way.

"The Chinese emigration to California was free and voluntary, confined to independent emigrants who paid their own passage money and were in a condition to look to their arrangements," Shih-Shan Henry Tsai notes. "The early Chinese in the United States were free immigrants, at the very worst coming on the so-called 'ticket-system' or on money borrowed at a high rate of interest."

According to the editors of *A History of the Chinese in California*, published by the Chinese Historical Society of America, a significant number of emigrants paid their own passage or were aided in making the trip by relatives and friends already in California. Travelers whose passage fee had been advanced to them were expected to repay the debt out of future earnings. Also, merchant brokers in Hong Kong advanced passage money, and agents in the United States were responsible for collecting the debt and finding work for the new immigrant.

Emigrants from the Pearl River delta would gather in Hong Kong in dormitories kept by the labor brokers while they waited for a ship to San Francisco—the primary port of disembarkation on the West Coast. British and American firms owned most vessels.

The arrival of Huie Kin in this strange new world was a familiar story, however unsettling it might have seemed to the peasant traveler from the Pearl River delta. Gunther Barth described the scene of arrival in San Francisco in the nineteenth century: "Noise and confusion accompanied the disembarkation on the wharves of San Francisco. Baskets, matting, hats, and bamboo poles covered a pier crowded with boatmen, agents of Chinese merchants, draymen, custom officials, and spectators."

The former fish buyer Fatt Hing went to the California goldfields and after two years of placer mining (the earliest form of gold mining, essentially panning for gold) decided to take the wealth that he had acquired and return to China. There he married and bought land. Eventually, like many other Chinese sojourners, he decided to return to California, but this time he was less successful at mining and instead went into the restaurant business. His story was the story of many a sojourner in Golden Mountain. Like a gambler who gets lucky, the sojourner who made a little money in Golden Mountain would often try again and more often than not fail.

Before Fatt Hing and Huie Kin and tens of thousands of their fellows arrived in California, Americans knew only two Chinese well, and these were the most famous Chinese-Americans of the nineteenth century. Unlike most of their countrymen who toiled anonymously on the Pacific Slope—working on the railroads, mining, running laundries and restaurants—they were household names. They were brothers who had married two American sisters—and had produced large families when miscegenation was considered an abomination, if not actually illegal. They owned black slaves and a considerable amount of land in rural North Carolina. Thousands of Americans who had never seen a Chinese person had not merely stared at them in wonder, but paid to do so. When Polly Bemis reached America the two were celebrities. They were even ambassadors of sorts; they had met Queen Victoria, Czar Alexander of Russia, the duke of Wellington, and Abraham Lincoln.

They called themselves the Bunker brothers (having borrowed the name from a friend) and when they weren't touring they lived on a remote farm in the Blue Ridge Mountains, ardent supporters of the Confederacy and (so their families would later claim, probably incorrectly) Baptists. Their names were Chang and Eng. Today, we remember them for a phrase their very existence inserted into the English language—a phrase still common, still heard. Chang and Eng were the "Siamese twins."

Born on a bamboo mat on a houseboat floating in the Mekong River near Bangkok, the brothers were brought to the United States at age seventeen in 1829 from their native Siam (they were ethnically Chinese) by wily promoters. Chang and Eng spent a lifetime in show business as professional freaks: "living curiosities," to borrow a phrase from P. T. Barnum, and P. T. Barnum would know. The father of American showmen, the "prince of humbugs," as the celebrated New York lawyer and diarist George Templeton Strong called him, helped make the brothers famous.

Word of their arrival and their "bizarre and wondrous condition" spread rapidly. Wild newspaper accounts stirred public interest. "We have seen and examined this strange freak of nature. It is one of the greatest living curiosities we have ever saw," noted the *Boston Patriot*.

Dressed in Chinese costume (at first), they played checkers and did somersaults and backflips to entertain the curious. Chang and Eng would also play checkers with any challengers, always besting them. They had also picked up an amusingly broken English fairly quickly and were able to chat with the crowds. Viewers were delighted.

Chang and Eng spent decades touring the United States and Europe, acquiring a strange and terrible fame by exhibiting themselves, and confirming, as the modern historian Iris Chang notes, "the popular image of all Asians as freaks of nature." They were of special interest to doctors, and from the day they arrived in Boston until their deaths five decades later, Chang and Eng were examined by the best physicians in the world to determine if they might be surgically separated.

When they arrived in Boston, they were examined by Dr. John Collins Warren, a legendary professor of anatomy and surgery at the Harvard Medical School and Massachusetts General Hospital. When they died, more than forty years later, the *New York Times* recalled that the chief reason for Warren's examination had been "for the purpose of giving a guarantee that they were genuine monsters and for the rest not in any way indecorous or unfit for exhibition—the main purpose, of course, of those who brought them from Siam."

A notice in the *New York Times* in 1860 hints at how America regarded Chang and Eng even after they had been in this country for more than thirty years.

BARNUM'S
AMERICAN MUSEUM
Under the personal supervision of . . . P. T. Barnum
EVERY DAY AND EVENING THIS WEEK
COMMENCING MONDAY, OCT. 15, 1860
Last week but one of the
ONLY LIVING SIAMESE TWINS
CHANG AND ENG, WHO, WITH TWO OF THEIR CHILDREN
will be on exhibition Day and Evening. Those who have ever seen these
most wonderful and extraordinary human beings, know them to be the
most interesting and curious of all objects, while those who do not, need
only to be told that they are TWO LIVING MEN 49 YEARS OLD, SO
INSEPARABLY UNITED AT THE PIT OF THE STOMACH that what
one feels the other does . . .

The "Siamese twins" joined the cast of oddities whom Barnum had presented to the public for decades, such as Joice Heth, a Negro said to be 161 years old and to have been George Washington's nanny; Jo Jo the Dog Faced Boy; and the Wild Man of Borneo. There were giants, midgets, bearded ladies, fat ladies, ladies who could stand in the palm of a man's hand, General Tom Thumb, the Ethnological Congress of Savage and Barbarous Tribes ("a collection of the world's uncivilized races"), and Jumbo the elephant. His exhibition of William Henry Johnson, better known as "Zip," a hulking black man with an oddly shaped head, possibly microcephalic, whom he breezily called the "Man Monkey," suggests that he was not above being offensive. Chang and Eng remained among his greatest stars, although they kept the shrewd promoter at arm's length. It should come as no surprise that Chang and Eng loathed Barnum.

Before the Gold Rush brought tens of thousands of "Chinamen" to the United States, the average American, if he had seen a Chinese person at all, might well have seen Chang and Eng and paid several dollars (a week's wages for a workingman) to do so. Virtually no Chinese were living in the country when the brothers arrived here. From the first, America loved Chang and Eng as freaks; and as freaks, America would support them. They experienced little real prejudice. They were simply too unusual; being strange trumped being Chinese. When they died nearly half a century later, there were so many Chinese on the Pacific Slope that labor agitators were stirring up the "Chinese must go" movement, which would eventually lead to federal prohibitions against the Chinese.

In 1860, Chang and Eng toured California—including the gold country—where they were well received and grandly accommodated at a time when the average Chinese immigrant would have risked stoning in the streets of San Francisco.

America's response to Chang and Eng says a great deal about feelings toward the Chinese in the first half of the nineteenth century. More than anything else, they were rarities. Occasionally travelers from the Middle Kingdom might literally wash ashore in an American port, as three sailors did as early as 1785 when they were marooned in Baltimore. No one knows what became of them. A few years earlier, a Chinese sailor died in Boston and the master of the vessel had him properly buried. There would in time even be theories that the Chinese had "discovered America" long before Europeans reached these shores. Chinese carpenters built ships for the British in the Pacific Northwest in the late eighteenth century. A Chinese man was baptized in Spanish California. A British sea captain with a Chinese crew sailed a Chinese junk made of teak from China to New York harbor in 1847, and New Yorkers were impressed. A number of Chinese youths came to Connecticut and Massachusetts to study at foreign mission schools in the early nineteenth century. And during the years before the Gold Rush, here and there a Chinese traveler would arrive and amaze Americans, most often performing as Chang and Eng did, in costume, in a country that largely regarded the Chinese as mysterious. Americans especially delighted in watching the Chinese use an abacus or chopsticks. Chang and Eng were not the only Chinese in show business in those days, merely the most famous.

No one did more to promulgate the stereotype of the Chinaman than the Yankee traders—New Englanders, chiefly—who in the late eighteenth century and the early nineteenth century opened the China trade and spent time in China's ports. One observed: "The first impulse of an American, when he sees for the first time a Chinese, is to laugh at him. His dress, if judged by our standards, is ridiculous, and in a Mandarin, a stately gravity sets it off for a double derision. His trousers are a couple of meal bags. . . . His shoes are huge machines, turned up at the toe, his cap is fantastic and his head is shaven except on the crown, whence there hangs down a tuft of hair as long as a spaniel's tail."

When there weren't very many Chinese in the United States, they were regarded as an unthreatening, harmless curiosity, not even really men but, as Barnum's publicity had dubbed Chang and Eng, "the most interesting and curious of all objects."

The week after James Wilson Marshall found gold on the American River the arrival of the first Chinese was documented in San Francisco, according to Hubert Howe Bancroft, the first great historian of California, who published the multivolume *History of the Pacific States of North America*. Bancroft was sure as to the precise date that the Chinese first arrived: February 2, 1848. Everyone who ever mused on this after him would cite his calculation, even those who, musing on the calculation, concluded that he was wrong. At any rate, the arrival of these Chinese travelers was a mere coincidence. They knew nothing of the gold strike.

"The first immigrants from China to modern California," Bancroft wrote, "were two Chinese men and one woman, who arrived by the clipper bark *Eagle* in 1848. The men went to the mines, and the woman remained as a servant in the family of Charles V. Gillespie, who came hither from Hong Kong." Bancroft, who was relying on Gillespie's manuscript memoir, did not record the names of the first "celestials." We know nothing about them. They arrived in the port of San Francisco and vanished. But no one who wrote about the Chinese in the American West after that failed to mention Bancroft's notation on the exact moment that the first Chinese appeared in California. Historians have long been puzzled. Just who was the first Chinese traveler to arrive?

In the end, perhaps what matters is not who was the first, but only that at first there were so few Chinese that no one bothered much about them. After the Gold Rush, however, there would come more and more, so that by the time Chang and Eng died on their farm in North Carolina there were, at least in the minds of many Americans, too many Chinamen in a white man's country.

In 1870, two years before Polly Bemis arrived in the United States, Colonel Albert S. Evans, a correspondent for the *New York Tribune* and the *Chicago Tribune*, described in great detail meeting the China steamer

Great Republic at the docks of San Francisco. The ship was bringing 1,272 Chinese into the country.

Next to the long, shed-covered wharf of the Pacific Mail Steamship Company, stretching far out into Mission Bay to the south, Evans saw huge steamers at anchor. Pushing his way through the throng of Asians, Americans, and Europeans who met every boat, shoving his way through the choke of wagons and carts and carriages, Evans was admitted to the *Great Republic* because he had a card from the shipping company's office, given to him as a courtesy.

Amid the mob meeting the ship, Evans noted as many as 100 Chinese merchants and representatives of the Six Companies. Evans described the *Great Republic*'s main deck as "packed with Chinamen —every foot of space being occupied by them—gazing in silent wonder at the new land whose fame had reached them beyond the seas, and whose riches these swart representatives of the toiling millions of Asia have come to develop."

Evans continued:

> As fast as the groups of coolies have been successfully searched, they are turned out of the gates, and hurried away towards the Chinese quarter of the city by the agents of the "Six Companies." Some go in wagons, more on foot; and the streets leading up that way are lined with them, running in "Indian file," and carrying their luggage suspended from the ends of the bamboo poles slung across their shoulders.

Later that evening, Evans reflected on the wild scene at the Pacific Mail Steamship Company wharf as the *Great Republic* disgorged its cargo:

> We can still hear the roar of many voices shouting in an unknown tongue, and see the stream of men in blue blouses, with shaven foreheads, and with long braided queues of glossy black hair and silk hanging down their backs. The strange odor of Asiatic tobacco, spices and opium which pervaded ship and cargo, still clings to our clothing, and finds its way into our nostrils. . . . We have indeed stood on the farther shore of the New World, and seen the human tides which have surged round the globe from opposite directions meet and commingle. . . . It was a sight worth living long and coming far to look upon— a scene to wonder at, to ponder over and reflect upon—to gaze upon once and remember through all the coming years of life—a scene such as our fathers

never beheld nor dreamed of, and of which our children's children only may
known the full import and meaning.

The cargo of the *Great Republic,* Evans reported in considerable detail, was exotic, hailing from Java, Manila, China, and elsewhere in the
Orient and including coffee and cassia, firecrackers, dried fish, cuttle-
fish, sharks' fins, hemp, porcelain ware, rice, opium, salted melon seeds,
pickled ducks' eggs, smoked oysters, tea, and silks. But its greatest load
of freight was human.

"Last week one thousand two hundred came by sailing vessels, and
behind them are yet four hundred million of the most patient, ready,
apt, and industrious toilers on the face of the earth," Evans told his
readers.

Among the arrivals on the waterfront were women from China. One
was the bride of a rich Chinese merchant, arrayed in the finest clothing.
Some fifteen or twenty Chinese girls destined for another sort of life in
Golden Mountain also came off the *Great Republic.* "The poor raft and
boat born women of Canton, trained, from childhood, to lewdness, and
as utterly ignorant of the ways of virtue or any sense of shame or moral
responsibility as so many blocks of wood—were landed also; some steamers bring them by hundreds in spite of the efforts of the 'Six Companies' to discourage the traffic," Evans reported.

The sex slaves Evans saw leaving the *Great Republic* were peasant girls
from the Pearl River delta—teenagers—not unlike Polly Bemis, bought
in China for small sums of money and headed for San Francisco's Chinatown to be sold:

These women signed contracts in China, to serve their masters a given number of years for their passage-money, board and clothing, and despite our laws,
will submit to live and die in a slavery more horrible than any other that ever
existed on earth; all efforts of our authorities to break it up having proved utterly
unavailing. As they land, they are searched in no delicate manner by the officers, and then received by their purchasers, and delivered to the charge of the
sallow old hags in black costume, with bunches of keys in the girdles at their
waists, who are called "old mothers," and who will hold them in horrible
bondage and collect the wages of their sin—if they who have no moral responsibility can be said to sin—for the remainder of their days.

The girls are dressed in silk or cotton tunics and trousers similar in shape
and color to those worn by the married ladies, but far less costly, are painted

gaudily on cheeks and lips, and wear on their heads the checked cotton hand-kerchiefs which are the badge of prostitution.

Their countrymen, Evans added, mostly laborers from the Pearl River delta, who crowded the docks looking for friends and relatives, howled insults at these girls as they were piled into wagons sent to carry them to the dens of Chinatown.

Men lifting sacks of rice in Chinatown at 921 Grant Avenue.
California Historical Society, FN-098I8.

Two

CHINATOWN

There are more things in San Francisco's Chinatown than are dreamed of in Heaven and on earth.
—FRANK NORRIS, *THE THIRD CIRCLE* (1909)

The city that would become San Francisco had begun as the village of Yerba Buena—meaning "good herb" in Spanish, probably a reference to the mint that grew wild thereabouts. Yerba Buena was a dusty, distant fragment of the once vast Spanish empire. As the middle of the nineteenth century approached, the old Mission Dolores and the Presidio, a fort established at the Golden Gate—the opening of San Francisco's immense bay—were crumbling reminders of a world that was now part of the newly independent nation of Mexico. The few hundred people scattered around the bay were a mongrel lot made up of Mexican cowboys, Christian Indians, shrewd Yankee shopkeepers, sailors who had jumped ship, adventurers, the odd mountain man, trappers who had crossed the continent, and even a few Mormons escaping persecution.

Occasional ships' captains or explorers, including Sir Francis Drake, Captain James Cook, and the British navigator George Vancouver, had cruised along this coast. Whether the visitors were English, French, Russian, or American, they never failed to comment on the magnificence of the bay and the shabbiness of this remote outpost. Whaling vessels occasionally stopped to replenish their stores after years in the icy northern Pacific, taking advantage of the splendid though little-used harbor. But Yerba Buena was largely a hide-trading and tallow port that capitalized on California's vast, nearly wild cattle herds.

"A more approachable harbor, or one of greater security, is unknown to navigators," observed Edwin Bryant, a former Kentucky journalist who visited in 1846, before the discovery of gold, when little was stirring in the village. Bryant, who chronicled his trip in *What I Saw in California*, shrewdly anticipated the great potential of the place:

> The position of San Francisco for commerce is, without doubt, superior to any other port on the Pacific coast of North America. The country contiguous and tributary to it cannot be surpassed in fertility, healthfulness of climate, and beauty of scenery. It is capable of producing whatever is necessary to the sustenance of man, and many of the luxuries of tropical climates, not taking in the account of the mineral wealth of the surrounding hills and mountains, which there is reason to believe is very great. This place is, doubtless, destined to become one of the largest and most opulent commercial cities in the world, and under American authority it will rise with astonishing rapidity.

The village that he reached was populated by just a few citizens. Isolation and indolence had taken their toll. California was not merely not yet a state; it was still part of Mexico. The Presidio, a modest and badly undermanned fort designed to protect the great bay, contained in its final days a tiny Mexican garrison consisting of a sergeant and a dozen poorly equipped soldiers. On several occasions, while attempting to fire salutes for visiting ships or dignitaries, the gunners blew up their antiquated cannons and injured themselves. Historians noted that it was necessary for the troops there to borrow gunpowder from visiting ships even to fire the salutes. The outpost was famous for fleas, too.

Mission Dolores, founded in 1776 as one of the northernmost of the twenty-one Spanish missions that ran up along the California coast to propagate Roman Catholicism among the heathen Indians, was about two miles from the village of Yerba Buena. *The Annals of San Francisco* described the old church in the early 1850s as a "whitewashed . . . huge and gloomy temple" reminiscent of a grand past. Edwin Bryant and his companions stopped for the night at the mission, and although they found hospitality the place was poor. "A more miserable supper I have never sat down to," Bryant recalled.

The writer Richard Henry Dana, author of the classic *Two Years Before the Mast,* which chronicled his time as a common seaman from 1834 to 1836, recorded a visit in the mid-1830s to Yerba Buena. He found the village a seedy, sleepy slice of old Mexico. By the time Dana, who had dropped out of Harvard and run away to sea, in hope that seafaring might improve his health, arrived on the California coast the mission system was unraveling.

"The Californians are an idle, thriftless people, and can make nothing for themselves," Dana reported, complaining that even in such a lush landscape they were incapable of producing wine and had to import it all the way from Boston at great cost. It was not very good wine, either, he groused.

California was nearly mythical. Few visited it. In its very early days, maps seemed uncertain of its dimensions and explorers even thought it might be an island, like the legendary Atlantis. Its few settlements were strung along the coast and largely linked to the mission system.

J. D. Borthwick, a Scottish writer and painter who arrived in 1851 and left a detailed account of his adventures in the new land, commented on California before the Gold Rush. Horace Kephard, who edited Borthwick's memoirs, included this explanation of California under the Spaniards, noting that they discouraged foreign visitors:

> California under Spanish and Mexican rule was a lotus-land of lazy, good-natured, hospitable friars, of tame and submissive Indian neophytes, of vast savannas swarming with half-wild herds, of orchards and gardens, vineyards and olive groves. There was no mining, no lumbering, no machinery, no commerce other than a contraband exchange of hides and tallow for clothing, merchandise and manufactures. There was no art, no science, no literature, no news.

But within a decade of the discovery of gold in 1848, San Francisco would become a city: an important, booming, and powerful city that would be at first notoriously lawless and, in the words of one of its biographers, famous as "the almost universal synonym for debauchery." Transformed practically overnight, San Francisco would soon contain citizens of the world, including large numbers of Chinese. More than 50,000 new arrivals from all over the globe were said to have streamed through the Golden Gate or come overland in the first year after gold was discovered. Most of them were not planning to stay but headed immediately to the goldfields.

Gold alone was the reason for the sudden and spectacular growth of San Francisco from its origin as an adobe outpost of old Spain—"a fragment of the grandest of colonial empires"—into a teeming metropolis with stately homes, theaters, and operas houses.

"Of all the marvelous phases of the history of the Present, the growth of San Francisco is the one which will most tax the belief of the Future. Its parallel was never known, and shall never be beheld again," Bayard Taylor, one of the most prominent journalists in the United States during the nineteenth century, noted. At age twenty-four, as a star reporter for Horace Greeley's *New York Tribune,* Taylor was sent to California in the summer of 1849 to write about what would become one of the greatest migrations in human history. His account of Gold Rush country, *Eldorado—Adventures in the Path of Empire,* published in 1850, would become a commercial and critical sensation.

The spectacular growth of the port city astonished Taylor: "When I landed there, a little more than four months before, I found a scattering town of tents and canvas houses, with a show of frame buildings on one or two streets, and a population of about six thousand. Now, on my last visit, I saw around me an actual metropolis, displaying street after street of well-built edifices, filled with an active and enterprising people, and exhibiting every mark of permanent commercial prosperity."

Taylor was also one of the first chroniclers to remark on what a hurry the gold seekers were in. Ships of all sizes, including Chinese junks, were abandoned by the dozens at the wharves, or beached and left to rot, because the crews were eager to head off for the "diggings." Some of the old ships were run aground and converted into ramshackle hotels for the new arrivals. One historian described the harbor and its beaches as "the Dead Sea Graveyard of All Ships." Colonel James J. Ayres, who entered San Francisco by ship in October 1849, remembered "a great forest of masts" as his vessel reached the harbor.

"During the year I had been absent from San Francisco that city had emerged from her primitive and chaotic state and assumed urban shape and form. Several imposing brick buildings had been erected on Montgomery Street, and frame structures had taken the place of canvas houses in every direction," Ayres wrote.

Writing in his memoirs at the end of the century, Ayres recalled that the village of tents he first encountered became a metropolis in a mere year's time: "There was bustle everywhere and the march of improvement kept step with the constantly increasing demand of a new city in full bloom. . . . Vessels from all parts of the world were constantly adding their contributions to the human hive. The harbor was covered with masts, and presented at that time a marine picture such as had never been seen. The desertion of sailors for the mines was so general that many vessels remained in the harbor idle for the want of crews to man them."

William McCollum, a forty-one-year-old physician from New York who arrived in July 1849, composed a series of letters home, published as *California as I Saw It*, observing that the spectacular growth of San Francisco was "a thing without parallel,—one that admits no comparisons, for there is nothing like it in the histories of cities." Included in McCollum's account were the recollections of a traveling companion of his—Lyman Bradley, who also found San Francisco growing explosively.

"Framed houses were often put up and enclosed in twenty-four hours," Bradley recalled. "Passing to-day, you would see a vacant lot, and passing again in forty-eight hours, there would be a store in which would be a large stock of goods, measuring off and weighing for customers; and so with buildings of other purposes. As many as forty buildings have gone up in forty-eight hours."

In 1859, Richard Henry Dana, by now forty-four and a maritime lawyer in Boston, would make a celebrated return journey to the site of his youthful adventures in the tallow and hide trade and find the city unrecognizable. Only the old Presidio and the crumbling Mission Dolores remained to remind him of a vanished world. Dana was astonished. The city was only ten years old, but he ate meals prepared by French chefs that were in his estimation as good as anything he had eaten in Paris, and he listened to a church choir he thought as good as any he had heard in Europe. He reveled in these changes. But he had a moment of nostalgia when, wandering along the city's transformed waterfront—which bore no resemblance to the shabby village of his first visit—he found a pile of rotting hides and an old Californian who told him the hide and tallow business that had brought Dana to this far coast so long ago was no more. Gold had changed everything.

"I have looked at the city from the water and islands from the city, but I can see nothing that recalls the times gone by, except the venerable Mission, the ruinous Presidio, the high hills in the rear of the town, and the great stretches of the bay in all directions," Dana noted.

The city that Dana revisited in 1859, with a population of more than 50,000, by then had a substantial Chinese presence. There were some 60,000 "celestials" on the Pacific coast by this time. Dana also commented that "The Chinese, too, are numerous, and do a great part of the manual labor and small shop-keeping, and have some wealthy mercantile houses."

In its early days, San Francisco was described as "the haunt of the low and the vile of every kind"—and had earned the name "Barbary Coast" after the African pirate lair. The city remained a somewhat lawless town when Polly Bemis was smuggled into the port in 1872. Prosperity brought only the illusion of law and order; there was still a very wild side to life. If nothing else, San Francisco was famously corrupt. Its reputation as a sinful and wicked place, however exaggerated when it became more prosperous, would not be entirely dispelled until the earthquake and fire of 1906 leveled the city.

The word "hoodlum"—a term for toughs who preyed on passersby— was said to have been coined here. A miner down from the Sierra Nevada with gold in the early days could have seen a woman have sex with a wild boar, according to that connoisseur of the low life Herbert Asbury, whose account—*The Barbary Coast*—is brimming with unnatural acts. And that was not the only unusual entertainment available to the out-of-town visitor. Vigilante justice in the 1850s was swift and deadly; there were public lynchings, and they were well attended, too.

Into this wild scene came the Chinese. Their early arrival in San Francisco was also remarked on in the *Annals of San Francisco*. In 1852, the annals estimated that 10,000 Chinese were in town and at least as many were on their way. The authors of the annals noted that "Chinamen" were both victims and a perceived threat: "Considerable apprehension began then to be entertained of the supposed bad effect which their presence would have on the white population. Large bands of Chinese were working at the mines upon conditions which were supposed to be closely allied to a state of slavery."

Concerns about "cheap Chinese labor"—an expression that would become a catchphrase—raised fears that the Chinese would supplant whites. The annals predicted that the white miner "might as well leave the country at once, since he could not pretend to compete with the poverty-stricken, meek and cheap 'coolie,' as so John Chinaman was now called by many."

Excluded from many other kinds of work and often prevented from mining, Chinese men dominated the laundry trade to such an extent that there were confrontations between Chinese laundrymen and white women who objected to the competition. The Chinese were largely pushed into the laundry business in the United States, primarily in the American West, according to the sociologist Paul C. P. Siu, who studied the origins of the Chinese laundry here. Siu noted that the initial scarcity of women on the frontier to perform the traditional chores associated with women—cooking and cleaning—led to the rise of the Chinese laundry. "These men were not laundrymen in China, and their usual occupation in China had nothing in common with laundry work. The majority of them were farmers and farm hands," Siu noted in *The Chinese Laundryman*. "The lack of women in the community created the great demand for household and personal services such as laundry work, cooking, hotel and restaurant keeping."

The Annals of San Francisco also made early note of a particular social phenomenon, the development of a "Little China" almost anywhere the Chinese settled. Indeed, that was much remarked upon by observers at the time. There would not be a city or town of any size in the American West—from San Francisco to Denver to places as lonesome as Winnemucca, Nevada, or the Comstock Lode boomtown, Virginia City—that would not boast a Chinatown.

San Francisco's Chinatown, where most Chinese who arrived after the Gold Rush congregated if they did not head for the mining country, was a nine-block labyrinth, a poorly lit maze of alleys and cellars brimming with life, good and bad, a world that seemed to outsiders both dazzling and depraved. Overwrought eyewitnesses, none of whom were Chinese, described the district chiefly as a realm of sin, a sewer of vice and corruption. For a girl like Polly Bemis, sold into slavery in China, it would have been the first stop in this strange and barbarous new country—and likely the last if she was unlucky.

"San Francisco's Old Chinatown was symbolical of the Far East," one popular chronicler, Alexander McLeod, observed. "Its tales of mystery, intrigue, plots and counterplots are legion." McLeod, whose highly romantic *Pigtails and Gold Dust* celebrated the intrigue of the place, found Chinatown "a picturesque stage for human drama, smuggling, blackmailing, and every high adventure." It was also, indisputably, McLeod pointed out, "the gateway through which poured a strange, mysterious, yellow-horde direct from the Orient during the gold rush days, and it was the end of the rainbow for thousands of Chinese Argonauts."

Benjamin E. Lloyd, the liveliest chronicler of Chinatown, described the quarter as depravity itself "mantled in dismal gloom." It was filled with opium dens, gambling parlors (Lloyd guessed that there were at least 150 gambling parlors), and brothels, and it was populated by slave girls, terrifying professional assassins called "hatchet men," and Chinese gangsters whom whites referred to as "highbinders."

The denizens of Chinatown, especially at night, were otherworldly. "Were it not for the sounds of life that strike the ear," Lloyd wrote, after a midnight stroll, "the imagination could easily transform these moving figures into the phantom host that watches and waits about the portals of hell, and the smoke and vapor that here rise, into the smoke of torment that ascends forever and forever from the fervid fires of that baleful region."

The district represented wickedness in every imaginable form. But it was also home to thousands of hardworking Chinese—neither hatchet men nor highbinders—who huddled together there for companionship and protection.

Chinatown was a city within a city, and home to the largest concentration of Chinese outside their homeland. Not an inch of space in this maze was wasted by the people, who lived virtually on top of one another in basements, cellars, dormitories, porches, lofts, garrets, and courts, Lloyd noted. Five or six people might be crammed into a room eight by ten feet. They even slept in shifts so that no bed would go to waste. The district's narrow streets were crowded, smoky, noisy, and dirty and were lined with brick and wooden tenements—fetid firetraps— overflowing with humanity the year Polly Bemis came into the seaport.

Cobblers and cigar makers did business in holes in the wall not much larger than a packing crate. Apothecaries sold exotic medicines, and other shops offered foodstuffs unknown to westerners. The butcher shops stunned visitors; nothing went to waste. The sidewalks were crammed with vendors peddling strange wares and Chinese delicacies. "The sidewalks are monopolized by them," Lloyd wrote, "with their little tables of fruits, nuts, and cigars; the cobbler, tinner, chair-mender, and jack-of-all-trades, claim, by squatters rights, a seat upon a box or a door-sill, where to ply their trades; the alleys, lanes, and by-ways give forth dense clouds of smoke from the open fires, where cooking is performed, and the house-tops are white with drying garments, fluttering from the net-work of clothes-lines that are placed thereon by enterprising laundrymen."

The smells—including burning opium—repulsed white Americans who came to gawk at this exotic and forbidden place. And the noise was overwhelming—firecrackers and other Chinese explosives were often set off, and well into the night the air rang with the sound of squeaking Chinese fiddles and kettledrums. Chinese holidays were ever wilder, Lloyd added.

"All this terrible racket of drums, gongs, bombs, and fire-crackers, is made for a purpose," Lloyd told his readers. The Chinese were fiercely superstitious and "this uproar is created therefore to frighten away from earth all bad spirits that may have gathered about during the past year."

Chinatown existed side by side with the booming metropolis of San Francisco, Lloyd observed, noting that "it is but a step from the monuments and living evidences of the highest type of American civilization, and of Christianity, to the unhallowed precincts of a heathen race, where unmistakable signs of a contrasting civilization are seen on every side."

Although Lloyd was fascinated with the demimonde, he found the Chinese "industrious and enterprising" and was impressed with their work habits. They were dependable laborers who showed up on time and got a job done. They could be relied on, Lloyd told his readers. They were frugal, shrewd, and hardworking. They paid their taxes and license fees on time. They made excellent house servants and cooks and were skilled at laundry, too.

Lloyd, who was among the first to assess the immense impact the Chinese were having on San Francisco and California, believed firmly that they contributed significantly to the state's prosperity despite their "heathenness":

Thirty years ago, San Francisco was a hamlet with scare a breeze of life in it. Thirty years ago, the State of California was a wilderness overrun by wild animals, and no less wild humans. It was an almost unheard of country. View the contrast. To-day San Francisco is a veritable metropolis; a city than which there is no other more prosperous, none with more comparative greatness, and none with a brighter future prospect, in the world. Why the progress of San Francisco, and State of California, in these three decades, is almost equal to the advance of other cities and countries during the years of a century!

Whatever alarmed Lloyd about the underside of Chinese life paled when he considered the contribution they had made in Golden Mountain: "We cannot see that the presence of the Chinese among us, in the past, has resulted in evil, but the benefits they have wrought are seen on every hand."

Common laborers made up the bulk of the Chinese population, but there was also an upper class, mostly wealthy merchants and shopkeepers who provided the goods and services needed by their poorer countrymen and also acted in many cases as labor brokers for the Chinese workers who were coming off ships from the Pearl River delta.

"There is a considerable number of respectable and wealthy Chinese merchants and shopkeepers in San Francisco, who have extensive business premises in Sacramento Street and in various other parts of the city. There merchandise, as might be expected, is chiefly the goods of their own country," the authors of the annals noted.

The annals described the Chinese upper class as "a credit to any community." "They are polite, shrewd, and learned gentlemen; and are sometimes generous. They can either talk the English language pretty fluently themselves, or by means of an interpreter can conduct any business transaction or private conversation." But the vast majority of Chinese were described in *The Annals of San Francisco* as "of a very inferior description," working as common laborers, laundrymen, and porters.

"The Chinese were generally carpenters, laborers, and keepers of rude shops and eating houses," William McCollum observed in the summer of 1849. "They were not, I should judge, your real 'celestials,' but a kind of half way 'outside barbarians,' who acquired a little knowledge of the world, by dwelling in the commercial marts of China. The shopkeepers were as keen as if they had taken lessons in our own Puritan, overreaching New England; and although the cooking in their eating houses, was generally of a strange hash medley, I saw no 'chop sticks'—no mourners of the canine species, for their martyred companions, no veritable rat tails in their soups."

Every Argonaut, it seems, had something to say about the Chinese. Albert Benard de Russailh, a French traveler who sailed from Le Havre in 1850 and arrived in San Francisco after six months at sea, offered this description of the Chinese in his journal:

There are many Chinese in California, and great bands are arriving every day. They come here with merchandise from their own country, sell it off without much difficulty, and thus pay their passage, and make enough money to go up to the mines. The city is filled with Chinese goods, which are usually sold cheaply, but which occasionally bring high prices.

The diary of his trip to California, published later, made special mention of the Chinese as not planning to stay in the United States:

As they are very saving and able to live on rice and tea, it does not take them long to gather together a few hundred dollars with which they return to China and live quite comfortably. They wisely limit their ambition; when the required sum has been horded up, they go home and lead lives of rest and comparative luxury; for they understand the value of the golden mean.

The *Daily Alta California*, the principal newspaper of San Francisco in the early days, observed in 1852 that reports of the gold strike had brought large numbers of Chinese to California and more were expected. In an uncharacteristic burst of optimism and good fellowship, the newspaper predicted that "the China boys will yet vote at the same polls, study at the same schools and bow at the same altar as our own countrymen." The newspaper plainly expected the Chinese to assimilate or at least hoped they would.

A celebrated example of the early acceptance of the Chinese, when they were a tiny minority, was the funeral ceremony in San Francisco in 1850 to mark the death of President Zachary Taylor. The "China boys"—as they were called—were given a place of honor in the procession and their presence in the city was viewed favorably. A frequently quoted thank-you note written by leaders of the Chinese community read:

Sir: The "China boys" wish to thank you for the kind mark of attention bestowed on them in extending to them an invitation to join with the citizens of San Francisco in doing honor to the memory of the late President Zachary Taylor. The "China boys" feel proud of the distinction you have shown them, and will always endeavor to merit your good opinion and the good opinion of the citizens of their adopted country. . . . Strangers as they are among you, they kindly appreciate the many kindnesses received at your hands, and beg leave, with grateful hearts, to thank you.

Two years later, the Chinese were still well thought of in California. The outgoing governor, John McDougal, speaking at a public gathering, described the Chinese as "one of the most worthy classes of our newly adopted citizens—to whom the climate and character of these lands are peculiarly suited."

It was easy for California to feel fond of the Chinese when they were few in number and were thought to be visiting only briefly, but that would soon change. In the spring of 1851, the *Daily Alta California* hailed the Chinese as "amongst the most industrious, quiet and patient people among us. . . . They seem to live under our laws as if born and bred under them." Two years later the newspaper declared, "The Chinese are morally a far worse class to have among us than the Negro. . . . They are not the kind that Americans can ever associate or sympathize with. They are not our people and never will be."

America would long remain conflicted about the Chinese. Thirty years after the start of the Gold Rush, at the height of the anti-Chinese movement, even the fiercely bigoted author G. B. Densmore admitted that the presence of the Chinese was irrefutably part of American life: "It would be easier to enumerate the occupations in which the Chinese are not engaged than those in which they are. Their handiwork is seen everywhere. A man who should undertake to live, without directly or indirectly contributing to the employment of the Chinese, would have a hard time of it." In Densmore's time, the Chinese did everything from running restaurants to rolling cigars and picking strawberries, from canning fruit to washing shirts. Densmore offered his grudging admiration, noting, "He performs his work quietly, is cheerful and inoffensive."

Although some of the livelier chroniclers of San Francisco speak of a "deluge of yellow men" pouring into the city, the actual migration of the Chinese was always modest. The presence of the Chinese in the American West was greatly exaggerated. At no time did they pose a significant threat to the majority population, because for every wave of immigrants from China there was another wave of returnees who either had made a modest strike in Golden Mountain and gone home to enjoy it or had tired of the new land. There may have never been more than 150,000 Chinese in the American West at the height of Chinese immigration.

But census figures were highly dubious, for many Chinese declined to answer questions, naturally distrustful of a government that did not appear to have their best interests at heart and that often taxed them unfairly. Most spoke no English even after years in the United States. In addition, significant numbers of Chinese lived in remote areas that were not yet states and where census efforts were imperfect.

In 1880, at the high-water mark of the "Chinese Must Go" agitation, there were slightly more than 50 million people living in the United States, according to federal census figures. The Chinese at that time numbered a little more than 100,000 and accounted for about one-fifth of one percent of the total national population. More than 6.5 million black Americans were living in the country at the same time.

But despite the modest number of Chinese actually here, there was never a shortage of publications or writers critical of the Chinese. "The Chinese quarter is very filthy. . . . John Chinaman undoubtedly is the dirtiest neighbor one can have. Sanitary measures are with him a sealed book; and the filthy habits engendered in youth and matured in manhood, acquired in his own country, have been brought here to the land of his adoption," Densmore complained. Yet Densmore noted that although Chinatown was filthy, the Chinese bathed daily at the end of the workday and changed into clean clothing. He also credited the Chinese with being thrifty.

Like many another chronicler of the Chinese, Densmore plunged into Chinatown. Nearly thirty years after *The Annals of San Francisco* blasted Chinatown and the Chinese, Densmore repeated most of the same criticisms, finding the quarter a filthy, crowded, mysterious firetrap, and noting that "a stranger would readily imagine himself in China rather than America."

But the best eyewitness to record the mysteries of Chinatown and the "heathen Chinee" remains the largely sympathetic and peripatetic Benjamin E. Lloyd. Lloyd remains down the years as mysterious and impenetrable as the Chinatown that fascinated him. He was hard at work the year Polly Bemis entered the port. He loved the seedy underside of the city, and he wandered the streets, mostly at night, traveling alone or in the company of an off-duty police officer or an English-speaking Chinese who acted as a guide and interpreter. He was curious, indignant, outraged, fascinated, and childlike. He could scold. He was a social reformer of a sort, but nothing was too strange for him. He vanished after his one book.

Lights and Shades in San Francisco contains some of the most vivid and detailed descriptions of the Chinese. Everything interested Lloyd.

He tells his readers that the typical Chinese worker wore durable clothing made from light blue cotton denim—similar to overalls but with the pants more fully cut. The shoes were made of cloth with leather or cork soles (although Chinese workers in the mining districts always bought boots and bought them in large sizes, too—this was often remarked upon). Those who were working outside wore a "Chinese umbrella hat" or a conical hat made of bamboo or rushes. The outer garments were made of similar materials and were shapeless and loose-fitting.

The Chinese lived frugally on rice, fish, pork, and whatever vegetables were easily obtained, Lloyd noted. He found the Chinese crude but successful agriculturalists. He admired their cuisine (though he found it strange). "There are no people in the world that enjoy eating more, or understand the art of preparing so great a variety of dishes, as the Chinese," he observed. He found them clannish. But he did not dismiss the things he did not understand, and his account is brimming with admiration for the Chinese.

In the mid-1870s, a coolie in California could live on $75 to $100 a year. Lloyd believed that most Chinese workers spent about $200 a year if they were not trying to save money. These Chinese worked for less because they had no familial obligations:

> If every "Chinaman" had a family to support he would have to demand for his services a price nearer to that white laborers are compelled to ask, and therefore he would not be such a formidable competitor to meet. But in the whole Chinese population of the Pacific Coast States of America there are probably not more than three hundred men who have families.

Lloyd found the Chinese to be "skillful in handicraft. Their woven fabrics of silk, satin and gauzes; their beautiful embroidery, delicate filigree work in gold and silver; their elaborate engraving on wood and stone, and carvings on ivory; their celebrated pottery and their brilliant colorings, are wonderfully wrought, and cannot but be admired."

He found them avid readers: "The Chinese as a class are great readers. The educated, in particular, are very studious—improving all their leisure time by reading standard Chinese works." Alas, Lloyd informed his readers, "What they read, is difficult to learn." Lloyd knew no Chinese; nor, it appears, did he have many connections with members of the Chinese community.

However, there was one source of information for Lloyd among the Chinese: Fung Afoo, "a Christianized Chinaman, who speaks, writes and reads English well, and who is very intelligent withal." Fung Afoo was the translator for the *Tong Fan Goon Po*—or *The Oriental*—a weekly newspaper published briefly for the Chinese in California by William Speer, the medical missionary who had served in China and returned to open a mission to the Chinese in San Francisco. With some 700 regular subscribers—at a rate of five dollars a year—the paper reported on news from China as well as American events that might have been of interest to the Chinese. The newspaper was heavily Christian in its editorial slant. In the tradition of the immigrant press, such as New York's *Jewish Daily Forward, The Oriental* also went to some lengths to explain American customs and laws to the immigrant. Fung Afoo had left China as a child and had traveled extensively in the United States, according to Lloyd, who noted: "He is perhaps as thoroughly Americanized as a 'Chinaman' can be—dressing in the American costume and conforming to many of our customs."

Lloyd often mentions signs, notices, and other bits of Chinese writing in his accounts of Chinatown, and it is probable that Fung Afoo served as his translator.

In addition to his detailed account of Chinese daily life, Lloyd was most fascinated by the city's underworld, and there was no shortage of oddities to attract his attention. He wrote about "night workers" ("for some must work while others sleep") and he wrote about "hoodlums"— he called them "ruffian[s] in embryo." He had observations on quack medicine and methods of suicide popular at the time (pistols were favored; they were easily obtained). He was fascinated with insanity and its causes, street preachers and styles of preaching, confidence games, and the city's newspapers. Earthquakes, quacks and quackery, Turkish baths, and divorce all interested him. He loved slang and "street echoes," the shouts heard in the street. He wrote about newsboys; collectors of rags, sacks, and bottles; tinkers who sharpened razors; tin menders. He also wrote about the rich and matters of commerce. But Lloyd loved the wild side of life. He specialized in what he called "the last stages of human degradation."

The remnants of the infamous Barbary Coast, which Lloyd called "a stagnant pool of human immorality," fascinated him, for it was even in his day the home of the criminal elements in the city, an area where they could escape what little law there was. In the days of the Gold Rush, going to the Barbary Coast meant taking one's life in one's hands, for "villains of every nationality held high carnival there," he recalled.

Lloyd's observations and knowledge of the demimonde remain some of the most frequently quoted and most vivid accounts of the city:

> Barbary Coast is the haunt of the low and vile of every kind. The petty thief, the house burglar, the tramp, the whoremonger, lewd women, cut-throats and murderers, all are found there. Dance-houses and concert saloons, where bleary-eyed men and faded women drink vile liquor, smoke offensive tobacco, engage in vulgar conduct, sing obscene songs, and say and do everything to heap upon themselves more degradation, unrest and misery, are numerous. Low gambling houses thronged with riot-loving rowdies in all stages of intoxication are there. Opium dens where heathen Chinese and God-forsaken women and men are sprawled in miscellaneous confusion, disgustingly drowsy, or completely overcome by inhaling the vapors of the nauseous narcotic are there. Licentiousness, debauchery, pollution, loathsome disease, insanity from dissipation, misery, poverty, wealth, profanity, blasphemy and death, are there. And Hell, yawning to receive the putrid mass, is also there.

Lloyd seems at times startled by his own descriptions, pausing at one point in the tale of the city to note: "We do not wish to say, or even imply, that San Francisco is the wickedest and most immoral city in the world; that her men are all libertines and her women are all fallen; that she has no noble sons and pure daughters."

Lloyd also understood the impact that the Chinese were having on the country and, unlike many of his contemporaries, he thought the presence of the Chinese a good thing. He did not believe that they endangered white workers' jobs but he did believe the Chinese must make a greater effort to assimilate. For a humble clerk, Lloyd displayed a remarkable understanding of the effects of Chinese immigration:

> Who knows, but that this opening up of the Chinese Empire, and pouring its hordes of queer inhabitants upon the surrounding nations, is but a part of the unwritten and mysterious history of the destiny of nations, that cannot be averted—another of the strange things that were to happen in the nineteenth century, the purpose of which will be revealed only in the future! Indeed, it is a mysterious power that controls the destiny of the world, whose sceptered hand is not seen except in the ages that are past.

Lloyd's *Lights and Shades in San Francisco* had the distinction of being almost completely ignored. The book was not reviewed. It was out of print for more than a century. But it was a shrewd and complex view of San Francisco and the Chinese that was far ahead of its time.

"Tremendous wealth and poverty existed side-by-side . . . but beneath the gold and marble veneer seethed another world populated by abused workers, exploited Chinese, alcoholics, gamblers, prostitutes, cutthroats, pettifoggers, and charlatans," Lloyd wrote.

Indeed, he could be immensely compassionate about the plight of the Chinese: "The hoodlum is the sworn enemy of the 'Chinamen.' Striking them down with their fists, jerking their queues, belaboring them with clubs and hurling cobble-stones at them, is their most favorite pastime," he observed. Gangs of hoodlums, Lloyd observed, roamed the streets waylaying drunks, savagely beating lone Chinese, assaulting women who were unescorted, and even mugging respectable citizens who were out late or traveling alone.

Lloyd was especially sympathetic in his assessment of the fate of Chinese women like Polly Bemis—virtually all of whom, he believed, had been brought to work as prostitutes.

"The most disastrous effects of this traffic in human flesh and blood [are] seen in the Chinese 'quarter' of San Francisco—in the Chinese houses of prostitution," Lloyd told his readers. "These women are purchased upon order in China, and brought to this country like so many cases of tea. After they are here, they are sold to the highest bidder—some being purchased by rich Chinamen, who maintain private harems —but most of them going into the custody of the proprietors of houses of ill-fame."

For all of his confusion and wonderment at the Chinese presence in San Francisco, one thing can be said about Lloyd—he understood all too well the fate of the women he saw coming off the ships from China.

Chinese prostitute looking down.
Photograph by Arnold Genthe.
Courtesy of the Library of Congress, Prints & Photographs Division, LC-USZ62-13459.

Three

SOLD

The debasement of women is a principle that appears to dominate all Chinese society. . . . Some writers have estimated that one-tenth of the women of China are sold as slaves.

JAMES A. WHITNEY, LLD
THE CHINESE AND THE CHINESE QUESTION (1888)

In China in 1853, when Polly Bemis was born, a female child was nearly worthless. A girl was just another mouth to feed; nineteenth-century commentators often noted that Chinese peasants commonly believed women did not have souls. Many females perished as infants, drowned or suffocated soon after birth. The streets of Chinese cities were often littered with abandoned babies. James A. Whitney, a lawyer regarded as an authority on the Chinese in the late nineteenth century, and author of *The Chinese and the Chinese Question,* estimated that 9,000 baby girls died every year in Peking, and no fewer than 30,000 across the country.

Those who survived were viewed as being placed on earth to serve men, and their lives revolved around drudgery. Few had any education or could read or write. Marriage was a matter of commerce, the best deal to be made. Men often had more than one wife, depending entirely on how many wives they could support.

Regarding the Chinese woman, Alexander McLeod noted, "The amusements and pleasures of her age were never permitted and were unknown to her. . . . Her whole education consisted in learning how to use her needle."

Life was hard for most women in this culture, even rich women, whose bound feet were a physical manifestation of their bound world. The formal Chinese patriarchal family system discouraged or even forbade "decent" women from traveling abroad; going to California, which was considered a barbaric place, was inconceivable. Writing in 1869, the Reverend A. W. Loomis noted that almost no Chinese emigrant—regardless of social standing—brought his wife with him to California (and this was two decades after the Gold Rush began). Loomis, who was sympathetic toward the Chinese, pointed out that Chinese custom required wives to remain home and that the Chinese did not think it was safe to bring their womenfolk to the United States. Increasing anti-Chinese sentiment reinforced this belief.

Most Chinese women living on the Pacific Slope after gold was discovered were prostitutes, with the occasional exception of the wife of a wealthy Chinese merchant. Even women who were not prostitutes might have been living as concubines, sexually submissive mistresses—a subtle distinction, but a form of sexual slavery nonetheless. Writing in 1870, two years before Polly Bemis arrived, William Speer estimated that there were about 8,000 Chinese women in California and that nearly all of them were prostitutes. Speer, who spoke Chinese, later opened a mission to the Chinese in San Francisco, where he had a medical dispensary for prostitutes. Here he saw firsthand the horrors of the sex slave trade:

> These women have been bought from their parents, guardians or owners at sums varying from thirty to two-hundred dollars each, according to their age, personal appearance and accomplishments.
>
> The majority of these poor women lead a dreadful life. . . . The diseases which are the consequence of their depraved life are too terrible to describe. Young and pretty girls presented masses of putrid and poisonous rottenness. And yet the haunts where they were found were partly supported by the money of profligate Americans.

It is possible that few women resented this fate. Women sold as prostitutes had been treated as merchandise in China and apparently believed this was necessary for their families to survive. Polly Bemis, in her occasional interviews as an old woman, never expressed any resentment or anger about her fate. Her life seemed perfectly natural to her. Her explanation of how she happened to be living in the remote Idaho mining country, a rare survivor of the sex slave trade, was matter-of-fact. It is quite possible that she thought nothing of it.

The prices paid for prostitutes in the San Francisco market varied with the age and quality of the "merchandise" and depended, of course, on supply and demand Herbert Asbury noted. Younger, stronger girls were preferred, but their price would drop if they were scarred by small-pox. Before the passage of the Chinese Exclusion Act of 1882, which suspended immigration from China, the prettiest Chinese girls could be purchased for a few hundred dollars each. But by 1870, when their importation was outlawed, it became difficult to smuggle them into the country and prices rose enormously.

During the early 1890s, prices ranged from about $100 for a one-year-old to $1,200 for a girl of fourteen, which was considered the best age for prostitution. Girls of six to ten brought $200 to $800. They would often work as house servants or grow up in a brothel before being forced to sell their bodies. By the end of the nineteenth century, when it became even more difficult to traffic in sex slaves, girls of twelve to fifteen sometimes sold for as high as $2,500 each.

The record price was probably $2,800 in gold (the equivalent of about $75,000 today), paid by Charley Hung and Dah Pa Tsin for a fourteen-year-old girl in 1898, according to one historian of the San Francisco underworld, Herbert Asbury. At whatever price a sale was made, the transaction was completed in regular form, and the purchaser received a bill of sale in which the girl was usually mentioned in a list of other commodities, which may or may not have changed hands. A typical document of this sort, concerning a nine-year-old girl, came into the hands of the Salvation Army in 1898 and was published in the *San Francisco Call*:

Bill of Sale
Loo Wong to Loo Chee

April 16—Rice, six mats, at $2 .... $12
April 18—Shrimps, 50 lbs., at 10c $5
April 20—Girl $250
April 21—Salt fish, 60 lbs., at 10c $6

$273

Received payment,
Loo Chee
May 1, 1898

The sex slave trade was a business, of course, so it made sense to keep records of the property transactions. The girl purchased for $250, along with rice, fish, and shrimp, was just one of the thousands of Chinese girls and women sold into bondage in the United States over half a century. Imported by the tongs, secret societies that specialized in criminal activity, these girls and young women came from cities and villages across China. What they had in common was desperation.

Being sold in China was the usual way for a girl or young woman to reach California and a life of prostitution. The story of how Polly Bemis came to be living in the Idaho high country in the 1920s was completely plausible. She was a rare survivor of a system that brought countless Chinese girls and women to the American West after the Gold Rush. There were many like her—"daughters of joy" or "one hundred men's wives," as the Cantonese called them—who had been bought or kidnapped in China and shipped as prostitutes to America.

Chinese peasants may not always have realized what fate awaited their daughters. Many believed they had sold their children as brides or as secondary wives for Chinese men in America, or else as *mooi-tsai* (indentured domestic servants), according to the historian Benson Tong. The *mooi-tsai*—a Cantonese term meaning "little sister"—worked as domestic servants in San Francisco while young but were frequently sold into prostitution when they became older.

Long after blacks were freed in the United States, practices involving Chinese women were tolerated in California and elsewhere in the America West that were, in essence, bondage. "It was generally supposed that slavery was abolished in the United States during the administration of Abraham Lincoln," Alexander McLeod noted. "Yet there existed for years, on the Pacific Coast, a slavery so vile and debasing that all the horrors of American Negro slavery did not begin to compare with it."

Like the black slaves who came from Africa, the Chinese women were victims not just of white foreigners but also, of their own kin and countrymen. The buyers of girls and young women who would be sold as prostitutes in San Francisco were sent into the countryside on the instructions of brothel owners in California. When there was a demand for prostitutes, the procurers—nicknamed "white ants"—went out from the port cities of Canton and Hong Kong that had been opened to the West following the Opium War. The slave brokers plied their vocation openly and with the full sanction of the Chinese government.

"When the agents did not find enough females to fill their orders, they sent subagents into rural districts to lure or kidnap girls and young women and forward the victims to them at the shipping ports," Lucy Cheng Hirata has noted. "Quite frequently those individuals who did the luring were returned emigrants from that community. The baits used included promises of gold, marriage, jobs, or education. Sometimes the victims were invited to see the big American steamer anchored at the docks, and while they were enjoying the tour, the boat would sail off to San Francisco. More often, kidnapping was carried out by force, and the victims were sometimes daughters of relatively well-off families."

In China, slavery touched both high and low households. A wealthy Chinese family might have twenty to thirty Chinese slaves, McLeod noted. Even the poor often had a slave. During times of hardship, peasants routinely sold girls—often the youngest child—to the highest bidder.

"One remunerative solution for relieving a family of its female members was prostitution: the family did not have to provide for the girl's upkeep and her sale or part of her earnings could help support the family. In times of natural disaster and war, families often resorted to infanticide, abandonment, mortgaging, or selling of children," Lucy Cheng Hirata writes. In the early 1860s, for example, the purchase price in China ranged on average from $50 to $100. But the market became so saturated in the decade after the Gold Rush, and peasants on the brink of starvation were so desperate, that the price in Canton dropped for a while to five dollars a girl, Alexander McLeod reported.

Whatever price she fetched in China, a girl would be worth ten, twenty, or even thirty times as much in Golden Mountain. The return on these investments was immediate and astronomic when compared with other options for making money. Only gambling and opium, the other chief vices of the Chinese in the American West, were as lucrative.

Prostitutes' entry into the United States began with a succession of humiliations. After arriving by ship in the port of San Francisco, they were searched "in no delicate manner" by customs officers, McLeod tells us. Then they were taken to "barracoons"—large holding pens—to await inspection and sale. Slave dealers operated a barracoon and salesroom in a basement on Dupont Street where between fifty and a hundred Chinese women were held at any given time. Such locations were chosen to offer safety "from the prying eyes of white men, and particularly of the white women who operated the Chinatown missions, and waged unceasing warfare against the slavers," Herbert Asbury wrote.

Then the girls and women, who were overseen by "sallow old hags in black costumes with bunches of keys in the girdles of their waists," according to Asbury, were sold at regular auctions, not dissimilar to those involving livestock. There was always a ready market for pretty young girls among the wealthy Chinese merchants along the Pacific coast, and there were always "special orders" for prosperous tradesmen, too. "A very considerable portion were sent into the interior of the state under charge of special agents, in answer to the demands from well-to-do Chinese miners and successful vegetable producers who wanted an extra wife or two," McLeod noted in *Pigtails and Gold Dust.* Polly Bemis was such a special order. She was not destined for auction but instead shipped into the backcountry of the Idaho Territory.

"When the sale began the girls were brought in one at a time to the auction platform. There they were stripped, punched, and prodded, and in most cases examined by Chinese physicians to be certain they were sound in wind and limb," McLeod recalled, adding, "Bids would fall thick and fast if the chattel were pretty and attractive."

Wealthy Chinese merchants and businessmen bought the best of these girls as mistresses and concubines. Some girls were sold to higher-class brothels; the less attractive prostitutes were sent to the so-called cribs. A crib was, as Asbury noted, "exactly what its name implies—a small, one-story shack some twelve feet wide and fourteen feet deep, divided into two small rooms by heavy curtains of coarse material."

The transactions stipulated that when a girl was sold, the price—in gold—be placed in her hands and then immediately given to whoever had sold her. "This procedure was to comply with the wording of the contract which she then signed stating that she had received money in her own hands, and that in return she had agreed to serve her master for a certain number of years," according to McLeod.

The economics of what was called the "slave girl" trade was simple. In addition to the purchase price, it cost between $50 and $150 for passage from China to San Francisco, depending on the level of accommodations. If a kidnapper snatched a girl, he collected a fee of about $185, according to Lucy Cheng Hirata. Bribes to Chinese and American officials did not exceed $100.

On arrival in San Francisco, the procurer could sell a girl for as much as $2,000—a substantial profit on a modest investment. Prostitutes could earn on average $290 per month and could be resold at a substantial profit if they were healthy and attractive. If a young woman was well maintained, her owner could easily net $5,000 profit in two years—an enormous return.

At a public hearing in San Francisco in 1892, one young Chinese woman who had been sold into sexual slavery offered this testimony about the financial transaction that determined her fate:

> I was kidnapped in China and brought over here (eighteen months ago). The man who kidnapped me sold me for four hundred dollars to a San Francisco slave-dealer, and he sold me for seventeen-hundred dollars. I have been a brothel slave ever since. I saw the money paid down and am telling the truth. I was deceived by the promise that I was going to marry a rich and good husband, or I should never have come here.

Her story was typical. "Prostitution is open and shameless in Chinatown," said the "Old Californian," the pen name for the author of *The Heathen Chinee, What He Looks Like and How He Lives, His Virtues, Vices, and Crimes.* The account was long on vices and crimes. Not many virtues were reported, and the accompanying illustrations of the Chinese were the sort popular at the time—grotesque caricatures with ratlike features and long queues down their backs. "These women are all bought for the loathsome trade they ply like so many cattle. . . . The unfortunates commence their careers in America as boughten mistresses of wealthy Chinamen. When their first master tires of them they are sold by him to another, and descend step by step till their last lover relegates them to the brothel. And after that? Look to the leper hospital," he wrote.

The Old Californian delighted in strange tales of the prostitution business and collected gruesome stories about sex slaves. One account involved a cagey elderly Chinese madam, Ah Leen, who had run a successful brothel in an alley off Washington Street in Chinatown. While back home in China on a visit, she purchased a girl, Chin Qui, whom she intended to import to San Francisco "on spec," as the account put it. The girl was very attractive and the price was $800: $400 down and $400 when she was delivered to the ship in Hong Kong harbor.

Ah Leen believed that she had made a good bargain and figured that she could sell the girl in San Francisco for $3,000. But en route to

California aboard the steamer *Peking*, Ah Leen realized that the girl was mentally disturbed.

"She had been duped. The prize she had purchased belonged in an imbecile asylum, not in a brothel," the Old Californian wrote.

The madam, however, found a way to recover from her misfortune. In San Francisco, Ah Leen promptly tricked a wealthy merchant who lived on Sacramento Street into buying the girl for $1,500 and nearly doubled her investment. The merchant, realizing his mistake but not wishing to lose face, decided to keep the girl. However, he found her behavior so strange that in the end he was glad to simply give her back to Ah Leen, who kept the sale money.

Ah Leen next took the girl to Sacramento, where there was a large and prosperous Chinese community, and sold her again—this time for $800 to an opium dealer, who on realizing that the girl was mad returned her to Ah Leen in exchange for $100.

The next trip into the countryside with the girl involved crossing the Sierra Nevada to Virginia City in Nevada, where again the girl was sold— following robust bidding—for $800. The Chinese miner who bought the girl returned her to Ah Leen within four days. Then, one of the earlier bidders on the girl, a wealthy storekeeper in Virginia City, acquired Chin Qui, unaware of what he was getting into. According to the Old Californian, "He already had a wife and when he took Chin Qui home found he might as well have purchased a wildcat. Chin Qui flew at the wife, tore her hair and made mince meat of her face. The house became a perfect bear-garden. The victim's rage knew no bounds at the manner in which he had been duped. Packing Chin Qui's clothes, he took her to San Francisco and delivered her to Ah Leen, who thus regained possession of her profitable purchase."

None of the unlucky buyers wished to make an issue out of the bad deal; they all feared loss of face, according to the Old Californian's account. However, news of the wild girl and her various purchasers became well known all over Chinatown, and Ah Leen realized that she could no longer sell her merchandise. Still, she had received $3,600— a profit of $2,800 over her initial investment—in less than six months.

The Old Californian writes, "So, one morning when the steamer was about to leave for China, a carriage drove on the wharf from which Ah Leen and her victim emerged. The plank was drawn, and the poor wretch left these shores, to probably find herself, on arrival in China, resold as an inmate of some Chinese bagnio. Such, in brief touches, is a picture of the social evils of Chinatown."

Many of the Old Californian's stories shed light on experiences that Polly Bemis may have had as a slave girl. Quoting the *San Francisco Chronicle* of the period, he recalled the testimony of a young Chinese woman the newspaper identified as Wong Ah Sing, who had recently appeared in police court during the trial of a Chinese man, Lee Chuen, charged with beating her.

Wong Ah Sing told the police court that she was twenty and that she had been sold into slavery at age ten in China, by her parents, for twenty dollars. Her purchaser, whom she called the "gray-haired lady," brought her and another girl of about the same age to San Francisco.

After a few months in San Francisco, she told the court, she was sold to a Dr. Li Po Tai for more than twenty dollars. After a few months of living with his family, the young woman said, she did something to displease one of his wives and was subsequently sold to another Chinese buyer for between thirty and forty dollars. This man, who kept a joss house, or temple, had her in his charge for several months. Then he gave her to a Chinese woman, a keeper of a house of ill fame, to settle a debt. From there she was taken to another house where she was sold to a man for $120. She was twelve years old at the time of that sale, and the man kept her as his wife for three years. Then he sold her to Lee Chuen for $160.

Wong Ah Sing testified that she had recently found out that Lee Chuen had tired of her and wanted a younger and prettier woman, and that he planned to sell her again to another Chinese man in rural California for $750. According to the testimony in police court, Lee Chuen had attempted to mutilate the girl when she objected to being sold. Mutilation, which normally involved disfiguring the face, would have resulted in her being reduced to domestic servitude or, even worse, sent to the infamous cribs, the tiny cubicles where Chinese prostitutes had sex with a constant stream of men for as little as twenty-five cents—and from which most prostitutes never emerged.

"I may as well state here, that this case was so far from uncommon that it excited only paragraphs of comment in most of the other San Francisco papers than the one I quote," the Old Californian noted.

Like many other writers at the time, he himself was fiercely anti-Chinese and an admirer of Denis Kearny, an Irish immigrant who was a celebrated labor agitator and the driving force behind the accelerating "Chinese Must Go" movement. But not all chroniclers of the plight of Chinese prostitutes were unsympathetic.

One of the most thoughtful was the eccentric historian of San Francisco's demimonde Benjamin E. Lloyd. Lloyd was both curious and concerned about the plight of these Chinese girls and women. "Not less than seven tenths of the Chinese women that come to California are imported to fill houses of prostitution. Some of them have led this life of shame in their native country, prostitution there not being looked upon as an infamous business, but followed by many as a legitimate avocation," Lloyd wrote in *Lights and Shades in San Francisco*.

On the other hand, he wrote, "Some (others) are sold into slavery for a term of years, by their parents or brothers, to obtain relief from pressing want. Those who purchase their services are aware that they are unprofitable in any other occupation, and, therefore, they must either accede to the desires of their masters or submit to most cruel personal abuse."

Lloyd was one of the first writers to explain the contract system under which most prostitutes were held in a kind of indenture, owing large sums of money to their owners. Most women came to San Francisco under a contractual arrangement of this kind, similar to the so-called contract labor system that involved coolies. The contract required them to perform prostitution services for a specified period of time. In theory, the prostitute could pay off her debt and get out of the business. In practice, few were ever able to do so.

"Most Chinese women, who could not read or write, could easily be duped into affixing their thumbprint to any document by the agent or party who was the beneficiary of the contract," according to Lucy Cheng Hirata.

Lloyd cites the following contract as typical:

For the consideration of $600 (or any sum agreed upon) paid into my hands this day, I, Ah Ho, promise to prostitute my body for the term of four (and any other number) years. If, in that time, I am sick one day, two weeks shall be added to my time; and, if more than one day, my term of prostitution shall continue an additional month. But if I run away, or escape from the custody of my keeper, then I am to be held as a slave for life.

(signed) "Ah Ho"

"Thus are the Chinese women of San Francisco kept in slavery for the most infamous purposes, brutally treated while in health, and if overtaken by sickness—which from the nature of the life they lead is sure to speedily come—are turned out upon the street, reviled by their countrymen, and find not relief except in a most agonizing death," Lloyd noted, holding out little hope for victims of the sex slave trade.

He added, "Sometimes a woman is reclaimed from these vile dens, and placed in a mission, or married to a Christianized 'Chinaman'; but her former master is full of resource, ingenious, and irrepressible, and sooner or later she is likely to be kidnapped and conveyed to a place of concealment, beyond the reach of her rescuers or the officers of the law, to continue in the disgraceful service."

The importation of sex slaves from China could never have functioned so smoothly, so efficiently, and for so long if bribery had not virtually been institutionalized in San Francisco in the years after the Gold Rush. Although prostitution would not be outlawed in California until 1914, there was growing concern about the importation of Chinese sex slaves, and this was increasingly restricted. The government began to crack down on the importation of "lewd or debauched women" by imposing closer scrutiny on emigrants both in Hong Kong and in San Francisco. This made it more expensive and complicated to import prostitutes.

But anything could be done if money changed hands. Bribes were factored into business transactions. They were simply an accepted way of doing business. Life was riddled with corruption at virtually every level, and that included the immigration office and the police department.

The tainted system that brought Chinese women like Polly Bemis to America included an elaborate network of procurers, importers, brothel owners, and highbinders, as well as corrupt police officers.

Consular officials and customs agents were also willing to look the other way. Emigrant women who were being brought into the United States for "immoral purposes" were coached ahead of time as to what to tell customs agents. Some were claimed as "brides" by legal Chinese residents in California. This was a common way to get a prostitute into the country. If she was detained by customs and immigration, a Chinese man, a legal resident of the country, would show up to claim her as his "wife." The young women were then released. Other girls and women were smuggled into the country in padded shipping crates or in secret chambers on ships.

The authorities, did, however, make some efforts to curb the sex slave trade. On July 12, 1864, the *Morning Call* reported an incident involving Captain William Y. Douglass and Officer Bernard Hagen, who boarded the ship *Clara Morse* on a Sunday morning when the vessel arrived in the port. Douglass and Hagen were a raiding party looking for contraband, and their visit to the *Clara Morse* yielded nineteen Chinese girls who had been stolen and brought from Hong Kong to San Francisco to be sold. Polly Bemis entered San Francisco on such a ship, although she escaped detection.

"They were a choice lot, and estimated to be worth from one hundred and fifty to four hundred dollars apiece in this market," the *Morning Call* told its readers:

> They are shut up for safe-keeping for the present, and we went and took a look at them yesterday; some of them are almost good-looking, and none of them are pitted with smallpox—a circumstance which we have observed is very rare among China women. There were even small children among them— one or two not two years old, perhaps, but the ages of the majority ranged from fourteen to twenty. We would suggest just here that the room where these unfortunates are confined is rather too close for good health—and besides, the most fresh air that blows on a "Chinaman," the better he smells.
>
> The heads of the various Chinese Companies here have entered into a combination to break up this importation of Chinese prostitutes, and they are countenanced and supported in their work by Chief Burke and Judge Shepheard. Now-days, before a ship gets her cables out, the Police board her, seize the girls and shut them up under guard, and they are sent back to China as soon as opportunity offers, at the expense of the Chinese Companies, who also send an agent along to hunt up the families from whom the poor creatures have been stolen, and restore to them their lost darlings again. Our Chinese fellow citizens seem to be acquiring a few good Christian instincts, at any rate.

The author of this account, a young journalist who worked for the intensely bigoted *Morning Call* for four months in 1864, was Mark Twain. He was still calling himself Sam Clemens then. Twain's arch editorial tone (apparent here) would eventually get him fired. The style is unmistakably his, although he did not sign the piece. He was the only reporter at the *Morning Call* that summer. In his posthumously published writing, especially the bilious *Mark Twain in Eruption,* he recalls his reporting days in San Francisco, leaving little doubt as to who chronicled the raid on the *Clara Morse*.

Alexander McLeod says that official attempts to clamp down on the Chinese trade in slave girls merely drove up the price of prostitutes. "Business was always open for those who wanted to purchase their wares," he said. "It did cause a rise in the woman's exchange. Girls that were originally sold for fifty dollars at Canton now brought a thousand dollars on the San Francisco market. Children purchased in China for five and ten dollars rose two hundred to eight hundred apiece."

The trade was controlled by the mysterious tongs, which would become a part of American folklore. In fact, these evolved out of Chinese secret societies like the Triad Society. They were essentially the Chinese equivalent of the Italian Mafia, and although they accounted for only a tiny percentage of the Chinese in the United States, they dominated all Chinese criminal activity. The organizations were "as distinctly American as Chop Suey" according to Eng Ying Gong and Bruce Grant, coauthors of *Tong War!*—a wildly romanticized account of the tongs in the United States published in 1930. (Other popular chroniclers also stress this.)

Tongs were essentially secret societies that protected the largely criminal interests and the lives of their members and allies, using violence when necessary and employing *boo how doy*—or hatchet men, professional killers who literally used hatchets. Popular accounts of the Chinese tongs—often written by American journalists aided by Chinese-Americans and purporting to tell the inside story—tended to emphasize the mystery, violence, and crime associated with tongs. The average Chinese-American was mild-mannered and hardworking, an inoffensive soul, so the account ran. But then there was the other side of Chinese life—the tongs, the hatchet men, a tiny, violent, mysterious subculture feared by the average Chinese and feared, too, by Americans.

One explanation for the development of the tongs was that Chinese immigrants did not feel the American judicial system would protect them. Grudges and grievances were settled privately. "The courts were not to be relied upon, but the vigilantes were, with their quick methods," noted the authors of *Tong Wars!*

Prostitution was a big business in the second half of the nineteenth century, so the tongs naturally got involved. The Hip Yee Tong, an organized criminal society that dominated sexual slavery, has been estimated to have imported some 6,000 prostitutes between 1852 and 1873—amounting to eighty-seven percent of the total of all the prostitutes brought into the country at that time. The trade in girls began about 1850, and by 1854 the Hip Yee Tong had imported 600 slave girls from China—a practice that would continue for the next two decades.

"The Hip-Yee Tong charged a $40 fee to each buyer, $10 of which were said to have gone to white policemen," Alexander McLeod reported. The traffic in Chinese females was so bustling by 1868 that the newspapers in San Francisco referred to it as the "importation of females in bulk," McLeod noted.

Despite the efforts of mainstream Chinese organizations such as the Six Companies—the Chinese benevolent societies that functioned as a sort of government in Chinatown—the criminal tongs that ran the prostitution business were not to be deterred. Americans, quick to be critical of the Chinese, generally confused mainstream Chinese activities—such as the workings of the Six Companies—with organized crime.

More than twenty years after Polly Bemis was smuggled into San Francisco, flesh traders posted public notices in Chinatown warning various Chinese businessmen and community leaders by name that they would be killed if they interfered with this lucrative business. "Your dying day is surely on hand," read one notice.

A few days later, the slave dealers posted other placards on billboards in Chinatown advising that twelve professional killers had been hired by the tongs to kill six members of the Chinese Society of English Education, which opposed the sex slave trade. Although no one was killed— perhaps because of increased security and police protection—the threats accomplished their purpose: law-abiding Chinese became reluctant to take on the tongs, as Herbert Asbury explained in *The Barbary Coast: An Informal History of the San Francisco Underworld.*

Prostitution flourished because of the enormous imbalance between men, both white and Chinese, and women in early California. Miners spoke of riding long distances to merely look at a woman. The disproportion was greatest among the immigrant Chinese, referred to as a "bachelor society"—men living far from home without women. When the Gold Rush began, and thousands of Chinese men streamed into San Francisco and headed out into the gold country, there were only a few Chinese women in all of California. And even thirty years later, in 1880, the ratio of Chinese men to women was roughly twenty to one. A decade earlier, 1,769 Chinese females over the age of fifteen were living in San Francisco—and 1,452 were prostitutes.

The fact that married or "decent" Chinese women were barred from traveling—and that there was a long and grueling ocean voyage between California and China—intensified the demand for women in the Chinese bachelor societies in the West. Even if working-class women had been able to leave China, they could not have found respectable work in California, because Chinese men performed domestic tasks for whites and ran restaurants and laundries. Traditional jobs that might have fallen to Chinese women under other circumstances were now closed to them. Scholars of the period note that the sex slave system may have, in some ways, strengthened Chinese society.

"The emigration of Chinese prostitutes helped to stabilize and preserve the family because Chinese emigrant males could thereby avoid liaisons which might lead to permanent relationships with foreign women," Hirata writes, and "the earnings of Chinese prostitutes in America helped to support their families in China. One such prostitute sent back as much as $200 or $300 after seven months in San Francisco."

As ninety percent of the early Chinese immigrants to the American West came from the Pearl River delta region, much of this money ended up there. Just as naturally, the women of these districts, which had been opened early to foreign trade, followed the men to California.

Some may have come willingly, but only a few—if any—of the Chinese women who came to San Francisco could have imagined what lay in store for them. Chinese prostitutes were rarely destined for the so-called parlor houses, the upscale brothels with clean linen, fine wines and whiskeys, and good furniture patronized by a better-off class of men who were always white. The prostitutes here, Herbert Asbury noted, were the "aristocracy of San Francisco's red-light district" who might earn as much as ten or twenty dollars for a brief encounter. Enterprising young women in these brothels might even strike out into business on their own or later become madams and manage parlor houses.

Most of the Chinese girls and young women were headed to the nightmarish cribs. Venereal disease was rampant there, and the customers were often violent. As many as six girls might work in a crib, standing at the doors or windows and calling out to passing customers, "China girl nice! You come inside, please?" For a prostitute, this was the absolute bottom of the business.

"These vocal enticements she varied with a more direct advertisement of her wares, a complete list of prices and services," Asbury reported. "Until the late hours of the night, in all the narrow, dirty by-ways of Chinatown, the plaintive voice of the Chinese crib girl could be heard crying in a shrill, monotone singsong: *Two bittee lookee, flo bittee feelee, six bittee doee!*"

Another eyewitness of the cribs was L. Vernon Briggs, a young medical student from Boston who was in San Francisco for a year in 1881, recovering from tuberculosis. Drawing on his late-night "tour" of Chinatown, he offered this scene to readers:

> The dens in which these unfortunates are kept in almost a state of captivity are situated in two or three of the connecting alleyways in the blocks bounded by Washington and Jackson streets. During the day the only signs of life are a few children playing in the filthy gutters, or an old woman or two discussing events with some of their countrymen who are connected with the houses as employees or proprietors.
>
> At night the scene changes; coal oil lamps shed an ill-smelling, sickly light through the tiny windows and doors, which are invariably protected by wire screens or iron bars. Each door is furnished with a sliding wicket a foot square, from which . . . protrudes the face of a gaudily painted damsel, whose rouged cheeks, blackened eyebrows, stiffly greased hair and vermilion lips present a curious contrast to the dingy boarding of the house and the hovel-like aspect of her surroundings. When the coast is clear of Caucasians the "cruiser on watch," as the women whose turn at the wicket it is are termed, displays her charms with shocking immodesty for the benefit of passing Mongolian Don Juans.

Women who wound up in the cribs, often at the end of their careers as prostitutes, were destined only to die, usually of venereal disease. In fact, diseased women and prostitutes from Canton and Hong Kong who had been "boat girls"—had sex with foreign sailors—were sent to the cribs immediately or sold as domestic help. "Chinese men generally felt that the most degrading thing a Chinese woman could do was to have sexual relations with a white man," Alexander McLeod recalled. Women who became sick or who broke down mentally or physically were doomed. They were dispatched to small, back-alley "hospitals" and left there alone to die, according to Herbert Asbury, one of many writing about the cribs who quoted this account from the *San Francisco Chronicle* in 1869:

The place is loathsome in the extreme. On one side is a shelf four feet wide and about a yard above the dirt floor, upon which there are two old rice mats. There is not the first suggestion of furniture in the room, no table, no chairs or stools, not any window. . . . When any of the unfortunate harlots is no longer useful and a Chinese physician passes his opinion that her disease is incurable, she is notified that she must die. . . . Led by night to this hole of a "hospital," she is forced within the door and made to lie down upon the shelf. A cup of water, another of boiled rice, and a little metal oil lamp are placed by her side. . . . Those who have immediate charge of the establishment know how long the oil should last and when the limit is reached they return to the "hospital," unbar the door and enter.

. . . Generally the woman is dead, either by starvation or by her own hands; but sometimes life is not extinct; the spark yet remains when the "doctors" enter; yet this makes little difference to them. They come for a corpse, and they never go away without it.

Writing in the *Overland Monthly* in 1869, the Reverend A. W. Loomis was horrified by the lives of Chinese prostitutes. Loomis quoted a public notice posted in the streets of San Francisco that had been translated from the Chinese for him. A man whose sister had been seized by Chinese bandits and sold into prostitution had put up the notice. He was pleading for her return.

After explaining how many of these girls and young women came to their fallen state, Loomis implored his readers to be sympathetic: "Therefore, reader, that shame-faced girl you sometimes see upon the street might be able to tell a story of her wrongs and sufferings which would moisten the eyes of those who seldom weep; and all of them deserve our pity."

Vegetable peddler in Idaho City, Idaho, late nineteenth/early twentieth century.
Denver Public Library; Western History Collection, X21518.

Four

◆

COMING INTO THE TERRITORY

The few Chinese women brought to this country being utterly
shameless and abandoned.
—AN OVERLAND JOURNEY FROM NEW YORK TO SAN FRANCISCO
IN THE SUMMER OF 1859 BY HORACE GREELEY

In the summer of 1872, as smallpox swept the countryside and the Blue
Mountains of Oregon burned with uncontainable wildfires, the girl who
would be known as Polly Bemis rode into the Idaho high country. She
came on the back of a saddle horse, freighted over the rivers and mountains along a trail impassable much of the year to the end-of-the-road
mining camp at Warrens, where a wealthy Chinese merchant had already
paid $2,500 in gold dust for her. Gold was the preferred currency. In those
days when Idaho was a territory, an ounce of gold was worth sixteen dollars. Polly, who never weighed more than 100 pounds, was worth a little
more than 154 pounds in gold dust that summer to the Chinese man who
had bought her sight unseen from a broker in San Francisco.

When she was a very old woman, Polly Bemis still remembered the
day she arrived at the end of the road—July 8, 1872. She got off the back
of the packhorse on the main street of Warrens—more accurately, a dirt
trail up through the mining camp. She dismounted in front of a saloon
owned by the man who had bought her. Some accounts say his name was
Hong King and some old-timers remembered him as "Big Jim." Then
someone said, "Here's Polly." She remembered that, too. "Here's Polly."

She told that story often. The man who greeted the girl from China—not by her real name but by the name that would stick—was Charlie Bemis, the Connecticut Yankee gambler who would eventually marry her.

It was a hot summer in the United States that year. Hundreds of people died in the eastern cities because of the heat, which simmered as the political conventions were going on. The Republicans met in Philadelphia and supported the incumbent, President Ulysses S. Grant, while the Democrats gathered in Baltimore and nominated Horace Greeley, the celebrated newspaper editor. Grant won. Greeley, who had done much to promote the lure of the American West and is perhaps as famous for that as anything else because of the advice often attributed to him, "Go west, young man," was exhausted by the campaign and died before the year was over. In rural Ohio, Zane Grey, who would go on to promote the lure of another American West with more than ninety novels, was born. There was smallpox in Oregon. In the backcountry, the Bannock Indians were still hostile, as many a party of miners moving into the territory still claimed by the tribe found out. The Blue Mountains around Walla Walla were on fire. There were bad fires all over the West in July and August, as usual. A rider into the territory could smell the faint smoke a long, long way off.

There were several ways to get to the high country in Idaho and several options to first reach Portland—the jumping-off point for the gold country. The steamers *Ajax* and *John L. Stevens* made regular runs to and from San Francisco. The Oakland and California Railroad came up from the Golden Gate, too—a trip of eleven hours and fifteen minutes. Many travelers still came overland. Some rode and some walked.

Many a sojourner came on foot, too, from San Francisco, more than 600 miles away. Two seventeen-year-old Chinese from a village in the Pearl River delta who survived in the Idaho high country for sixty years, panning the riverbeds for gold that just never came, told an interviewer in 1923 that they entered the United States in San Francisco and then came up the coast to Portland on a steamer. From there, they made their way into the mountains on foot, carrying everything they owned suspended from long bamboo poles and jogging or trotting about twenty miles a day. The West was full of such sojourners in those days, when the completion of the transcontinental railroad scattered thousands of Chinese laborers across the countryside.

Portland had the second-largest concentration of Chinese in the West then. From there, many Chinese headed to the Pacific Northwest mining districts, which included parts of the present states of Oregon, Washington, Idaho, and Montana.

The steamers from San Francisco moved up the Pacific coast and the Willamette River to Portland, a five-day trip. The arrival of the steamer was an event recalled by J. W. Hayes in a memoir published in 1911:

> "Steamer day" was a joyous occasion and the pomp and ceremony attending the arrival of the ocean steamer was not easily forgotten. A cannon was fired announcing its arrival and bulletins at the telegraph and newspaper offices gave out the exact time of departure from Astoria and its passing up at Oak Point, Kalama and St. Helens. A large crowd always met the incoming ocean steamer and the usual runners were out.

From Portland, the way inland was farther upriver. The Oregon Steam Navigation Company's boat for Lewiston, an important trading center on the frontier, left every Monday at five A.M. The trip on the river could take as long as a week and was tough and expensive.

In its heyday, the Oregon Steam Navigation Company operated six sternwheelers on the lower river and four on the middle river; navigation on the upper river was just beginning. Eventually, the company bought out the portage owners and replaced the mule-drawn cars and stagecoaches with narrow-gauge railroads to carry travelers around the stretches of rough water.

During the height of mining activity on the Clearwater River, east of Lewiston, the steamboat company provided fairly regular service from Portland to Lewiston. But after new gold strikes in the Boise Basin had lured miners south, and drained the region of much of its population, the steamers stopped coming.

Given the enormous sum for which Polly Bemis was sold, it is likely that she traveled upriver from Portland to Lewiston on the weekly steamer. From Lewiston, the staging area for all commercial ventures in the region, she would have climbed onto a horse and traveled by pack train to Warrens. About the time she arrived, the Chinese had begun to settle in the region, and there were many Chinese pack trains serving both the Chinese and the non-Chinese in the mining camps.

Lewiston—which tried briefly to be Idaho's capital, before losing to Boise—was the quintessential boomtown, described by one local chronicler as a mining town without mines. It was built at the confluence of the Snake and Clearwater rivers, on land stolen boldly from the Nez Perce Indians.

Joaquin Miller, who would be later best known as the "poet of the Sierras," spent some time in this country in the early 1860s, working as an agent for a Pony Express line. He recalled:

> Lewiston, built of boards and canvas, looking sickly and discouraged, stood shivering in the wind of October . . . and winced under volleys of pebbles that struck the sounding houses with such force you might have thought an unseen army was bombarding them. The town looked as if it had started down from the mountains above, ragged and discouraged, and, getting to where it then was, had sat down in the forks of the river to wait for the ferry. The town looked as if it ought to go on—as if it wanted to go on—as if it really would go on, if the wind kept blowing and the unseen army kept up the cannonade.

Early histories of the town noted that complaints about hogs running loose became so frequent that the city council outlawed swine on the streets but found it could not enforce the law. In the mid-1870s, loose horses and cattle were a common nuisance.

"Cattle of all kinds roam the streets, oft-times taking possession of the sidewalks to the exclusion of pedestrians," the *Lewiston Teller* noted, adding that "a cow treed several school girls on their way home to lunch." And on another occasion, the *Teller* told its readers: "An anxious inquirer asks whether upon meeting a cow on the sidewalk, it is proper to give her the inside or the outside of the walk?" As might be expected with so much livestock, the streets were full of raw sewage and sinkholes.

Henry Leland, writing in the *Lewiston Signal* of June 6, 1874, scolded: "What a horrible condition some of our leading streets are in—boots, shoes, tin cans, shavings, paper boxes, etc., etc., scattered about town in all directions. All these, together with loose gravel and rock, make the streets look very bad. And a few bits would employ a 'Chinaman' or two to make a decided improvement in the way of cleaning." The city council passed on using "Chinamen" and instead put city prisoners to work cleaning the streets.

The Chinese packers of Idaho County wintered in Lewiston on the Snake River, where the weather was mild and there was a sizable Chinatown. One of them, Ah Choy, had a pack train consisting of seventy-five horses, strong, sinewy cayuses, ideal for this grueling work. Ah Choy went into the packing business during the decade after Polly Bemis came into the country, but his operation was typical of the transportation needed for the mining camps to survive. It was on the back of one of these horses—perhaps a saddle horse, more accustomed than a packhorse to carrying a rider—that Polly Bemis made the last leg of her journey in July 1872.

The U.S. mail promised delivery along the whimsical, winding route of 170 miles from Lewiston to Warrens via Florence, in about three and a half days. The mail carrier, riding horseback, left Lewiston at six A.M. on Monday and was scheduled to reach Warrens at noon on Thursday. But pack trains took much longer to travel this distance. Well into the 1880s it took a pack train from Grangeville, the Idaho County seat, ten days to reach Warrens. Eventually a toll road would be established to allow wagon traffic, but in the early days this was it.

When the snow began to melt in the mountain passes in the spring, Ah Choy readied for his first seasonal trip into the interior, according to the historian Melvin Wikoff:

> Ah Choy personally supervised the loading. A crowd always gathered to observe this entertaining spectacle. Chattering Chinese attendants chase the frisky animals, attempting to throw the aparejos (a saddle designed to hold pack goods) onto their backs. The horses bucked and cavorted, providing excitement for the crowd and making loading a difficult task for the packers. When the train was ready to depart people lined the street to watch this popular English-speaking freighter begin his journey. He rode his bell horse and led his pack string down the main street of Lewiston. The crowd watched as he gave orders to his Chinese employees in his native tongue and listened to their verbose responses.

To pack a horse or a mule was not a one-man job. The animal often had to be blindfolded or hobbled (its feet tied together to keep it in one place). The pack was secured on a packing saddle with weight distributed equally on either side of the horse or mule to make the animal as comfortable as possible. The 300-pound load was secured with a diamond half hitch. With two men rounding up the horses or mules in the morning, an experienced packer could load this string quickly, often as soon as an animal was brought to him. Pack trains ranging from a few horses to several dozen strung together—tied head to tail to prevent bolting from the line or falling down steep slopes—moved from one grazing and water stop to another.

Anything could be packed into the backcountry for a price. Rates ranged from a few cents to as high as eighty cents a pound at Lewiston, depending on demand, travel conditions, and the materials involved. Mules carried seemingly unbelievable weights; items as large and as heavy as anvils and even pianos made the trip. A history of Lewiston's early days quoted a Mrs. Sarah Rowley, a pioneer of 1873, who recalled that another pioneer woman had come into the country on one side of a mule with her cookstove strapped to the other side.

The packing sheds along the Lewiston waterfront were the site of the town's first business district. Here hundreds of horses and mules were fed, harnessed, and loaded for the trails that led up to Florence, Warrens, and Dixie. In addition to the pack trains, the ferry business was highly lucrative here, for travelers inland had to first cross the river with all their equipment.

One of the most celebrated Chinese packers in Idaho County was called Pie Biter because of his taste for freshly baked pies, according to Wikoff. Described by historians as "a fat Chinese," he successfully ran a string of sixty or more cayuses to the various mining camps between 1878 and 1889, hauling merchandise into the high country from Lewiston.

"He was eminently popular with his countrymen and seldom left Lewiston without capacity loads," Wikoff notes. "In spite of Pie Biter's popularity, his claim to prominence was found in his insatiable appetite for pies and not in his skill as a packer. Lewiston had several bakeries at this time, but Pie Biter believed that Skookum's bakery produced the tastiest pies. When he was in town he had a standing order for at least twelve pies daily. Pie Biter was especially fond of huckleberry pie (when it was in season), Dutch apple, and lemon pie. He usually ordered four of each."

The *Lewiston Morning Tribune* told its readers that "when the pack train pulled out for the mines with Pie Biter on the bell horse, a wooden box hung from the side of the saddle. Therein the boss kept his sustenance of life—pies. When the train wended its way south of Snake River Avenue, thence over Normal Hill, Pie Biter would give orders to the others with his mouth full of pie, sputtering and laboring and sometimes giving vent to his feelings in Pidgin English. All the way on the long trip he munched pie, occasionally quaffing from a cask of Chinese whisky."

The *Lewiston Morning Tribune* also recalled that Pie Biter was capable of practical jokes at the expense of his fellow Chinese immigrants.

On one occasion he issued a decree in Lewiston's booming Chinatown, saying the emperor had ordered that work be stopped for a week or two. "While his competitors rested and heeded the manifesto, Pie Biter took over the freight business and won many new friends in the mining camps by giving them uninterrupted service," the newspaper noted.

There were as many as nearly two dozen registered Chinese packers in Idaho County in 1880—most running pack strings of twenty-five animals that included horses and mules. An old pioneer, Billy Williams, recalled packing as a boy for a Chinese freighter named Ah Kan who hauled freight to Warrens with a string of packhorses.

"He purchased chickens, eggs, and bacon from the farmers on Camas Prairie to take with him to the mines. About four dozen chickens, housed in coops of spruce, were taken each trip. The eggs were individually packed in boxes of oats to protect them from breakage," Williams recalled.

Williams was paid fifty cents a day for his labor while a fifteen-year-old friend was paid one dollar per day. The work included two meals. Descriptions of pack trains and overland travel at the time indicate that the travelers rose early—four A.M.—to eat breakfast and pack the train, which normally took two to three hours depending on the number of horses and mules involved. Billy Williams's trip from Mount Idaho to Warrens with the Chinese packer took three to four days.

The summer Polly Bemis arrived in Portland, the Chinese population in the state was on the rise. It would triple during the decade when she immigrated. In 1870, the census takers found 3,330 Chinese living in Oregon, but by 1880 there were 9,510. Census figures were always a bit dubious in the counting of "Chinamen," but those were the figures reported. The Chinese population in Oregon, and in neighboring Idaho, which was still a territory and did not become a state until 1890, was overwhelmingly male. These sojourners were working on the railroad, mining, doing common labor such as ditch digging and roadwork, running laundries and restaurants, or working as domestic help, cooks, and dishwashers. Most of the immigrants were in their late teens, twenties, or early thirties. In 1872, there were 460 Chinese residents of Portland, but nine times as many Chinese were scattered through the countryside. In some sections of the Idaho Territory, the Chinese outnumbered whites.

Although gold was first discovered in Oregon in 1852, placer mining—panning for gold—did not begin in the eastern part of the state on the Powder and John Day rivers until a decade later. Oregon had become a state in 1859, but its eastern part remained largely unsettled. Placer mining opened the country, bringing "Chinamen" to work in the mines and on the railroads. The completion of the transcontinental railroad in the late 1860s had thrown thousands of Chinese workers into the labor market, and agitation against them was fierce during the summer that Polly Bemis rode into the mining camp in Warrens.

In Oregon, much as in California, the attitude toward the Chinese was turning antagonistic. The Chinese were by law restricted or even prevented from owning property or working a mining claim, but they were (along with blacks and others) required to pay a state poll tax of five or six dollars (or work it off on public road construction). They could not vote, however, and they were generally persecuted.

"We observed, in squads, the ubiquitous 'Chinaman,' moving from mining locality to mining locality, fleeing from the kick of one and the cuffs of the other, with no fixed abiding place to be called his permanent home," observed Captain John Mullan while traveling through Oregon at the time.

Portland's Chinatown reflected what one chronicler called a "floating proletariat"—a highly mobile workforce that by necessity went where there was work. Much of the Chinese community left Portland in April for the mining country, returning in September. Most Chinese workers found employment through Chinese labor brokers based in Portland or through others in San Francisco or in the Pearl River delta in China.

David Newsom, a celebrated pioneer in Oregon and author of *The Western Observer,* had a lot to say about "the Chinamen." Newsom, who had made the overland trek on the Oregon Trail to the Willamette River Valley, had traveled 2,575 miles from his farm near Springfield, Illinois. The trip had cost him serious money—nearly a dollar a mile, he would later report. Although he was a farmer born and reared, Newsom was also a longtime contributor to America's newspapers, primarily the *Illinois Journal* of Springfield. Like many an eyewitness of the Chinese migration, Newsom was largely favorable in his observations about the "sojourners."

"The necessity of hiring 'Chinamen' at low rates—just what they ask—is forced upon us. And these Chinese will work every sort of labor we wish them to perform. And they will stick to their jobs! I have never seen a 'Chinaman' drunk, and I cannot say that of our white folks," Newsom reported back to his readers in Illinois.

He noted that Oregon's housewives preferred Chinese servants and cooks in their homes and kitchens: "Nearly all the cooking and drudgery in the hotels and boarding houses are done here by Chinese. 'Chinamen' are scattering out all over Western Oregon grubbing and clearing up the brush lands ready for the plow, at one-half the rates charged by whites—Chinese board themselves in all cases. We know this is a delicate question to discuss, and so was once the question of human slavery."

Newsom wondered what was to be done, noting that threats of violence were made regularly against the Chinese and whites who dared to hire them: "The popular voice is against hiring or trading with Chinese— When the popular voice in China is against Christianity and dealing with us, we do howl. If we set the Chinamen down as *all fools,* we miss the mark. For shrewdness, good laws, firm government, well-ordered police regulations, and rigid justice to offenders, they are ahead of us. Just as well treat the Chinese in our country, so will they treat our people in China." For a humble farmer Newsom shrewdly understood the hypocrisy of the issue. Americans complained bitterly if their merchants and missionaries were interfered with in China but failed to see that they were not offering courtesies and safeguards to the Chinese in the United States.

Newsom clearly disapproved of how Americans treated the Chinese:

They come here to labor and amass a little wealth, and then return to the Flowery Kingdom, and live in ease. To talk of mobbing them out of the country is preposterous. Our commerce and people are admitted to China as of the most favored nations of the earth. We have no more right to maltreat, murder or drive out the "Chinamen," than we have the Germans, Irish, Scotch, French, or English people. If the Chinese violate our laws, they are amenable to them, as our people are in China. Is it wrong or a violation of any law or treaty, for these people to immigrate to the United States and work at low rates, or sell their products here at under rates? And as to corruption in morals, they only follow out the promptings of human nature, not restrained by Divine grace. In our own high, favored Christian country, we find that lewd fellows commit every degree of crime known in history.

David Newsom was not the only sympathetic observer of the Chinese in the American West at that time. The very month that Polly Bemis passed through Portland, close readers of the *Oregonian* might have noticed a brief item in it. The public library in Portland had purchased two copies of a new book, an entertainment about the American West. It was already very popular in the rest of the country. Readers curious about the Chinese streaming off the ships that came upriver to Portland might have found something to interest them in its pages. The book that was all the rage that summer was Mark Twain's rollicking account of going west, *Roughing It,* and Mr. Twain had things to say about the Chinamen.

"They are a harmless race when white men either let them alone or treat them no worse than dogs; in fact they are almost entirely harmless anyhow, for they seldom think of resenting the vilest insults or the cruelest injuries," Twain observed in a tone that would reappear later in "A Pen Warmed Up in Hell."

Under the heading "A Humorous Book," the *Oregonian* noted:

> We have received from H. W. Cutter a copy of Mark Twain's new book. This production of the noted humorist goes under the title, *Roughing It.* It is a large book of nearly 600 pages, and is to be read for diversion. It is a funny record of personal experiences and humorous anecdotes. Those who desire the book can leave orders with Charles Holder, corner First and Washington Streets.

Included in what would become a classic of western travel writing were Twain's memories of the Chinese as he encountered them on the Pacific Slope—first in the Nevada mining country and then in San Francisco. His memoir was rooted in a trip he took in the summer of 1861 with his older brother, Orion, leaving from Saint Joseph, Missouri—a departure point well known to many travelers into the West—and crossing the countryside in a Concord coach in about three weeks. Twain's brother had secured a position as secretary to the territorial governor of Nevada, and Twain went along for the ride.

Written a decade later (he does not appear to have taken any notes), Twain's firsthand observations of the Chinese, made in the early 1860s in rough-and-tumble Virginia City, were full of irony and indignation. Having later seen even more of the Chinese and the abuse they suffered in San Francisco, Twain did not restrain his outrage, providing a rare voice in defense of the defenseless:

> They are quiet, peaceable, tractable, free from drunkenness, and they are as industrious as the day is long. A disorderly Chinaman is rare, and a lazy one

does not exist. So long as a Chinaman has strength to use his hands he needs no support from anybody; white men often complain of want of work, but a Chinaman offers no such complaint; he always manages to find something to do. He is a great convenience to everybody—even to the worst class of white men, for he bears the most of their sins, suffering fines for their petty thefts, imprisonment for their robberies, and death for their murders. Any white man can swear a Chinaman's life away in the courts, but no Chinaman can testify against a white man. Ours is the "land of the free"—nobody denies that—nobody challenges it. [Maybe it is because we won't let other people testify.]

Roughing It, in so far as it applied to celestials and sojourners, had competition that summer in the American West. Twain's book was critically and commercially popular, but its success was nothing compared with that of a comic poem sweeping the country. The poem had been written by Twain's old friend from his days on a newspaper in San Francisco Bret Harte. At the time, it is far more likely that Americans would have known this poem than Twain's musings on the Chinese. Harte's verse was originally titled "Plain Language from Truthful James" but, if we remember it at all, we remember it as many Americans did for decades, as "The Heathen Chinee." It was published in September 1870 in the *Overland Monthly,* the first serious literary journal in the American West and a showcase for the talents of Twain, Harte, Ambrose Bierce, and later Jack London. "The Heathen Chinee" was a bit of comic verse written by the celebrated chronicler of the California Gold Rush. It was slipped into the magazine on deadline to fill space:

> WHICH I wish to remark,
> And my language is plain,
> That for ways that are dark
> And for tricks that are vain,
> The heathen Chinee is peculiar,
> Which the same I would rise to explain.

> Ah Sin was his name;
> And I shall not deny,
> In regard to the same,
> What that name might imply;
> But his smile it was pensive and childlike,
> As I frequent remarked to Bill Nye.

It was August the third,
  And quite soft was the skies;
Which it might be inferred
  That Ah Sin was likewise;
Yet he played it that day upon William
  And me in a way I despise.

Which we had a small game,
  And Ah Sin took a hand:
It was Euchre. The same
  He did not understand;
But he smiled as he sat by the table,
  With the smile that was childlike and bland.

Yet the cards they were stocked
  In a way that I grieve,
And my feelings were shocked
  At the state of Nye's sleeve,
Which was stuffed full of aces and bowers,
  And the same with intent to deceive.

But the hands that were played
  By that heathen Chinee,
And the points that he made,
  Were quite frightful to see,—
Till at last he put down a right bower,
  Which the same Nye had dealt unto me.

Then I looked up at Nye,
  And he gazed upon me;
And he rose with a sigh,
  And said, "Can this be?
We are ruined by Chinese cheap labor,"—
  And he went for that heathen Chinee.

In the scene that ensued
  I did not take a hand,
But the floor it was strewed
  Like the leaves on the strand
With the cards that Ah Sin had been hiding,
  In the game "he did not understand."

In his sleeves, which were long,
He had twenty-four packs,—
Which was coming it strong,
Yet I state but the facts;
And we found on his nails, which were taper,
What is frequent in tapers,—that's wax.

Which is why I remark,
And my language is plain,
That for ways that are dark
And for tricks that are vain,
The heathen Chinee is peculiar,—
Which the same I am free to maintain.

Generations of Americans would read Bret Harte's romantic tales of the gold country such as "The Outcasts of Poker Flats" and "The Luck of Roaring Camp." But to Harte's lasting chagrin—he would later say that this was not merely the worst poem he ever wrote but the worst poem anyone ever wrote—every American that summer and for a long time afterward seemed to know "The Heathen Chinee." Recited in bars, sung by corner boys, quoted in the halls of Congress, Harte's little piece of doggerel inspired songs, musicals, theatrical productions, and countless illustrations and caricatures. Imitation being the sincerest form of flattery, Harte had many imitators, too. Later, an attempt by Harte and Twain to turn the poem into a theatrical production failed miserably and destroyed a friendship that had begun when the writers were young and unknown. But "The Heathen Chinee" would turn out to be not merely one of the best-known poems wherever English was spoken (the British loved it) but one of the most misunderstood.

The poem was satiric, mocking two dishonest white miners who attempt to cheat a Chinese coolie, Ah Sin, in a card game. Ah Sin, who appears to the miners to be a sucker, shrewdly turns the tables on them and beats them, causing them to roar with indignation (and physically abuse him). Bits from the poem such as "we are ruined by cheap Chinese labor" and "the heathen Chinee is peculiar" became catchphrases that delighted Americans of all classes well into the twentieth century.

Bigots, Know-Nothings, the "Chinese Must Go" gang, Irish day laborers, and white supremacists quoted the verses. Fools cited it in Congress as a dire warning of the "yellow peril." Congressman William Mungen of

Ohio, a self-proclaimed Civil War hero, introduced the theme into the *Congressional Record*—unaware, it appears, that the poem was satire. Ulysses Grant, then president of the United States, delayed his administration's discussions of matters relating to the Chinese on these shores and to relations with China because the poem was on the lips of every American. It was especially popular among the illiterate and was repeated like a comic song or jingle or among conservative politicians, nearly all of whom, down the years, appear too dense to have understood its intent.

While Harte was clearly satirizing the ignorance and prejudice of Americans, the poem misfired and became a rallying cry for racists. Its enormous popularity explains much about how America regarded the Chinese in the years after the Gold Rush. For if Chang and Eng represented the nation's notion of the "Chinaman" before gold was discovered, as a harmless freak, the wily Ah Sin of "The Heathen Chinee" was the epitome of the "Chinaman" after the Gold Rush: a crafty rascal who was not to be trusted. The poem was long misunderstood. Patrick Morrow, a modern critic of Harte's work, observed nearly a century after its controversial success: "The poem is not a plea for red-blooded Americans to stamp out the Yellow Peril, but an effort at social criticism."

"Perhaps no literary event in America caused so great and so immediate an effect as the appearance of 'Plain Language from Truthful James,'" William Purviance Fenn noted, speaking before the Convocation of the College of Chinese Studies in June 1933 in Peking. Fenn, a professor and head of the department of foreign languages at the University of Nanking, reminded his audience that "the poem spread with such startling speed that its phrases were soon on all lips; like the latest jazz hit, it passed from mouth to mouth until it became common property."

In discussing how misunderstood Harte's verses had become, Fenn commented that "the poem was accepted by the great mass of readers as corroborating their own preconceptions in regard to the essential sinfulness of their yellow neighbors and rivals."

Even more than his popular short stories, the poem (for which he was paid twenty-five dollars) made Harte a celebrity, but in the end it ruined his life. Riding on its fame, he left the West, the site of his early success and his best work, moved East, and later went to Europe. He never again received significant critical or commercial acclaim. And he never returned to the United States—he spent more time in exile than he had spent in the Gold Rush mining country that made him famous, haunted to the very end of his life in 1902 for writing something that embarrassed him.

In Portland in 1872, Judge Owen Nickerson Denny was often busy in the court. For in addition to Bret Harte's comic verses, if Americans knew much about "the Chinamen" it was from reading the newspapers, and virtually all newspaper accounts portrayed the Chinese as thieving, shifty, and untrustworthy. Two Chinese laborers, Ah Fook and Ah Non, appeared before Judge Denny on a charge of entering the residence of a Mr. Baum with "burglarious intent," as the *Oregonian* termed it. The newspaper did not explain the judge's decision, but Ah Fook was found guilty and Ah Non was released.

Crimes purportedly committed by the Chinese were much in the news that summer. Quoting the Montana press, the *Oregonian* noted that "Chinamen, to the disgust of the white burglars, are monopolizing the house-robbing business in Montana. A correspondent wants them exterminated, thereby furnishing the high-heeled, black mustached robber an op-portunity to ply his vocation without coming in contact with cheap Chinese labor."

Cheap Chinese labor. More echoes of Bret Harte and his little poem, then less than two years old but alluded to often in the popular press, es-pecially in the *Oregonian*, which loved allusions and puns. Even the trade of house burglary was ruined by cheap Chinese labor that summer. No one was safe. The "Chinaman" was plainly annoying to the average citizen.

A Chinese cobbler who plied his trade in the open, repairing boots and shoes in Portland on a Sunday, for example, drew the ire of the *Oregonian*, which described his offense in considerable detail.

"The Asiatic has a profound contempt both for the sacredness of our Christian Sabbath, and the public accommodation," the *Oregonian* observed. (The Chinese cobbler was blocking the public way, too.) "If he must labor, let him show some respect to this country and its insti-tutions by working in doors, and not seat himself in a conspicuous place, attract a crowd, and by that means inconvenience the public travel. Let him be tutored, if he is a new recruit; and be made to respect our laws if he knows better. It is a nuisance, and we call upon the police authori-ties to suppress that Asiatic forthwith."

The *Oregonian* was much conflicted in the matter of the Chinese. The week after Polly Bemis arrived in Portland, it reported, in considerable detail, an assault on two Chinese coolies: "Three little rascals were up before Judge Denny yesterday on the charge of having assaulted a 'Chinaman' without the slightest provocation, and for cutting off the cue of another Celestial."

The account naturally alluded to Bret Harte's poem:

> It seems that these young vandals were down at an Indian camp below the city on Sunday, rambling around. Pretty soon two "Chinamen" came along past where the boys were. One of the youngsters proposed to his companions to have some sport at the expense of the "Johns."
>
> This was of course readily agreed to, "and they went for the heathen Chinee."
>
> The three little rascals beat and kicked one of the Chinese men and then cut off the cue of the other "Chinaman."
>
> He remonstrated and protested but no mercy was found in their heart (sic), and after cutting off an important portion of his religious belief, they let him go in peace. To lose his cue any "Chinaman" regards as a great sin and disgrace; so this cueless heathen sought for redress and vengeance for the burning indignity heaped on him.

Judge Denny's handling of the matter (he would later serve as a diplomat in China and Korea) was praised by *The Oregonian*!

> On hearing the testimony in the case the Court rendered a most righteous judgment by sentencing the young hoodlums to the city jail, each for the term of twenty-three days. Served well right. Let this serve as a warning in the future.

The Chinese sojourners written about in the *Oregonian* in the summer of 1872 were all invariably mysterious. They all were said to smoke opium. They could be unexpectedly violent—especially among themselves. They stole, too. No chicken was safe. They were accomplished liars. This newspaper delighted in reprinting accounts from other western papers about Chinese involved in violent affrays. The *Montanian* reported that summer, from a wild Montana mining boomtown with a large Chinese population, on a "Chinese Duel." This was one of the longest and most detailed stories concerning the Chinese to appear in print that summer, and it provided a blow-by-blow account of a hatchet fight between two Chinese laborers.

The fight, involving Mung Gee and Ching Ho, was entertainment for *Oregonian* readers. The account implies that the fight was over a

Chinese woman, a not uncommon occurrence in the so-called bachelor societies of Chinese laborers:

> Throwing aside their outer garments, and each arm(ed) with a huge knife and an ugly looking hatchet, they face(d) each other for the fray—the woman, meantime, viewing the preparations with unconcern. For a moment they stare at each other like wild beasts over disputed prey, and then sprang forward with uplifted weapons.

Mung Gee got the worst of it but was expected to live, the newspaper reported. Ho fled the scene, fearing arrest. But "Chinamen" who hit other "Chinamen" with hatchets were not much of interest to what little law and order there was in the territories in those days. The *Montanian* noted:

> Although horribly mutilated Gee may possibly recover. The wound in the neck is not so deep as was hoped, and the jugular vein was unfortunately missed, but his facial attractions will always lack their usual amount of cheek, and his genial voice will be marred by the absence of nearly all his front teeth. The section of his left ear is the only relic the authorities have of Ho, and even that will be relinquished to the medical faculty on application.

An unsuccessful attempt by Chinese immigrants to smuggle opium into Portland aboard the bark *Manila* was the lead story in the city news on August 6, 1872. "For ways that are dark, and tricks that are vain the heathen Chinee is preeminent," the *Oregonian* noted, imitating Harte's comic verses. "But with all his subtle cunning and ingenuity, John sometimes miscalculates and gets caught in his endeavors to evade." Smugglers were discovered to have hidden twenty-five pounds of opium in the false bottoms of wooden chests that were unloaded by customs officials.

By the end of the summer, as the weather cooled in the high country, Chinese laborers began descending on Portland. Construction along the line of the Northern Pacific Railroad was halted for the winter season and hundreds of "celestials"—as the newspapers always called them —came down to camp on the east side of the Willamette River where the Oregon and California Railroad trestle work crosses the flat.

"Their frail canvas tenements, now smoked and stained by long exposure, can be seen to stretch along for several hundred yards," the *Oregonian* observed.

There were "Chinamen" everywhere that summer, according to the *Oregonian*. Some 100 of them were grading and excavating a road on the west side of Portland. And every steamer out of San Francisco brought more "celestials" into the Pacific Northwest.

Some days, dead "Chinamen" came to town, too. The ship *Fanny Troup* came into Portland one day with the body of a dead immigrant on board. "The 'Chinaman' is said to have been killed by an accident at some point along the line of the Northern Pacific Railroad. We were unable to learn the circumstances of the unfortunate occurrence."

The *Oregonian* frequently reported on dead "Chinamen" by way of commenting on the Chinese and their customs, which Americans then found odd. For example, the Chinese at that time did not like someone to die in a house or any sort of dwelling, believing it brought bad luck, and so they placed the dying outside, a practice that Americans found cruel.

A Chinese laborer found dead by his fellow workers on L Street between Eighth and Ninth in East Portland was identified as Ah Woyu, and he was about thirty-five, the newspaper noted. He was a road worker with a gang of Chinese laborers in East Portland:

> For several days past he had been complaining, and on Thursday evening it appears that his comrades, becoming convinced that Ah Woyu would die, compelled him to leave the hut where they were stopping. He did so and passed the night in some brush near the house. The following morning he was found lying dead, wrapped up in some old blankets.

The coroner could not be found to examine Ah Woyu. He was only a "Chinaman." But his comrades placed his remains in a pine box. Dead sojourners were shipped home to China. It was the custom.

There were mad "Chinamen" in the country that summer, too, the *Oregonian* told its readers. One, named Lin Lee, was taken into custody "acting in an insane manner. He was rushing up and down the streets brandishing a long knife and threatening summary vengeance on whoever chanced to come his way," the newspaper reported.

Taken before Judge Hamilton, Lin Lee was deemed insane and sent to an asylum. "The poor lunatic was very violent while on the way to the asylum, requiring the united strength of the Sheriff and several 'Chinamen' to hold him on the seat. The physician who made the examination is of the opinion that the cause of Lin Lee's insanity was the excessive use of opium."

When there was a shortage of Chinese mischief locally, the *Oregonian* reprinted stories of "Chinamen" up to no good elsewhere in the West:

> *The Enterprise* tells the story of a white girl being whipped at Oregon City by a "Chinaman," for which "John" was arrested and fined $15, and was going to pay it but his boss told him to go to jail and he (the boss) would pay him full wages while "John" worked out the penalty of the law. Most "Chinamen" would be well satisfied with such an arrangement.

In Portland, a Chinese man was arraigned before Judge Denny on a charge of assaulting H. Fleckenstein with a knife. After an examination of the case the suspect was held to answer before a grand jury. In default of bail, he was taken into custody.

A few days later, under the headline "Team Frightened," readers of the *Oregonian* learned:

> Several "Chinamen" engaged in flying a kite yesterday, ventured too near the team of a farmer which stood before Quinn's fish market. The tail of the kite passed very close to the heads of the animals. A pair of badly frightened equines was the result. They ran down Washington to First and then turned up First. Some half a dozen venturesome individuals vainly endeavored to stay the horses in their impetuous career; but they continued on up Madison Street, and then made a straight line for the suburbs. We have been unable to ascertain results.

The *Oregonian* did not contain many reports of Chinese women that summer, for there were not many Chinese women in the country in those days; but there was one, Lin Foy. News of her presence appeared in the *Oregonian* when a charge of having stolen $100 from one Charlie Lee was brought before the court.

The redoubtable Judge Denny was once again presiding and, finding an absence of evidence, he dismissed the case and discharged the defendant. We know nothing more about the woman or where she went or if Charlie Lee ever got his $100 back or if it had even been stolen in the first place. Lin Foy was described by the *Oregonian* as a "courtesan," for that was a job, too, in those days when there was smallpox in the countryside and the Blue Mountains were on fire.

Hydraulic mining operations at Chinese Gulch, Colorado, 1869-1879.
Denver Public Library; Western History Collection, Duhem Brothers, photographers, X18575.

Five

THE END OF THE ROAD ... WARRENS

Life wasn't worth much in those wide open days. The bark of a revolver
was nothing to be alarmed over in the villages along the way because that
was the way quarrels were settled.
       —WILLIAM E. WARDEN, MAIL CARRIER TO WARRENS,
              IN AN INTERVIEW, 1941

When there was gold in those hills, Warrens was the end of the road,
and Warrens remained the end of the road when the gold was gone. In
the Salmon River Mountains of central Idaho, a steep and lonely country heavily forested with lodgepole pines, the road still ends at Warrens;
a traveler does not pass through on his way to anywhere else. A man
had to want to come to Warrens in the boom times, and it was always
gold that brought the traveler to the end of the road.

James Warren found gold on Summit Flat near Warren Creek in
1862, and the site of his discovery was variously known as Summit,
Warren's Diggins, Warren's Camp, and Warrens. It is known as Warren today, and it remains at the end of the road. The original town was
about four miles up Warren Creek from the current site. Historians of
the period described its founder, James Warren, as "a shiftless individual,
a petty gambler, miner and prospector." He would soon be joined by
others fitting that description.

James Warren left Lewiston, Idaho, on August 1, 1862, on an expedition along the Salmon River basin. The countryside was alive with

hostile Indians but that did not impede gold seekers. Greed is a great source of Dutch courage. Warren was back in less than a month with tales of gold deposits at a site he named Warren Meadows. The historian Hubert Howe Bancroft recalled that "when the news was brought to Florence, a stampede ensued, and men left rich diggings, worth twenty dollars a day to the man, to rush to the new discovery. But a different kind of men settled at Warrens, mostly real miners, satisfied with taking out fifteen to twenty dollars a day."

Before the snows came that year, the little mining camp and its neighbor Washington saw their population jump from half a dozen miners to more than 2,000 prospectors. In its heyday, 6,000 miners worked the placers in Warrens. The Chinese were among the last to arrive. At first barred from the area, the Chinese were eventually allowed to come in the spring of 1870. White miners wanted to sell worked-over claims to the Chinese.

The popular historian of Idaho Robert Gresham Bailey, writing about how the Chinese were discriminated against in the territory, noted that "very few times were they permitted to take up mining claims in the first locations. They usually had to work for others or work over ground which the white man in his hurry had merely skimmed for the cream. But so painstaking and thrifty were the Chinamen that they secured fortunes where others would have starved to death."

The federal census of that summer recorded 362 "celestials" in Warrens. The Chinese population in the area would rise to 738 in 1880 and drop to 278 in 1890; by the turn of the twentieth century only twenty-two Chinese remained at what was then called Warren.

Chroniclers of the Chinese experience in the nineteenth-century West always note that "celestials" were discouraged from mining if their presence threatened white miners. Sometimes that discouragement was violent. "If one of the yellow men tried to trespass on the rights of a white man, he was strung up by his pigtail to the nearest cottonwood tree," the mining historian William S. Greever noted.

The world that sprang up in a mining boom town like Warrens was the United States in 1862 in miniature. The Civil War was some 2,000 miles away, but the sentiments of northerners and southerners—thrust into close proximity in the mining camps—were also evident here. The political allegiances of the residents were reflected in the settlement of two towns in close proximity—one called Washington, for Union loyalists, and the other, named Richmond, for supporters of the Confederacy.

Warrens was a rough camp, a hodgepodge of log cabins and later clapboard shacks, thrown up quickly and cheaply. Nothing was painted. Painting was a waste of time, and there was no paint in any case.

Mining cabins—often designed for a single occupant—were simple structures built of logs with bunks against the back wall. Many were windowless. Chinese miners dug holes in the ground or in the side of a hill. Mattresses consisted of fir boughs covered with blankets. A dry-goods box nailed to the wall was the cupboard. The cabin had a fireplace and a simple table. Cheap pictures, prints, or illustrations cut out of magazines or newspapers were the only decoration. Union sympathizers tended to have a picture of Abraham Lincoln on the cabin wall; Confederates favored Robert E. Lee or Jefferson Davis. A quick glance at the illustrations on the wall of a miner's cabin established the political sentiments of the occupant.

Labor expended on tasks other than mining was also wasted time, in the minds of most men at the end of the road. The roofs of many of these buildings were covered with sod or earth. The streets were merely trails through the mining camp. In the winter, the camp was frozen solid for more than six months. Depending on how ambitious the residents were, a kind of rough sidewalk of boards and planking might be set down to allow pedestrian traffic to move across a sea of mud, which thawed and froze and thawed and froze and eventually turned to dust in the summer. The streets in front of these shanties were a mire of mud, manure, and firewood. The carcasses of dead animals might be strewn about, leaving a robust tang in the air in hot weather. Hogs rooted about the camps. This was the scene that confronted Polly Bemis when she rode into Warrens in the summer of 1872.

Fire was the scourge of such a community, as every building was made of wood, an explosive tinderbox, and any fire not quickly extinguished could burn down several buildings in minutes. Whole mining camps burned to the ground in a few hours and were rebuilt in a matter of weeks. In the summer and fall, wild forest fires could rage in the mountains, the billows of smoke visible for great distances. Only time, Mother Nature, and rain would extinguish such blazes then.

Mining camps like Warrens were hardscrabble worlds, inaccessible for half the year, high in the Idaho mountains. Warrens was nearly 6,000 feet above sea level; the air is thin and sharp there. Twenty and even thirty feet of snow might accumulate at a mountain pass, shutting the community off from the outside world for weeks or months. Temperatures in the winter could fall far below zero—on January 8, 1876, a temperature of fifty-five degrees below zero was recorded. In the summer, the temperature could soar as high as 114 degrees, as it did on July 27, 1872, at Slate Creek. The first pack trains of spring often did not reach this distant country until June.

Well into the twentieth century, freighters hauled materials into these outposts on the backs of horses and mules when the narrow trails that snaked through the mountains were passable. The inaccessibility of the place was much commented on even then. (Today, the road to Warren is still not fully paved and is not free of snow until June.) Sometimes only men could make this trek, carrying whatever they could on their backs. Much of the year the trails were not passable. First there was too much snow, then there was too much mud, then the mud froze, and then it snowed again. In the mining camp of Florence, it snowed all day on the Fourth of July in 1862.

Winter lasted forever or until summer, and summer was not long at those altitudes. Keeping warm in winter was full-time work, and the danger of snow blindness, which could leave a man defenseless, was real and worrisome. Because the winters were so long and hard and because very little mining could be done in those early days, many miners left the high country before early November, returning in the spring from homes in Oregon and elsewhere. To winter over in a place like Warrens was difficult, lonely, and dull.

"Though the snow lay deep on all the roads and trails from December till April, there was but little interruption to the tide of travel that went on. All winter long men were daily leaving Oro Fino on snowshoes with heavy packs on their backs for the distant mining camp, Florence in the Salmon River country being the principal point that attracted them. The whole country above Lewiston lay buried under a thick mantle of snow with the exception of some narrow river bottoms favored by lower altitudes," William Armistead Goulder noted in his memoirs. Oro Fino (Spanish for "fine gold" and sometimes written as one word by Americans) is in the Clearwater River country in north-central Idaho and was the site of the first gold discovery in 1860.

Goulder recalled how "with temperatures far below zero much of the time, travel was dangerous during the winter months, but miners traveled nonetheless. It seemed like a fit of madness for men to undertake to battle with all the difficulties and dangers that attended this transit on foot across snowfields for a distance of one hundred miles, and with heavy loads on their backs, but there were hundreds who did not hesitate to confront the task. Nearly every week would bring some returning pilgrim or messenger from Florence to Oro Fino."

The mines bore names like "Lucky Boy," "The Bull Dog," "Whiskey Gulch," "War Eagle," and "Little Giant." The men who named these mines had their own fanciful monikers, such as "Club-Foot George," "Rattlesnake Jack," "Snapping Andy," "Three-Fingered" Smith (he had a little accident with a shooting iron), "Cougar Dave" (he spent a lifetime shooting the big cats), and "Pony" Smead (who was said to have either won a squaw in a card game or traded a horse for her). It was a hard world and these were hard men, "free from the trammels and restraints of Sunday-school influences," Goulder noted.

Bernard DeVoto, the Pulitzer Prize–winning historian, believed the living conditions in the mining camps contributed to this lawlessness. "Except in war, and Southern prison stockades, Americans have never lived so vilely and degradingly as in the mining camps. All the barbarities of other frontiers, diet for instance, must be thought of as greatly magnified here," DeVoto observed.

Observations such as DeVoto's on mining camps in the American West were common. In the 1860s, the wandering Irish-born journalist J. Ross Browne was reporting on life in Virginia City, Nevada, the quintessential mining boom town. In a letter to his daughter, Lucy, Browne declared that "in all my travels on the four continents, I have never before visited such a desolate, comfortless, miserable region, and never experienced such a series of mental and physical privations. It is absolutely frightful to think of it." He could easily have been describing Warrens, which was even bleaker and more primitive.

Browne described a scene that evokes most western mining camps:

Frame shanties, pitched together as if by accident; tents of canvas, of blankets, of brush, of potato-sacks and old shirts, with empty whisky-barrels for chimneys, smoky hovels of mud and stone; coyote holes in the mountain side forcibly seized and held by men; pits and shafts with smoke issuing from every crevice; piles of goods and rubbish on craggy points, in the hollows, on the rocks, in the mud, in the snow, every where, scattered broadcast in pell-mell confusion, as if the clouds had suddenly burst overhead and rained down the dregs of all the flimsy, rickety, filthy little hovels and rubbish of merchandise that had ever undergone the process of evaporation from the earth since the days of Noah. The intervals of space, which may or may not have been streets, were dotted over with human beings of such a sort, variety, and numbers, that the famous ant-hills of Africa were nothing in the comparison. To say that they were rough, muddy, unkempt and unwashed, would be but faintly expressive of their actual appearance.

When the mining strikes in California and Nevada were played out in the 1860s, prospectors looking for gold came to Idaho, and along with this next wave of Argonauts there came, too, the camp followers—cardsharps, whores, thimbleriggers, road agents, and rascals of all kinds. In the early days—the 1860s—justice was pretty much homegrown in the mining camps of Idaho. So-called miners' courts were the law of the land, if there was any law, and these were informal affairs.

It was a violent world, too, and hard men sometimes needed hard punishment. A historian of early Idaho, Cornelius J. Brosnan, recalled that a hanging was referred to as a "midair dance." And while not strictly legal, hangings were not uncommon in the early days, for, as Brosnan recalled a miner exclaiming about an execution, "If a man ain't good enough to live here, he ain't good enough to live anywhere."

Violence broke out on a whim, and the criminal code was enforced erratically. "The annals of murder appall one not by their brutality but by their triviality," Bernard DeVoto noted. He added, "Life has become so cheap that it is barely worth saving—or even taking." A man could be sent to the prison over in Oregon for fatally shooting his wife—he might even have to serve a couple of years behind bars—but a man could be lynched following the briefest session of a miners' court for messing about with someone's placer mine in the diggings. Stealing horses was a sure way to die at the end of a rope.

The local historian Margaret Day Allen described something of the character of the miners and their sense of justice:

The miners tended to be a rough lot and yet many historians have praised their honesty, hospitality and generosity. A miner seldom locked his cabin even though he might leave boxes and cans of gold dust standing about. One miner might shoot another and get off on a pleas of self-defense, but to steal another's gold or rob his sluice box was unpardonable.

Justice was queer, swift, and violent, but then so was life in the territory. In the early days in Idaho, official vigilance committees—local posses of vigilantes and miners' courts—dealt with offenders harshly and quickly. Criminals were tried in secret and sentenced in secret. They did not attend their own trials. There was rarely an appeals process.

"This was not a society, it was the atomization of society," DeVoto wrote of the mining camps. In explaining frontier justice to readers in the early twentieth century, W. J. McConnell recalled an early pioneer from Arkansas who had told him that "when a man was killed in his state, the authorities empanelled a jury, not for the purpose of determining whether the accused was guilty of killing the man, but to ascertain whether it had been a fair fight. If the latter was shown by the evidence, the verdict of the jury was 'Bully for the boy with the glass eye.' Yet these same men would hang a horse thief without compunction."

McConnell recalled that in the early days of Boise County not one of the accused murderers, and there were many, was put to death for his crime. But criminals of all stripes were everywhere in Idaho in the days of the gold strikes. The territory was a powerful magnet for toughs who came into the country as soon as word of the gold strikes reached the outside world. The lure of gold and the certain knowledge that law and order had not yet reached the end of the road were great inducements for the lowlife.

"Our gold fields had scarcely become known to the world before bands of desperadoes, who had made crime a profession in California and Nevada, came flocking to the newest Idaho camps," Brosnan recalled. "Their chief business was robbing stages, stealing horses and cattle and murdering miners. So well organized were these roughs that if a judge, jury, or miners' meeting attempted to punish one of their number, other members of the 'gang' could be counted upon to wreak a brutal vengeance upon the men who presumed to bring the ruffian to justice."

Frustration that arose because the criminal class was going unpunished ultimately led to the vigilante movement. According to McConnell, "Neighbors did not know one another, hence, as was wise, they hesitated to suggest an organization designed to oppose lawless methods, lest the men approached might be a member of the banditti. There being no church nor society organization with which the better classes could affiliate, it was every man for himself. The road-agents had the only perfect organization and it shielded its own. But a time came when conditions were altered."

McConnell also pointed out that some of the attempts to curb lawlessness in the Idaho backcountry resulted from the presence of Masons in the region. This fraternal organization provided the structure and secrecy necessary to ensure some form of justice, however harsh.

"The punishment that followed conviction was swift, sure, and generally terrible. Since there were no jails, these convicted outlaws usually left the camp 'at the end of a rope.' (Immediate banishment from a mining camp [and] flogging were lesser options. But the death penalty was robustly used against desperadoes.) The mysteriousness and severity of the Vigilante tribunals overawed the most desperate criminals, and they usually began to conduct themselves decently or fled to districts where the strange sign of the Vigilantes was not in evidence. As soon as local and territorial laws became effective, the career of these 'popular tribunals' was, of course, at an end," Brosnan noted.

The *Chicago Tribune*'s chronicler of the Wyoming mining camps and boom towns of the era, James Chisholm, a Scottish immigrant, filed long, gory accounts of lynchings. "'It's a sign of good times,' they say here, when people begin to do a little hanging," Chisholm cheerily wrote to his newspaper from Cheyenne in March 1868. He had no shortage of "midair dances" to describe. He told his readers that in a place where law and order was in its infancy, the locals had decided to take matters into their own hands. It does not seem, from Chisholm's accounts of vigilantes, that many innocent men were hanged. All early histories of Idaho, detailing the activities of vigilantes in the territory, reach similar conclusions.

Another early chronicler, Byron Defenbach, musing on crime in the Idaho mining country, noted that "a mining camp at its inception resembled the circus. It was transient; it was a little world of its own. It formed an environment sparkling with excitement, spectacular, full of illusions, unreal. Until the last acre had been prospected, until the element of high chance had given way to the prosaic certainty of measured returns, a mining camp was an opium-eater's dream."

"The criminal element ruled, first one community and then another," Defenbach wrote. "These awful stories of murder and rapine are ours; their telling is necessary to a true history of the state; their reading is essential to a proper understanding of the country which in so short a time has changed from a community dominated by outlaws and desperadoes, to a peaceful and law abiding commonwealth."

Judge James Poe, a veteran of the boom time in Warrens, recalled that he once stood on a bar in a saloon and made an impassioned plea for a client's life (the man was charged with robbery). Poe, who was a business associate of the aforementioned "Three-Fingered" Smith, must have been an eloquent speaker, for his client was spared the rope and later was convicted of robbery and sentenced to a short term in the penitentiary.

But miners at the end of the road were not hungry merely for justice or a sense of order. Life was hard there in many ways. There was little to eat whenever the pack trains could not come into the country. In the early days of Idaho, a boom town like Warrens would have been nearly exclusively male, and virtually every occupant—white or Chinese—would have been engaged in some form of mining or in providing a service that miners needed. A boom could bring a mob of 5,000 or more to a village of tents and shacks, and a boom elsewhere could clear a camp out in a month. Between 1860 and 1980, more than $4.4 billion in gold and silver was mined in central and southern Idaho in camps with names like Muldoon, Yellow Jacket, Buffalo Hump, Seven Devils, Orogrande, Viola, Yankee Fork, and Dixie.

"Wild bouts of gold fever swept across the Idaho Territory," recalled Thomas Donaldson a pioneer who later wrote the classic *Idaho of Yesterday*. A gold strike at Loon Creek, about fifty miles northeast of Idaho City, set off a stampede from Boise—then the only place passing for a city in the region. One of the members of the Idaho supreme bench came to see Donaldson, the morning after news of the strike reached the community. This judge had borrowed an old horse and was leaving for the high country. He paused only to ask Donaldson to get some continuances for him on a couple of cases. Only a few men then remained in Boise, although the gold strike proved to be worthless and the rest of the town eventually drifted back, disappointed.

But Warrens was always a boom or bust town, up or down, flush or flat, dead broke or slapping leather. In the course of a century, more than $16 million came out of the ground here in this rough village at the very end of the road, but it sometimes came hard.

In her history of this region, *Pioneer Days in Idaho County,* Sister M. Alfreda Elsensohn noted, "Warrens has been described as a roaring placer camp in the sixties, dead in the seventies, revived in the eighties, dead again in the early 1900s, and resurrected in the 1930s." Charlie and Polly Bemis were there for nearly all of those busts and booms.

In 1865, three years after the first gold strike, at least 1,500 miners, as nearly as anyone could count, were scratching at the ground in Warrens. Within two years, the population was said to be down to about 500, but by 1872 a wave of Chinese workers—there were plenty of extra "celestials" drifting about in those years following the completion of the transcontinental railroad—boosted the population up to about 1,200.

When the ground was nearly played out and the whites no longer wanted the claims, the Chinese took over. They were patient and industrious, and they would make an old, long-played-out claim pay, even if only a few dollars a day. Chinese miners would often resift a piece of ground that had been mined, to collect the gold dust that had been missed.

"Celestials always worked placers; they carefully washed claims which the white men had abandoned as paid out, and were satisfied with profits of two or three dollars a day," Thomas Donaldson recalled. "They worked more hours than any miners I ever saw and, poor souls, were often the victims of Christian extortion and discriminations." Donaldson noted that it was not uncommon for Chinese miners to be forced by unscrupulous whites to pay the annual license fee as often as four times a year.

But by 1890 even the Chinese had pulled out of Warrens. There were about 150 souls at the end of the road, and there was not much to draw a fortune seeker, although some later attempts to mine the ground would be made. On the day Polly Bemis died in 1933, the newspapers reported that yet again someone was planning to mine at Warrens. Dreams of wealth die hard, even in a hard world.

The first method applied in mining here, as during the early Gold Rush in California, was placer mining, essentially panning for gold using a metal pan to sift the gravel from a streambed, using water. The miner usually stood in the water, which was often bone-chillingly cold. Gold, which is heavier than gravel, settles in the bottom of the sifting pan. This was the most primitive and least complicated way to mine for gold. The traditional method of "panning" for gold involved filling a pan with pay dirt, adding some water, and shaking the pan to create a whirling motion that separated the gold from the gravel.

Cornelius Brosnan estimated that a prospector could take between $70 and $100 a day out of a streambed by placer mining, with little capital investment and a few tools—a pick, a shovel, and a pan (often the same pan used by the miner to bake his bread).

The second development in prospecting for gold was a technique involving a "rocker" that resembled a baby's cradle. Essentially, the miner separated the gold by using this rocker. It was a more elaborate form of panning for gold and allowed a larger volume of pay dirt to be sifted. The third development, an extension of the rocker, was the introduction of the sluice box, another method akin to panning for gold. Mining would eventually become more complex, utilizing hydraulics, but in the early days it was hands-on and labor-intensive.

Placer mining was a seasonal occupation. Miners worked only seven months of the year at the higher altitudes, leaving the district as winter approached and returning in the spring when the snow melted and the streams were flowing.

Most of a miner's life was mere subsistence. Everything enjoyable at the end of the road—whether it was a Chinese dancing girl, a demijohn of whiskey, fifty pounds of flour, or a six-month-old copy of the *Springfield Republican*—had to be brought in on the back of a pack animal. Where the trails would not accommodate four-footed traffic, men filled in, but men could not carry everything.

Three hundred pounds was considered an average load for most pack animals, and gleanings from the *Lewiston Teller* give a reader more than a century later some idea of what kind of freight moved into the mountains.

June 18, 1886: The Grostein and Binnard pack train took in 22,500 pounds of freight to Warrens on their last trip, and made the passage in eleven days,

beating the Benson train by twenty-four hours. The G and B train started from
Mount Idaho on its second trip to Warrens on Wednesday last. Included
among the freight was a big demijohn of whiskey weighing 560 pounds.

July 23, 1886: The G and B train came in from Pierce City via the Clearwater ferry and Lawyer's canyon last Monday and loaded 20,000 pounds of
Grangeville flour and started for Warrens yesterday.

September 16, 1887: Benson's pack train left here for Warrens Monday
with about 25,000 pounds of freight.

The prices of materials hauled in on pack trains were extremely high.
A newspaper that might cost a nickel or dime in the outside world would
sell for $2.50 here. It was a seller's world, but the market was whimsical
and unpredictable. A merchant in a boom town could ask top dollar for
anything needed, but news of gold elsewhere could siphon off his customers in a week, leaving him with a stock that had to be sold at cost or
at a loss.

Miners who ate in boardinghouses—and ate at the pleasure of the
boardinghouse keeper, usually a woman—were accustomed to paying
three dollars a meal. Biscuits, flapjacks, cornbread, fried pork or ham,
beef, and beans were staples. Boardinghouses, saloons, and cheap Chinese restaurants were the preferred places to eat. Bakeries often doubled
as restaurants.

Wages give some perspective on the high prices of goods and foodstuffs brought into the Idaho Territory. Miners were averaging five
dollars a day, carpenters four dollars, bricklayers from five to eight dollars, and common laborers three to five dollars. Farmhands earned fifty
to sixty dollars per month; schoolteachers, male or female, earned
seventy-five dollars to a hundred dollars per month. Chinese house servants averaged forty dollars per month, white servants sixty dollars.
Doctors charged three to five dollars per visit.

The Idaho that Charlie and Polly Bemis lived in was erratic. Every man
was his own boss. Given the vagaries of mining, today's pauper might be
tomorrow's millionaire. The workforce was transient and undependable.

"With scarcely ten minutes' warning, men could, and did, change
their vocations," Thomas Donaldson remembered. "In the blink of an
eye, churchmen, merchants, laborers, lawyers, would turn miners. The
term 'miner' included anything from a bishop to a gambler, a child of
six to a man of eighty; it meant any person capable of handling a pick

and shovel. The education of 90 percent of the miners begins after they have made a location, or staked a claim."

Donaldson, who arrived in Idaho after the Civil War, compiled a detailed account of wages and prices: "Food, with the exception of meat, was very dear. Vegetables sold by the pound; potatoes brought from one dollar and twenty cents to four dollars a short bushel, and apples were often eight dollars a bushel. California fruits were fifty cents a pound, with oranges at fifty cents each and lemons as high as a dollar in price. Flour was comparatively cheap, for mills were in operation in Boise, and wheat was grown within easy hauling distance. Green corn, pumpkins, and squash were plentiful, but watermelons and cantaloupes, now so plentiful in Idaho, were luxuries."

Alonzo Brown, an early prospector in the Florence area, recalled that his three-dollar meal included bread, bacon, beans, and dried-apple sauce. "Later in the summer they had butter and potatoes," he remembered. In the 1860s, during the first big gold rush, a bottle of mustard could cost five dollars and a pound of tea five dollars. Eggs were a dollar each. W. J. McConnell, who would later become a United States senator and in 1893 the third governor of Idaho, wrote in his memoirs an account of selling a melon for what was then considered an enormous sum.

McConnell was in the mining camp of Buena Vista Bar one Sunday in August 1863 when an emigrant family arrived from Missouri. (Many new arrivals were fleeing the Civil War at that time.) Two members of the party were beautiful girls, and the miners were vying for their attention. McConnell was selling melons, which had been hauled on pack animals for about twenty-five miles over mountain trails and were considerably more expensive than his customers realized. One large melon weighing thirty-two pounds was eight dollars—or twenty-five cents per pound. Melons in the East normally sold for four or five cents a pound. But, McConnell recalled, the young miner who bought this fabulously expensive melon for the two young ladies—probably the first two women he had seen in a long while—did not complain. "And in extenuation of the investment of the young man," McConnell mused, "it is also fair to state that he thought she was worth it."

McConnell remembered well the roadhouses in the Payette Valley where prospectors en route to the mines stopped to eat or, more likely, drink. "They all served meals consisting usually of bread and meat, generally bacon, with brown bread and black coffee, all for the nominal sum of one dollar each. These houses were invariably kept by unmarried men, and most of them were orderly and well conducted."

Strong drink, McConnell also reflected, was never far from the thoughts of the thirsty traveler. The Payette Valley Road was famous for its alkali dust, which could easily cause "an excessive thirst" in a traveler. "Nothing but some kind of alcoholic beverage seemed to assuage, and even that relief was a temporary one, hardly lasting from one house to another," McConnell noted. The operators of the roadhouses were familiar with "the malady, and were prepared to promptly relieve the sufferings of all comers. These prescriptions were administered for 'two bits,' or twenty-five cents each," he added.

The fare was plain and simple in the mining camps, Cornelius Brosnan noted. In Idaho in the days of the Gold Rush, fish and game were plentiful if anyone had the time or inclination to hunt. But hunting was considered as frivolous as painting a house, even if it resulted in some game for the table. Men came into that country to dig for gold. In addition to the staples, herds of cattle were often driven in on foot, and beef became one of the most plentiful and, of course, one of the cheapest articles of food. On account of the lack of vegetables, miners frequently suffered from scurvy, a serious disorder caused by a deficiency of vitamin C, and a common problem in the early days when men might go for months without eating any fruits or vegetables.

Potatoes, which had been brought into the country before winter set in and stored deep in the ground to prevent freezing, were one source of vitamin C. "When the scurvy broke out in the camp, the tubers were packed on men's backs from fifteen to twenty miles and distributed among the sufferers from the cruel complaint. Uncooked potatoes sliced up and soaked in vinegar were far from affording a very appetizing dish, but it proved a sovereign remedy for scurvy," William Armistead Goulder remembered.

During the middle to late nineteenth century, Americans—most of whom performed manual labor—consumed on average 4,000 calories per day, about twice what is now consumed. But there were not many fat men at the end of the road. Mining was calorie-burning labor—even harder than farmwork, which burned on average ten calories per minute. Life in this world was a dawn-to-dark regimen of work, though the Sabbath, if observed, was largely reserved for recreational pursuits or just doing the laundry.

No source of complaint was more frequent than the absence or want of mail. News from home, "treasures richer than any the mines can yield," was on the mind of every miner in every camp. Goulder remembered Sunday in the mining camps when the express mail rider from Walla Walla arrived: "They are letters from the dear ones in the distant homes —letters in which the kisses are yet warm and the heartbeats yet audible."

The delivery of mail was itself often an amazing feat. In the winter, mail was brought into these areas by couriers who used snowshoes and even skis. One fabled mail courier was Israel B. Cowan, a small, wiry man who carried express from Lewiston to Pierce City in the winters of 1863 and 1864 on his back. He made the trip of eighty miles in ten days—despite his clubfoot, which left a unique signature in the snow. "At the end of each trek, as he approached Pierce City, the merchants and miners would walk down the trail to meet him and help carry the letters, newspapers and freight in his pack," Margaret Day Allen recalled in *Lewiston Country*. His stamina and reliability were legendary. One miner wrote to a friend, "With Cowan bringing the mail, even tho crippled, your letters will reach me."

But this was dangerous work. Mail carriers were often buried in snowslides. On some occasions, packers suffering from snow blindness because of reflected light walked single file in groups behind the only member of the party who could see. "People thought nothing of trekking long distances on foot in winter, and the perils of the trail were taken for granted," Allen reported. Miners froze to death, or their limbs became severely frostbitten, requiring crude amputation.

In his memoirs, Goulder graphically recounted an incident when three members of a party of four travelers had to abandon the fourth during a dangerous winter trek in extremely cold weather. The three reached safety, barely, but the fourth died of exposure from spending a night out when temperature fell far below zero.

Men who could not keep up were often left to die, and Goulder noted that in this case and in many others "the instinct for self-preservation proved too strong for the exercise of any nobler feeling."

The newspapers and word of mouth warned potential prospectors not to come unprepared to end-of-the-road stops like Warrens. There was little or nothing to buy in such places. A man would have to fend for himself, and settle for rough living.

Construction materials brought from the outside were also expensive. "In 1870, I paid twenty-seven dollars for a barrel of cement worth one tenth that in the states," Donaldson remembered. "Nails were twenty-five cents a pound. The absolute dearth of hardwood in the territory necessitated the importation of ax handles, spokes, and good furniture. Much of our furniture, necessarily, was homemade."

The miners themselves were a motley, ragtag assemblage. They wore broad-brimmed felt slouch hats, rarely shaved, and kept their hair long. They favored heavy gray or blue flannel shirts. A large bandanna or kerchief was tied around the neck. The pants or pantaloons were tucked into the tops of high, hobnailed boots and were belted at the waist. Most miners carried a six-shooter, Cornelius Brosnan noted.

Bathing was infrequent among the mining class, but the Chinese laborers—as observed along the line of construction of the transcontinental railroad—sluiced themselves off with a hot water bath at the end of the workday and changed into clean clothing, in marked contrast to their white compatriots.

Most miners were young, although older veterans of the California Gold Rush came to Idaho in the 1860s. Once they figured out the dangers of the more obvious dietary problems, like scurvy, the miners found life in this new Eldorado healthy. "In the daytime, they worked in a clear, electric air; at night they were lulled to sleep under mountain pines," Brosnan recalled. The occasional deaths in these camps were almost all a result of violence and shootings rather than sickness. "Infectious diseases were practically unheard of," Brosnan noted. Rheumatism, pneumonia, and scurvy were the most common complaints.

There was a market for anything and everything in those Idaho mining camps. There are frequent accounts of entrepreneurs bringing in wagonloads of cats from Oregon, either as house pets or to keep down vermin such as mice and rats. Thomas Donaldson recalled such an entrepreneur in his memoirs: "In the days of strikes and high prices at Florence, an embryo financier named Blevins hauled a wagonload of riffraff cats from the Willamette Valley, Oregon, appreciating the fact that miners wanted a reminder of home. He was quite right in his assumption; Dick Whittington had ne'er a more lucrative feline tour. Blevins trailed for Bannock, now Idaho City, and retailed the cats at ten dollars a head, payable in gold dust."

In winter, ironically, entertainment was more readily available. For the miners who remained in the high country the chief employment, as one holdout wrote home, was getting their firewood, cooking and eating their grub, assembling in small squads, and poking fun at their neighbors "who are disposed to work around and on their claims to some extent. Altogether they seem to be a happy community."

This was not just any day, however—it was Christmas. The writer went on:

> Riding on snow shoes downhill, occasional stag dancing and playing jokes upon each other form much of our amusement. A few are engaged in preparing claims for hydraulicing, some are engaged on quartz mines. We have had two quite sick in camp, both seem now to be convalescent. Our newly elected county officials keep bachelor hall at the Raymond Saux saloon building. It is said that our Sheriff and Auditor do up the cooking in commendable style and one of our merchants draws water. Whether or not he is also the hewer of wood I have not yet learned. We have two of the tender sex of our own race in camp.

The snow was about thirty inches deep in the valley along Warrens Creek and at higher elevations, four feet deep on average. There was not much mail. The last post brought only one letter and one paper to the camp.

But it was Christmas, nevertheless, and the letter writer reported:

> Our boys are doing up Christmas brown, by dancing, singing and making themselves merry generally. Christmas Eve was the occasion for a general oyster stew; some of course had to take strong beverages to wash the oysters down, fearing they would not settle by dancing. One hundred and fifty men in Lewiston cannot outdo the fifty of this camp in enjoying themselves.

"The principal mining-camp recreations were gambling, drinking, dancing and theatricals," Cornelius Brosnon reported. "Gambling was the master passion. The brilliantly lighted saloon, with its enticing music, its social cheer, and its babel of strange voices, proved a magnet for the mining community. Many a California miner was reminded of the days of 'Forty-Nine' when he heard the familiar cry: 'Make your game, gentlemen, make your game—all down—no more—game's made.'"

Drinking was common and drunkenness was only a minor transgression. Whiskey was the favorite drink and was taken straight and at a gulp. Although many young men resisted, or were not overcome by the temptations offered at the gaming tables and bars, it is true that gambling and drink blighted many a promising career. Dancing and theatrical troupes were also diversions, and billiards furnished "an innocent form of pastime," Brosnan noted.

Reading, book discussions, and recalling experiences "back home" were common forms of entertainment in the evenings, along with discussions of mining techniques. "Among the favorite out-of-door sports were foot-racing and horse-racing," Goulder recalled. "The long winter evenings were devoted to the reading of the few books that could be found in the camp and in overhauling the old newspapers that had accumulated in the cabins while the express had been able to make regular trips. A man named Harris kept a little newsstand in Oro Fino that winter, and among the treasures on his shelves was a nearly complete set of [Sir Walter] Scott's novels. My comrades agreed to buy and pay for the books if I would agree to read them aloud evenings while they rested in their bunks and did the listening."

There were other favorite (and unexpectedly sedate) diversions. Much time, Goulder recalled, was given over to playing chess or to organized debates. Goulder remembered the weekly meetings of the Oro Fino Lyceum and Debating Club. The Civil War was a frequent topic of discussion.

The *Lewiston Teller* of August 26, 1887, reported that Leroy T. Weeks preached the first Methodist sermon in Warrens in Bemis's Saloon to a quiet, attentive audience that summer. The collection plate totaled $17.75. A year later, the Reverend J. D. McConkey, according to the *Lewiston Teller* of August 24, 1888, arrived back from Warrens "and speaks very highly of the hospitality of which he was the recipient while in the camp. He held religious services on Sunday and was very gratified at the large audience which assembled on the occasion and proposed to repeat the trip and stay longer next summer."

According to an article that McConkey himself wrote at the time of his visit to Warrens, there were 100 white and 300 Chinese miners in the mining camp. McConkey said Warrens consisted of forty long buildings, a Chinese gambling shop, a school with eight pupils under the leadership of a Miss Riebold, and six families. The rest of the town was almost entirely male (three-quarters of that population Chinese). Religious services, when an enterprising parson risked the trip into the high country, were held in what had once been a brewery. There were also two stores in the mining camp. According to McConkey, travel to Warrens was largely via Weiser.

Winter also changed the population of a remote mining camp like Warrens. Chinese miners here at the end of the road might well outnumber whites during the winter. William Armistead Goulder recalled a resulting incident in the Oro Fino district in the early 1860s. "The few white men remaining in camp were overwhelmingly outnumbered by the Chinese, who had been coming into the country steadily and buying up and reworking claims that had been worked and considered worthless by white miners." On finding themselves in the majority, the Chinese soon decided to assert themselves in a way that was unexpected, Goulder remembered:

> Among the first intimations that we had of the disposition on the part of the celestial inhabitants was, that on the slightest provocation or fancied offense they would gather in groups behind their cabins and begin practice at a mark with their revolvers. Others would bring out their long knives, take possession of any grindstones that happened to be near, and begin to sharpen up and polish those long, ugly, dagger-like blades. But little attention was paid to these demonstrations, as they were, too evidently, only very stupid and cowardly efforts at intimidation. It could be noticed, however, that the "Chinamen" generally were becoming more and more surly and insolent. At least one of them, a little bolder than the rest, prepared a stick of stove-wood by boring a hole into it and filling the hole with powder, and then managed to get the piece of wood into a room where some of the white miners were assembled.

The explosion damaged the building and injured some of the miners.

According to Goulder, "This was bringing things somewhat near a climax and seemed to call for something to be doing on the part of the white men." The Chinese miner who had perpetrated the offense was put on trial, found guilty, and sentenced to hang. But Goulder and others in the camp successfully urged that the sentence be reduced to flogging— twenty-five lashes were finally agreed upon. The prisoner was then punished and ordered to leave the camp. The incident appeared to have some effect on the Chinese miners, Goulder noted: "This episode ended all warlike demonstrations or apparent desire for hostilities on the part of the Chinese population in the camp. Diplomatic relations were promptly restored, and everything moved along as if nothing unpleasant had occurred."

The incident, however, became widely known outside the camp and was misunderstood, Goulder remembered: "The news had spread that the white miners at Pierce City had brutally attempted to murder an unoffending 'Chinaman,' who had barely escaped with his life, and then had been driven into the snowy wilderness in the depth of winter."

But not everyone in Warrens was going to church or participating in book discussions. This was always a dangerous place, where the risk of violence and robbery was ever present. L. P. Brown, a well-respected pioneer often quoted by the historian Sister M. Alfreda Elsensohn, described the early days in Idaho as "a fearful time, full of danger for life and property, the trails were waylaid by highwaymen, who were not eager to work and sought only to plunder the innocent and inoffensive; the most atrocious crimes were committed and no person felt secure, day or night." Even as late as November 1897, an enterprising fellow wearing a grain sack for a shirt and grain sacks over his boots robbed the Warrens mail on Steamboat Creek at a place called the Big Corduroy. The *Lewiston Teller* estimated that $4,000 was taken. It was the end of the season, the snows would soon be coming, and the pack trains would not make the trip into that country until very late spring.

The backcountry was full of highwaymen or road agents, as they were called in those days, robbers who knew that many travelers down from the mining country were carrying substantial amounts of gold dust. Even in the hard winter, road agents continued to work the countryside. "Miners, prospectors, and traders were all carrying more or less money," recalled Goulder, "and many of them were making the transit back and forth between the camps in companies of two or three persons and often a single lone traveler. The gross yield from these sources was not a very large item for the 'agents,' but they managed to make it pay expenses while waiting for the more lucrative trade that was sure to come with the opening up of regular travel that would follow as soon as the hard winter was over."

Goulder recalled an incident when an old Irishman was robbed while making his way in a snowstorm from Florence into Oro Fino. The road agents took his gold, but the old man pleaded for his watch, a family heirloom given to him by his father in Ireland. The road agents were amused by his plea and granted his wish.

"A watch is something we have no earthly use for. We do not need a watch or watches," the road agent said, adding, "Everybody is watching us."

Chinese girl in front of brothel in Chinatown.
Photograph by Arnold Genthe.
Courtesy of the Library of Congress, Prints & Photographs Division, LC-USZ62-13459.

Six

SOILED DOVES

Amusement may be extemporized in some form of personal combat or the baiting of animals, but only whiskey, whores, and gambling can be counted on.

— Bernard DeVoto, *Unregarded Inheritance from the Frontier*

They were "soiled doves," "fancy ladies," and "sporting gals." They were "Cyprians," "trollops," "tarts," "daughters of joy," "frail sisters," and "sisters of misery." They were "the fair but the frail" or, in French, "filles de joie." They were "camp followers," "courtesans," "cottage girls," "common women," "scarlet women," and "strumpets." They were "sluts," "chippies," and "whores." The Chinese, in addition to calling them "one hundred men's wives," used the Cantonese term *lougeui,* meaning "always holding (her legs) up," just so that there would be no confusion about what they were doing in the American West.

Prostitution and gambling were rarely separated in the nineteenth-century West, and in rural Idaho during the Gold Rush they were conjoined, the first almost always complementing the second. Open a saloon and the gamblers and the sporting gals would follow.

In California at the time of the Gold Rush, young, pretty dealers in San Francisco's saloons and casinos almost always hinted at sex, if only as an enticement to wager. Many saloons and casinos employed attractive young women as hostesses—and miners in town for a spree would pay them merely to talk. Talk was not cheap—a conversation cost the equivalent of an ounce of gold.

"Women who are chosen from among the most attractive, are employed to take care of the gambling tables, and naturally they [men] gather in a circle around them," observed Etienne Derbec, a French journalist who was in California in the early days of the Gold Rush. "How can you resist the smile of a lovely lady who invited you? There was a house which they [the gamblers] used not to frequent, and which is doing a brilliant business since white hands are rolling the dice, and dealing with cards, or turning the wheel of fortune."

Warrens, though, when Polly Bemis arrived in the summer of 1872, was not San Francisco. There were no fancy sporting houses in Warrens; there were no fine parlor houses and no brothels with good furniture, chandeliers, champagne, and fresh linens. There were few dwellings resembling houses in the scattering of unpainted wooden shacks and log cabins when Polly got off the back of that saddle horse. Warrens was the end of the road for whores, too.

"Dance hall chippies," the first women to arrive at the end of the road, were not schoolmarms or librarians. They were not the wives of preachers, for there were no preachers in Warrens. These were societies without children, too. A mining camp needed a whorehouse before it needed a library or a school.

Saloons, gambling establishments, and dance halls or hurdy-gurdy houses were the center of life in mining camps. The hurdy-gurdy was a stringed musical instrument, a form of hand organ that produced music when the handle was turned. The historian Anne Seagraves notes that the hurdy-gurdy was first used in Europe—Germany was probably its birthplace—and became a popular musical instrument in America during the 1800s. Most dance halls used these machines for music, and that is why they were called hurdy-gurdy houses, as Seagraves explains. The women who worked as dance partners in a hurdy-gurdy house were called hurdy-girls or hurdies. A gambling hall at a mining camp might import some hurdy-gurdy girls for the amusement of its patrons.

Saloons and hurdy-gurdy houses, as described by Seagraves, were "long, narrow frame buildings with a bar on one side and dance floor on the other. A hallway with several small rooms was in the rear. These rooms were rented to the customers who wanted more than a dance, and to the hurdy-gurdy girls who chose to entertain a man after, or during, working hours. Not all of these girls were prostitutes; most earned a good salary from dancing and serving drinks."

The dancing itself was free, but the customer was required to pay a dollar for a drink for himself and his partner after each dance. The girls drank cold tea so that they would not become intoxicated and be unable to dance. "A popular hurdy could take the floor with 50 men or more during the evening, which meant she earned at least $50, half of which she gave to her employer," Seagraves reports. "But a good hurdy-gurdy girl, in the right sort of saloon or dance hall, could clear $100 on a good night—ten times what a hard-rock miner might make in a day. It was a good wage for that era and unless the girl was greedy, she had no need to use a room. In many saloons and dance halls in the West, the attraction of dancing girls or hostesses was not primarily sexual. The girls were there to keep the miners talking, drinking, spending money and gambling. The matter of sex for sale was entirely up to the girl."

But many hurdy-gurdy girls had to be imported at considerable expense and effort, and they didn't come to a remote locale like Warrens merely to charm the local miners. Although many later chroniclers of this era in Idaho tended to play down the sexual nature of these arrangements, hurdy-gurdy girls in far-off places like Warrens were often prostitutes, who entertained men in hotels, boardinghouses, or even the infamous cribs.

Some prostitutes "did well on the mining frontier, especially during the boom days, when competition was limited and prices were high," the historian Julie Roy Jeffrey observes. A gambling establishment might increase its business if it had girls, and such girls could be specially ordered (particularly among the Chinese) from San Francisco or even all the way from Hong Kong. The recollections of George Bancroft, a prominent mining engineer who knew Charlie and Polly Bemis and wrote a short memoir about their friendship, suggest that this may well have been how Polly reached Warrens in the summer of 1872.

The demand for their services in the American West brought prostitutes from the East: New York City, New Orleans, or even Europe. They became pioneers, too, understanding what gold in the hills meant for them as well.

French whores did exceptionally well, and observers often noted that simple streetwalkers from France reinvented themselves as high-class courtesans on the Barbary Coast. Entire shiploads of prostitutes arrived in San Francisco in the early days. Julie Roy Jeffrey noted that prostitutes may have made up twenty percent of the female population in California in 1850, and in the early mining camps they outnumbered respectable women twenty-five to one.

The popular image of whores with hearts of gold and opulent bordellos bears little resemblance to the life of a prostitute in a mining camp in the second half of the nineteenth century. Even if prostitutes made good money, it was quickly spent, the historian Anne M. Butler has noted in *Daughters of Joy, Sisters of Misery*. "Money, when they got it, went quickly for material possessions and did not contribute an appreciable improvement in the standard of living." For most prostitutes, life was hard and often short.

"The picture given of prostitutes in court records and newspapers is one with few happy endings," Jeffrey points out. Prostitution was associated with violence, drink, drugs, and youth (some prostitutes were apparently in their early teens), as was a growing social hostility.

"Of all the human wrecks caused by the maelstroms of vice and dissipation," said Nevada's *White Pine News* in 1869, "there is none so sad to look upon as that of a young and beautiful woman. We saw such a one in Hamilton. She was young, perhaps not twenty, but intoxicated—beastly drunk. She had staggered in through the back door of a gambling den, and had been ejected from the room into the backyard . . . where she fell, amid the jeers and ribald jests of the rabble, the mass of whom were doubtless less refined and no more virtuous than even the degraded target of their vulgar wit. In this helpless, maudlin mood, she began singing, in sweet and plaintive tones, the very words above all others most suited to her case: 'Once I was happy, but now I'm forlorn.'"

Bernard DeVoto, who was born near the end of the nineteenth century in Utah, when the memory of the Wild West was still fresh, offered a frank view of the prostitute, whom he described as "a female dehumanized by the manic cruelty of her customers." DeVoto emphasized the profession's brutality, coarseness, and violence, noting that "an unmistakable strain of cruelty runs through Western prostitution. Literature and horse opera have completely disregarded it." His portrait of the typical prostitute was unsparing in its cruel detail, and he found attempts to romanticize such women "preposterous."

"The frontier whore, that is, was often so degraded that it is futile to look for the equivalent in the waterfront dives of far ports," DeVoto observed. "She was an old bag for whom her profession could provide no employment in any place where the first steps toward social stratification had been taken. Or, very often, she was a child who had become physiologically a woman within the year. Or she was any other female whom circumstances had exposed to the utmost conceivable debasement and depravity."

In DeVoto's estimation, such women often became, as a result of ill treatment, as violent and vile as their worst customers. A brothel was a dangerous place, too, for customers as well as the girls who worked there. The newspapers in the West were regularly full of accounts of knife fights and shootings involving prostitutes.

"Fighting, drunkenness, and mayhem filled the air of the brothel. Even the most ordinary customer might unexpectedly turn on a prostitute, or some hapless inmate could get caught in the cross fire of feuding customers," notes Anne M. Butler. "The most routine encounters unpredictably erupted into scenes of murder or maiming. A quarrel over a woman caused two men to fire at each other in a dance hall. In Deadwood, the paper complained about the numbers of women appearing bruised and blackened in the dance halls."

Charges of assaulting prostitutes were routine on court dockets in the American West in the late nineteenth century. But prostitutes weren't always victims; they frequently consorted with criminals, assisting in murders and armed robberies.

"The social behavior of persons participating in prostitution ranked among the most disruptive and vile on the frontier," Butler notes. "A frontier setting and the basic ingredients in prostitution were not conducive to the production of genteel decorum. The corrosive, degrading experiences of the women wore away the most desirable human qualities and often produced hardened, embittered personalities. Only those who could absorb the elements of the institution into their own being could survive."

The official attitude toward prostitution was quite tolerant: local authorities regularly fined the doves but did not run them out of business. The anti-vice movement tended to come with civilization, and by the early twentieth century the American West cast a colder eye on the world's oldest profession. Red-light districts and "tenderloins" were regulated, and fines were used to control vice (however corrupt such practices might have been).

In larger towns or cities where there was some semblance of law and order, prostitutes were easy targets for graft. They were subjected to nearly constant shakedowns by the police and other local officials. Substantial portions of their earnings went toward merely keeping the authorities satisfied.

"Saddled with a gloomy professional existence and subjected to a complex payoff structure, the prostitute's career became one of sordidness and corruption. The combination of so many powerful negative forces served to produce a population of women notable for the coarseness and violence of their lives. Their interaction with customers sank to the lowest levels of depravity. The grasping nature of their economic interests, and the incipient suspicion with which customers and prostitutes viewed one another, reduced the possibilities for enobling social and sexual relationships. . . . As a result, violence and crime dominated the social contacts of prostitutes with customers," Anne Butler observes.

The system that brought Chinese prostitutes to the American West in large numbers also kept them subservient, the historian Butler notes: "Oriental women carried with them to North America the societal hierarchy that they had lived with in China. The Chinese called upon the system of controls as they knew it in their own country to create an American Chinese society based on rigid institutions." It was a system dominated by a tiny merchant class. According to Butler, "The Chinese overlords . . . carved out a society within a society as they continued to dominate the Chinese emigrants; among them were Oriental women imported for prostitution. These women simply moved from one controlling hierarchy to another."

There was a class system among prostitutes, and the Chinese in the rural West were mostly at the bottom of it. Brothels rarely had Chinese girls working alongside white women. Chinese prostitutes worked for Chinese pimps, although their customers often were white. White prostitutes loathed their Chinese competitors, just as white miners hated Chinese miners. At the top of the scale of "fallen women" were the mistresses, courtesans, and concubines—these words were used frequently to describe expensively kept women, private companions for the wealthy, whether white or Chinese. At the bottom of the scale were the occupants of the cribs—as they were called in San Francisco—or "hog farms" or "hog ranches" as they were called on the frontier. These notorious dives were often located near military installations or forts. Poor women and prostitutes past their prime, often diseased, had sex with soldiers and teamsters for small amounts of money. A patron would be likely to contract venereal disease in the bargain.

Between those extremes were dance hall girls, hurdy-gurdy girls, and parlor girls who worked in brothels. A parlor house—a well-maintained brothel—with clean linen and a madam to run the shop and servants might be operated like a decent hotel.

Almost no women in this old profession worked alone. A prostitute was owned or maintained or kept by a pimp. Debt often was the root of this relationship. She may also have been a drug addict. Alcoholism was endemic. Her pimp may have been her legal husband; marriage does not appear to have removed a woman from prostitution. Or a prostitute might have been owned by a procurer who kept a group of girls like a string of racehorses. The daughters of whores often became whores.

One infamous "hog ranch," near Fort Laramie in Wyoming, was named Openly Lewd and catered to a rough set of soldiers and travelers. "The Openly Lewd was a wild place where the rot-gut flowed and gun and knife fights were common," Michael Rutter, a historian, writes. Rutter notes that the celebrated Calamity Jane, Martha Jane Canary, a larger-than-life figure in the West during the late nineteenth century whose exploits were much embellished, worked here when she was taking a break from being a teamster.

Near Fort Fetterman, also in Wyoming, was the "particularly seedy and dangerous" One-Mile Hog Ranch, Rutter says. "You didn't go to the One-Mile unless you were armed. More than one man was murdered in its confines for a careless comment or his pocket change. If the Openly Lewd at Laramie was rough, the One-Mile was a battle zone. Most of the girls were no longer girls but nearing thirty—which was getting long in the tooth for this profession. Several of the ladies admitted they hadn't backed up to a bar of soap in nearly a year—the same could probably be said for the soldiers, so the playing field was even."

Historians note that desperation or the hope of quick money often drove young women into prostitution. According to Anne Butler, "Within the working world, women found that few jobs awaited them, and the existing ones offered less than lucrative pay. These problems enlarged in a frontier environment that catered to masculine workers.

Here women desired not only employment but some of the boom profits attached to the burgeoning frontier enterprises. From this combination of elements, a substantial prostitute population emerged on the American frontier."

Prostitution was also a last resort for women whose previous occupations were threatened by immigrant labor from China. For women in the West, many conventional women's occupations—such as being a laundress—were not options. The Chinese held those jobs.

"Because Chinese laundrymen provided a less expensive service, 'celestial' washhouses could undercut the prices asked by white women," Paula Petrik, a historian of Helena, Montana, notes. "Helena's laundresses challenged the Chinese on January 27, 1866, when they published a notice in the *Montana Radiator* warning the Chinese washermen to leave town or be visited by a committee of laundresses who would enforce its wishes."

One modern historian, Li-hua Yu, notes that the *Idaho Avalanche* of Silver City published a complaint from a woman who objected to Chinese laundrymen:

> What are the chances for getting employment in your city? The Chinese barbarians have captured Boise and will soon rule the whites. I would like to know if this is a free and independent country? If so, why should the "Chinamen" carry on their bull-dozing operations? I went to Boise city to try and get employment but the answer at each house was, "We've got a Chinaman." I inquired the amount of wages paid. The answer was usually $8 a week. I asked several of them what they would give a good cook and house keeper if they could get a white woman. The reply was about $4 per week. I left them disgusted, and subsequently met a friend, Mrs. ———. She wanted a girl if she could get one having just discharged her Chinaman. I asked what she would pay a good cook. She said $3 per week; she said she had given her Chinaman $7, but he was much better than a white woman. I bade her good day, with a tear in my eye, wishing I was a Chinaman.

Having no skills and few options, women could still, regardless of age, sexual appeal, or attractiveness, find work as whores. Often women whose husbands had abused and abandoned them went into the business willingly. One madam in Denver recalled how women entered the trade:

I never took a girl into my house . . . who had no experience of life and men. That was a rule of mine. Most of the girls had been married and had left their husbands or else they had become involved with a man. No innocent young girl was ever hired by me.

Not everyone understood what awaited her on the frontier. Gamblers, pimps, and dance-hall owners would meet a stage from the East that was carrying girls who had been brought West with the promise of high wages and a good life, Miguel Otero has recalled mining camp life in the mid-nineteenth century: "But when they reached their destination, they would find themselves forced to accept a life of debauchery or famine among the riffraff."

"It is probable that most of the girls who came out were pretty stupid, who had unrealistic dreams of fabulous wealth and position," note the historians Vardis Fisher and Opal Laurel Holmes.

In one large mining town—Helena, Montana—about half of the fifty-three women who could from census records and other sources be identified as prostitutes in 1880 were Chinese. But although Chinese prostitutes were as numerous as those in any other demographic group, white prostitutes might have greater independence and even achieve financial success, such as owning property.

"Men controlled prostitution in Helena's Chinatown," Petrik notes. "There is no record, for example, of any Chinese woman owning property or appearing in any criminal court action on her own behalf. In the social structure of the sexual marketplace, Helena's Chinese prostitutes were at the bottom."

The Chinese in such a world were helpless. An experienced French prostitute might make her own way in a city or a town, often operating on her own, selecting her clients, and eventually owning her own house. A Chinese peasant girl like Polly Bemis, who did not speak English and was a complete stranger in this hard, new land, did not have that option. From the moment of her sale in China and resale in San Francisco, she was trapped in a system of debt from which there was nearly no escape except by death or by the highly rare option of marriage, almost always to a Chinese man.

But marriage was almost inconceivable for a Chinese prostitute because a suitor would have to pay off her debt. The system under which Chinese prostitutes were indebted was rigged against them. Girls who became ill, or who missed work because of their menstrual cycle, had days or even months added to their contract. Venereal disease and pregnancy could result in lost wages, too, and contract extensions.

"It must have looked like a life sentence," Rutter observes. Prostitutes who escaped were further penalized, for they were required to pay for all the costs involved in their capture, plus the revenue lost.

"Some contracts state that if a girl attempted to escape, she agreed to be a prostitute for the rest of her life," Rutter notes. And, he says, the cultural demands on such Chinese girls and women were often sufficient to keep them working as prostitutes: "Women were so steeped in the tradition of honor and family fidelity that they hardly ever ran off. If a woman did escape or didn't do her job, she knew her behavior would bring dishonor upon her family. This was especially true if she was sold to pay family debts."

According to Rutter, it was not uncommon to have five, ten, or even twenty years added to an original contract, and as a result the girls or women were doomed. When they became too old to be attractive to male customers, they were often required to work as maids, cooks, or laundresses. "In California, some women were sold for $50 to $75 to farmers, and they worked in the fields until they died," Rutter adds.

A study of Helena, Montana, quoted by Petrik, indicated that most of these Chinese prostitutes "lived with men, identified variously as a servant, a restaurant keeper, a baker, and an acrobat; one Chinese fancy lady lived with seven Chinese cooks." These men, were, in fact, pimps; and most often, Petrik notes, the census enumerator described them as "loafers."

Glimpses of this world and the fate of Chinese women in it are horrifying. Newspaper accounts of the misfortunes of the Chinese were often written in a tone of arch amusement. On September 29, 1866, the *Idaho World* reported, under the headline "Celestial Love," "A China woman died suddenly on Friday morning in a wash house on Wall Street. Her history, as we hear it, is as follows: She lately arrived in Idaho City— belonged to a Chinaman whom she did not like—knew another Chinaman who she did like—tried to join No. 2 and was prevented by No. 1—per consequence, took poison and left No. 1 a disconsolate Celestial." This brief item captures the sentiments of the majority of the population concerning the Chinese. They were curiosities. They were strange. Their customs were unusual. They were difficult to understand, literally and figuratively. They were not taken seriously. They provided editors of newspapers in the West with an endless supply of odd man-bites-dog stories. Newspapers across the West routinely reported stories of Chinese women—many simply identified as prostitutes—committing suicide. Overdoses of opium and laudanum (a liquid form of opium) were the preferred means of escape. Drugs were easily obtained and not regulated. Occasionally, when drugs could not be found, some despairing prostitute would hang herself, as two young women attempted to do in a jail in Idaho. They were revived. The loss of such girls was seen entirely as financial and as a loss of face for the owner, an investment gone bad.

Chinese peasant girls tended to leave no record of their passing and no glimpse into their lives, but Josie Washburn, who spent a lifetime working in or operating brothels in the West during the late nineteenth century and the early twentieth century, believed that suicide was common among these girls. Newspapers provide ample evidence of this and were often the only grim reminder of the number of Chinese prostitutes in the West and the hopelessness of their lives.

"This unhappy girl ends all her earthly griefs by committing suicide. Suicide in the underworld is of such frequent occurrence that it does not attract the attention of the public unless there is something sensational about it," Washburn observed in her memoirs.

In Nevada, which had a sizable Chinese population, the *Virginia Evening Chronicle* of September 11, 1875, noted: "A Chinese woman, on H street, attempted to commit suicide last evening by taking opium. In the stem of an opium pipe is a small bowl in which the juice and dregs of the drug collect. It is a powerful narcotic, and a small portion of it is sufficient to produce death. The woman drank a quantity of it and was soon insensible. Dr. Heath was summoned and applied a stomach pump and administered emetics. The Chinamen kept the woman on her feet, moving about all night, and to-day she is in a fair way to recover."

Mark Twain's old newspaper the *Territorial Enterprise* reported on November 13, 1875, under the headline "A Celestial Suicide," the case of a prostitute who killed herself with laudanum. Her disconsolate owner "appeared to be greatly excited. Rings of white were constantly visible round both of his eyes, and he exhibited signs of mental distress that

would be safe to say the woman was one who had cost not less than
$800."

The *Territorial Enterprise* of March 15, 1868, offered another sad
account, headlined "Suicide of a Chinawoman":

> Yesterday officer Downey, who has special charge of Chinatown, as the Chi-
> nese quarter of the city is called, was informed by a Celestial that a Chinawoman
> had poisoned herself with opium. . . . As soon as the Doctor examined the body
> he said life was extinct—that she was gone. "Where gone to?" queried some
> of the long-tailed "Johns"—the whole front of the house being blockaded with
> them at the time. In order to make himself understood the Doctor was ex-
> plicit and said: "I think she's gone to China." The "Johns" received this an-
> swer with a roar of laughter, showing plainly enough that they understood
> what was said.

In a world where there was often little law and order, the fate of
whores was of little interest to the authorities. Besides dying by suicide
or from disease, many prostitutes were frequently killed by their pimps—
this despite the fact that many of the pimps were legally married to the
women and lived off them.

In the rural West, particularly in the mining camps, venereal diseases
were rampant, virtually incurable, and often the primary killer of prostitutes. Chinese prostitutes were frequently cited as the source of venereal diseases. A report of a special committee of the board of supervisors
of San Francisco on the conditions in Chinatown offered ample evidence about concerns over venereal disease, and ready speculation about
who was to blame.

A Dr. Tolland who testified before the board of supervisors said he
had seen boys as young as eight and ten years old who had contracted
"the worst cases of syphilis I have ever seen in my life" from Chinese
prostitutes. Tolland blamed these prostitutes for virtually all the venereal diseases contracted in the city. The report concluded, "Chinese
prostitution exists among us as the basis of the most abject and satanic
corruption of human slavery." The special committee not only blamed
Chinese prostitutes for venereal disease but went on to blast the Chinese as a source of crime and corruption, citing gambling and opium.
The Chinese community was also said to be the source of most of San
Francisco's health and sanitary problems. Although the report was over-
emotional and racist, the picture it painted of the life of a Chinese pros-

titute, while not intended to be sympathetic, made it clear that these women were victims.

The majority of prostitutes on the frontier were young. Figures available from surveys and census takers indicate that most prostitutes were between fifteen and nineteen years of age, or between twenty and twenty-nine. Very few were older than thirty-five.

A survey of prostitutes in the Wyoming Territory in 1880 found nearly identical age patterns among prostitutes. "From among the known prostitutes buried in Cheyenne between 1875 and 1890, eight were fifteen to thirty years old, four were thirty to forty, two were over forty, and the ages of two were unknown," Anne Butler reports.

The average age of a Chinese prostitute was twenty-eight, which was rather old for a prostitute in the West, although prostitutes ranged in age from teenagers to a few who were in their forties. Age was the great enemy of the prostitute, for as women aged their ability to attract customers slipped away.

The treatment accorded sporting gals varied widely on the frontier. Thomas Donaldson, the old pioneer of the Idaho Territory, offered these surprisingly positive observations on the life of a woman in a mining camp:

> With all the intermingled good and bad in the early days of Idaho, the average of social life was good. Divorces were not frequent, although the marital tie was once in a while stretched by people who wanted to be free. Some of our men and women did not care to have their former marriage conditions touched upon. I have been in mining camps where the ten or twelve respectable women were far outnumbered by common women. But all women were given respect and consideration by Idaho men.

Donaldson's memoirs, *Idaho of Yesterday,* written at the end of the nineteenth century, when the author was in Philadelphia, paint a rosier picture of the life of a prostitute than many of his contemporaries or modern historians offer. His recollections of the treatment of prostitutes borrow something from the gallantry shown to such fallen women in Bret Harte's stories. Donaldson recalled:

> Men were not suffered to abuse common women any more than they were suffered to abuse respectable women; any and all acts of cruelty to females met with prompt retaliation, within or without the provisions of the law. Eastern

people, raised in the midst of what are termed—often erroneously—moral surroundings, where external piety is in vogue at least one day in the week, cannot comprehend the gallantry, yes, the chivalry, with which men of the frontier, removed from the customs and restraint of older communities, treat women of all classes. Men thus situated see in every woman the image of perhaps a mother, a sister, or a betrothed; they see this image even in the worn features of those poor women who, as much sinned against as sinning, must at one time have been gentle and innocent. This reverence—and it existed in the largest and smallest town of the territory—was not an encouragement for vice: it was the form and name of the object which begot this veneration.

William Perkins, a pioneer quoted by Julie Roy Jeffrey, noted an astonishing feature about prostitution in early mining society. A number of the "soiled doves" who paid "a nominal tribute to virtue," mainly by behaving decorously in public, were considered socially acceptable during the early years of the Gold Rush. At San Francisco's first piano concert, in 1849, the front seats were reserved for the "doves"; a respectable man could appear openly in their company with little risk to his reputation; and the women were "treated with the greatest respect and gallantry the same as would be extended to the most respectable women by men in general." The mining frontier's sexual demography and the ability of some prostitutes to observe "all the exterior rules of respectability" explains this social phenomenon, so shocking to conventional moralists.

But that acceptance was not available to most prostitutes. One glimpse into the world of Polly Bemis comes from the poetry, translated by Marlon Hom, that the Chinese left behind them, testifying to the hard life on the frontier for prostitutes and the hopes they held for escape.

> The sufferings in a Cheun tower [brothel] are unbearable.
> To leave it is to be spared from sorrow.
> To be a prostitute is to be dirt cheap, and worse.
> Today, happily, I've met a fine young man.
> I vow to eternity;
> I will withstand even poverty.
> The domestic life may lack the luster of the gay quarters;
> But it's far better than living in a green mansion as a hundred men's wife!

The poems written about such young women always spoke of the hope of finding a nice young man who could rescue the girl from the life of a prostitute.

A green mansion is a place of filth and shame,
Of lost chastity and lost virtue.
Most repulsive is it to kiss the customers on the lips
And let them fondle every part of my body.
I hesitate, I resist;
All the more ashamed, beyond words.
I must by all means leave this troupe of flowers and rouge;
Find a nice young man and follow him as his woman.

The fate of such an unfortunate was sealed unless she became the mistress or concubine of a wealthy Chinese. When Polly Bemis dismounted from the saddle horse in Warrens in the summer of 1872, she was already in debt. Someone owned her. She acknowledged this half a century later in an interview. The only way out of the rough life for a girl like Polly, as the Chinese poem advised, was to find a nice young man. In a fashion, however odd the circumstances, and at a time when intermarriage between whites and Chinese was unheard of, Polly Bemis did just that.

Illustration of "The Heathen Chinee" playing cards from a musical album.
The Bancroft Library, University of California, Berkeley - f M1619.H4 1871.

Seven

FOND OF PLAYING CARDS

Life was at best an uncertain game, and he recognized the usual percentage in favor of the dealer.
—BRET HARTE, "THE OUTCASTS OF POKER FLAT"

In 1901, Robert Gresham Bailey, an itinerant printer bent on adventure who had come to what little remained of the Wild West, hired a "prospector-packer-cook-miner-guide-horse-wrangler" to take him into the still remote interior of Idaho. There were few roads. Much of the area was accessible only on horseback, and Bailey was advised not to go into the backcountry alone. The Nez Perce and the Bannock Indians were long subdued, but a man could have an accident. The old-timers still carried a handgun with them for an emergency—chiefly to shoot themselves if they broke a leg.

Bailey, who would later become a celebrated popular historian of Idaho, recalled that he first bought a half-wild horse from an enterprising fellow, Billy Palmer, who specialized in spirited mounts: "One dark brown horse especially attracted my attention, and this one I picked out as a first choice. The animal weighed about 900 pounds, but was so broad and compactly built that he looked 200 pounds less in weight than he actually was. My judgment was good in one way. Later the horse proved to be sure-footed and an exceptionally good packer."

Just starting out was an adventure because the horse that Bailey and his guide, Joe Randall, were trying to pack was half wild. First, it had to be blindfolded; then it had to be hobbled, its feet tied together to pre-vent kicking; and finally it had to be hog-tied. Palmer had agreed as part of the transaction to pack the horse that first day; if he hadn't, Bailey recalled, "the horse would never have left Grangeville."

The packing proved lively, drawing a crowd. "When the rope was pulled from his feet and the blind removed, although a 200-pound pack was diamond-hitched securely to his back, the horse seemed to be on his feet in one jump," recalled Bailey. "And then the fun began. We had a wild west circus of our own. That Cayuse executed every bucking jump known to the range, and I am not sure but that he had a few of his own never before seen. After a few minutes of this he quieted down and for that day gave no more trouble. But every day we had to go through the same routine performance."

Bailey and Joe Randall later went up over the old Nez Perce Trail, the same route taken nearly a century earlier by Lewis and Clark and the Corps of Discovery when they came through Idaho headed toward the Pacific Ocean. The route took Bailey and his guide to Harpster and then Elk City and over to Orogrande and the Big Creek section near the Buffalo Hump, and then down to the mouth of the South Fork of the Salmon River.

A man could still have an adventure in the high country, in those days, even without riding a half-wild horse, and Bailey and his packer had a few. One day, one of their string of packhorses carrying fifty pounds of dynamite lost its footing and rolled 200 yards down a mountainside. The horse was no worse for wear, but Bailey noted drily: "It was a ticklish time for Randall and myself. Dynamite when in the condition of that on the horse explodes very easily from shock."

At Crooked Creek, the two travelers met their first human in several weeks, a boatman who operated a ferry there. He took them and their belongings across the Salmon, making several trips. "When all was over I asked him what I owed him and his answer was 'nothing.'" Bailey said the ferry operator refused repeatedly to take any payment for his ser-vices and invited the travelers to stay with him. "We spent the evening at the house of our host, and I was regaled with stories of adventures from real life more lurid than is usually found in fiction. Midnight came all too soon."

Bailey's host was Charles A. Bemis, a well-known gambler who had long operated a saloon in nearby Warrens. Bemis entertained and fascinated his visitor, but Bemis's wife proved even more interesting to the historian. Bailey never forgot meeting her. "Our host introduced us to his wife and while I did not say anything, of course, I did a lot of thinking when I noticed the woman was Chinese."

What a Chinese woman was doing living in a cabin with a gambler on the remote Salmon River was a question that would interest Bailey for the rest of his life. This would be the first of Bailey's many visits with Bemis and his wife; their stories of "romance and adventure" became part of Bailey's *River of No Return: The Great Salmon River of Idaho.*

Written in 1935, shortly after Polly Bemis died, Bailey's rambling history—in which, he insisted, he "purposely avoided entering the realms of fiction"—contained a detailed account of how Charlie Bemis and his wife, Polly, came into the mountains in the days of the great mining booms. Bailey's version of how Charlie Bemis and his Chinese bride came to be together was based on numerous interviews with Bemis and others who knew him.

Bemis was descended from Yankee storekeepers in the Connecticut River Valley near Hartford who were long settled in New England. The family was prosperous in the mid-nineteenth century, and the reasons Alfred Bemis and his son Charles headed West remain unexplained. But there was gold in Idaho in those days and that was inducement enough for many to travel there. Neither father nor son ever returned to Connecticut. In those days, when a man went West to seek his fortune, he might never go home again.

As a young man Bemis got an early taste of the rigors of placer mining and concluded that there might be other ways to make money in the Idaho Territory. No one who ever spoke of Bemis said he worked hard. How much actual gold mining Charlie Bemis ever did is unclear. There were those who later would swear that he never lifted anything heavier than a deck of cards. But gold mining is a business that attracts other interests, and there were many diversions, even in the Idaho backcountry, for miners. Easy come, easy go. Bemis found other ways to keep busy.

Bemis is described in some accounts as well educated, and he prospered at some ventures. Early newspaper reports referred to him, in the parlance of pioneer times, as "one of our solid Muldoons." This reference to a popular nineteenth-century wrestler implied that Bemis was a force to be reckoned with, a successful businessman and taxpayer. But Bemis was really a gentleman of leisure from the very start.

"Not liking hard work, he took to the saloon business early in life," recalled his old neighbor in the Idaho backcountry Peter Klinkhammer. "I do not believe he ever had much money at one time. He was a gambler and could make money and spend it too."

Bemis was always something of an idler. He had soft hands, the hands of a gambler. He played the violin, too. Old-timers remembered Bemis as a layabout. When he wasn't gambling, he whiled away his days playing cribbage or talking to miners down from the diggings to get supplies.

Photographs of Bemis—all taken when he was an adult and some at the end of his life—show him bearded and brooding. He had admirers, but he was also reputed to have a bad temper and he spent the last decades of his life a wounded recluse.

What stories Bemis may have told the men in Warrens we do not know exactly. The winter nights were long in that country and the mining camp at the end of the road was snowbound six or more months of the year. There was plenty of time to spin a good story. Whatever the case, many men in Warrens thought Bemis was someone or had been someone, and Connecticut was so far off and unfamiliar that it might as well have been Europe or the moon. And so in the memories of the miners and men who lived in the mining country of central Idaho, Charles A. Bemis had come from something.

The exact date of his arrival in Idaho is uncertain. His father appears to have come first (records indicate that Alfred Bemis was in the territory in 1863) and perhaps sent for the son, who was only fifteen that year. It is also possible that the younger Bemis accompanied his father and that, because he was a minor, the public record did not note his presence in the territory. The Civil War was going on, and it was a strong motivation for easterners to visit Idaho or other points west if they wanted to avoid military service.

Bemis came from South Windsor, near the state capital of Hartford on the Connecticut River, one of the earliest places settled in New England. His grandfather Daniel Bemis was a doctor in East Hartford and active in local politics. His father owned a store in South Windsor and served as town clerk and postmaster over the years. By the standards of the times, the Bemis family was solidly middle-class or even upper-middle-class.

Charles A. Bemis (the name is often spelled Bemas, Bemus, etc.), the eldest son of Alfred Bemis and Marian Amanda Foster Bemis, was born on May 1, 1848. His father was then twenty-nine and his mother twenty-one. Alfred Bemis was listed as a "manufacturer" in Connecticut state records. The son was originally also named Alfred, but Charles appears to have been added to distinguish him from his father. The 1850 census listed him as a two-year-old living in South Windsor. That year, Alfred Bemis and his wife had a second child, a son, William Foster Bemis, who became a storekeeper in Connecticut.

Bailey provides a somewhat different account of Bemis's past, one that may reflect the bias of a greenhorn easterner. Bailey's relationship with Bemis dates from 1901, when he made his first packhorse trip into the backcountry. Bemis would have been fifty-three that year; Bailey was twenty-seven. "As was the case with all youngsters born in the bleak New England states, his early life was one of hardships and privations," Bailey wrote in his rambling history. According to Bailey, Bemis "when yet a young man . . . went to the seacoast, got a job on a sailing vessel and nearly a year later found himself in San Francisco. Tales of rich gold diggings in Idaho were beginning to trickle to 'Frisco, and when young Bemis learned of this he decided that Idaho was the place for which he had been looking." Bailey makes no mention of Bemis's father, but that may be explained by the fact that he met Charlie Bemis a quarter of a century after the elder Bemis's death.

Idaho's "golden age" of mining came in the early 1860s. Elias Davidson Pierce, who traded with the Nez Perce Indians at Lapwai, was probably the first gold seeker in what would become Idaho. While hunting with Indians in the winter of 1860, Pierce found gold, just enough to convince him that there was more to be found. The following summer, Pierce and a small party of gold seekers began prospecting along the Clearwater River. Idaho lore has it that here, on October 1, just before sundown, Wilbur Fisk Bassett took a few pans from Canal Gulch just above its confluence with Orofino Creek, a name that would be synonymous with the mining country. The discovery netted Bassett and the exploratory party a few hundred dollars in gold dust and also led to an outbreak of gold fever, with news of possible riches trickling out into the Pacific Northwest and then California in the next year.

Idaho had its gold rush. Within five years $3.4 million was taken out of the ground in the area around Pierce (as the first mining town was named) and the nearby mining camp of Orofino. There were subsequent gold strikes in Elk City and along the Salmon River at what became Florence. Near there, in the summer of 1862, James Warren found gold in the mining camp that would bear his name. By the end of 1866 the site at Warrens had yielded about $6 million in gold. Charlie Bemis and his father came to this camp at some point in the early 1860s.

According to Bailey, Bemis "made his way to Lewiston, and thence by various stages of travel through the different mining camps until he landed at Warrens, when that camp was at the height of its glory. Gold was everywhere in evidence, though the really rich diggings were owned by the few and the mass of the newcomers had little opportunity to make a stake."

Bailey's recollections of Charlie Bemis differ slightly from those of virtually every other chronicler, especially in regard to his work ethic: "Bemis was ambitious, thrifty, a hard worker and ever on the alert to better his condition." In the backcountry, Bailey recalled, there were sufficient distractions for Bemis: "Saloons were plentiful, the hurdy-gurdy houses offered their lure of painted women, and the gambling houses called lustily to those who would pass an evening of forgetfulness. Bemis took his pleasures as did his friends. He was no better or worse than the average adventurous miner of the early days. His one great passion was gambling, and his friends say he was ready and willing to wager everything owned when the fever of the game was upon him. Sometimes he had a good stake, and at other times it was a struggle for existence."

George Bancroft, the mining engineer who knew Charlie Bemis and eventually his Chinese bride, did not think much of his skills as a miner, finding him completely unqualified and unsuited to mining in this hard country. Bancroft, who was also the mining editor of the *Rocky Mountain News* in Denver, would have been a fine judge of a man's mining abilities, and so his recollections are all the more significant:

> He [Bemis] had neither the physical strength nor the natural aptitude to build sluices or dig gold gravel. He went to work in the mines however and he acquired some good claims. His instincts brought him back to the comparative comforts of Warren's whenever it was possible to come. He was fond of reading and playing cards.

Bancroft recalled that Bemis was soon well known for his gambling prowess throughout the Idaho mining country. He was the town's best poker player and found that he could win far more money playing cards than by mining. He leased his claims and devoted himself to card playing, which was not as stigmatized at the time as it would come to be.

According to Bancroft, Bemis was an honest and fair gambler who ran a good saloon:

> He was absolutely square and entirely fearless. While there is no record of his having shot a man, his fearless personality, coupled with his skill at shooting, enabled him to maintain order without getting into trouble.
>
> By and by he bought a place of his own. There was a small bar in front and a bedroom in the rear, but the place was mostly given over to roulette wheels and card tables. Like most keen gamblers Bemis cared little for drink. He prospered and was on the road to riches.

Thomas Donaldson recalled in his memoirs the boom and bust times that when Idaho was still a territory and gambling was done openly and under license. "In the early seventies we classed gamblers as gentlemen or loafers. The cheap sports, the 'tin-horn' gamblers, were driven out by vigilantes prior to 1868," Donaldson wrote in *Idaho of Yesterday*. Donaldson's book describes the role Charlie Bemis played in Warrens and the social standing a "good, honest gambler" enjoyed in the West:

> Our regular faro or poker player was considered as respectable as a reputable merchant, for they were honest in all things but their occupation; and the majority of them pursued straighter courses in gambling that our businessmen did in their lines under the guise of respectability.
>
> Many of our gamblers moved in polite society and were very popular. Eastern people find it difficult to reconcile gambling with respectability, but when custom permits a thing—when, in fact, gambling takes the rank of an industry—the social crime disappears. The high class of our gamblers, generally designated "sports," seldom drank, never cheated at cards, never lied to or swore at a man or woman. Their credit was the highest everywhere.

There was nary a remote mining camp in the Idaho Territory in those days that did not play host—sometimes quite permanently—to resident cardsharps. In a nearly all-male world, a world remote, tough, and lonely, men who gambled for a living—for what is mining but a kind of gambling?—gambled for pleasure, too.

"The great popularity of gambling games in the frontier West and the perceived need for the professional gambler were inevitable and predictable. In that historical time and place everyone was to some extent a gambler. All who fought for fortunes in the West were betting on the land, the future, and themselves," William Armistead Goulder recalled in his memoirs. "It was a period of great enthusiasm and optimism, for all were convinced that huge rewards awaited those with nerve enough to take a risk. For those too impatient to wait for the claim to produce a bonanza in gold, the cattle to multiply, or the town to develop, the gambler's table offered an opportunity for instant riches. It was a time of almost unlimited personal freedom and it was a loose, tolerant society with few to say that gambling was a sin, a crime, or a folly."

The enthusiasm for gambling was shared by the Chinese. No chronicler of the Chinese experience in the second half of the nineteenth century—from the Chinese-speaking missionary the Reverend Otis Gibson to Mark Twain to the modern Chinese-American historian Iris Chang—has failed to comment on the Chinese compulsion to wager.

"About every third 'Chinaman' runs a lottery," Twain said. Indeed, in gambling shacks across the West, from dusty railroad towns in the Nevada desert to the Montana high country, loud, excited groups of Chinese bet on dice, lots, and tosses of a coin. Historians frequently cite the editor in Montana who complained about the noise, which began after dark: "We don't know and don't care how many years they claim to have been infesting the earth, and only wish they would go to bed like decent people and stop playing their infernal button game of 'Foo-ti-hoo-ti,' so a fellow can get a nap."

"Gambling was as addictive for Chinese railroad workers as whiskey among their white counterparts," Chang notes, pointing out that the modern game keno derives from a nineteenth-century Chinese gambling game, *pak kop piu*. Gambling was the chief vice in a "bachelor society" of young Chinese men, although prostitution and opium provided other diversions.

"Gambling was the greatest passion, especially to the Chinese, who drank less than many other ethnic groups and did not dance at all. Therefore, gambling houses rather than saloons or dance halls became the preferred place to mitigate hardships and sharpen pleasures," the historian Liping Zhu has observed.

Liping Zhu and others often noted that the Chinese rarely played Western gambling games such as poker or euchre (hence the joke in Bret Harte's little poem). The games most popular among the Chinese were fan-tan (a counting game), *pai kow* (Chinese dominoes), and *pak kop piu* (Chinese lottery).

John Philip Quinn, a reformed gambler of some renown in the late nineteenth century, said that although the Chinese were extremely avid gamblers, they did not take to poker. Poker, in Quinn's estimation, was too American a game for them. "The Chinese evince no disposition to learn any of the gambling games in vogue among the whites," he reported. "They have no idea whatever of poker, faro, roulette, chuck-a-luck, or any of the other amusements which play such sad havoc with the fortunes, the morals and the reputations of their brethren of fairer skin."

There is, however, considerable evidence that the Chinese and whites occasionally mingled at the gaming tables, especially in remote mining camps. In Virginia City, Montana, a mining boom town, in the 1860s and 1870s, whites gambled with the Chinese. But in California, Alexander McLeod found that white gamblers preferred the ubiquitous Chinese lotteries over the gambling parlors. It would appear that the language barrier and the unfamiliar games of chance kept many white gamblers away, although that was not always the case.

"White neighbors were welcome at the gambling tables," Larry Barsness observed of Montana's mining camps during the boom times. "Those miners who had picked up 'a slight acquaintance with the jargon of chow chow' found that they could make a little money here."

The customs of the pioneer days, when gambling was openly conducted, died hard. Liping Zhu has pointed out that in Idaho gambling remained a legitimate form of entertainment until the 1890s, when the state legislature outlawed it: "However, people simply defied these laws. Some newspapers openly defended gambling activities, claiming that 'the anti-gambling law will be hard on the old timers of this state—not so much on those who have acquired the habit of gambling as a business, but those who through the long winter evenings have driven dull care away in the favorite Idaho game known as solo—played for . . . drinks or cigars.'"

But not all Chinese gambled for recreational purposes. "During the heyday of mining activities, professional gambling was prevalent in the mining towns. Quick Chinese minds and hands could make easier money at the Chinese gambling tables than in the placer fields. In both the 1870 and 1880 census returns, professional gamblers constituted the third largest Chinese occupational group," Zhu points out. In the Boise Basin (south of the Warrens district) gambling was particularly endemic: "There were five individuals running gambling houses and nineteen employees working there in 1870; in 1880, there were nine owners and

thirty gaming experts. Such a considerable number of parasites in the
camps indicates the relative wealth of the Chinese community."

Like those of their white neighbors, Chinese gambling dens were
places of violence, too. "Gambling houses were the chief Chinese killing fields. The majority of Chinese homicides were gambling-related.
Arguing over bets or debts at the table, gamblers quickly drew weapons
on each other," Zhu notes.

No account of the mining days in Idaho, whether focusing on white
or Chinese miners, fails to mention how central gambling was to the
day-to-day life of the residents. And no account of how Charlie Bemis
came to win his wife in a poker game in the Idaho mining country fails
to mention how much he enjoyed a game of chance.

Bailey frequently quoted old-timers as his sources, having great confidence in veterans of the pioneer days, many of whom were still living when
he arrived in the Pacific Northwest in the late nineteenth century. "I contacted and talked with hundreds of old timers who crossed the plains in
covered wagons," Bailey noted in the preface to *River of No Return*. "And
with many others who drifted West from different directions . . . and lost
no opportunity to get as much information from them as possible."

Charlie Bemis was such an early pioneer, in Bailey's estimation, and
his account of how Bemis won Polly in a poker game is vivid, spun out
of his interviews with the old gambler at the remote ranch on the Salmon
River.

The game was poker. The setting was a saloon in the mining camp
of Warrens. The key players were Bemis and an unnamed "Chinaman"
—sometimes identified as Hong King or Big Jim—who was something
of a local power broker and Chinese gambling czar.

The wandering Scottish journalist James Chisholm's account of the
Wyoming Gold Rush of the period captures the scene of the frontier saloon
where Charlie Bemis and his Chinese opponent would have faced off.
Chisholm describes "the flaring gambling tents—the dance houses—the
eternal strumming of old banjoes—the miserable females who have to
dance all night till the broad day light, with about as much hilarity as so
many prisoners in the treadmill—the game of Faro—the game of three
card Monte—the game of Roulette, Black and White—the hundred and
one games too numerous to mention—the perpetual tumult and uproar
and din of mingling cries—'all down, all set, make your game—seven of
diamonds and the red wins'—'Come now boys I only want one more

couple for the next set'—quarrels, cursing, drinking and the flash and bang of pistols—shameless pimps, shameless women, broken gamblers, thieves—depravity that flaunts its banner in the broad daylight—such are a few of the memories that haunt the vacant chambers of the brain."

According to Bailey, the poker game between Bemis and "the Chinaman" was the title bout in the mining camp and eclipsed all other action that night. "Old timers tell of one evening long to be remembered when every game in a big gambling house stopped dead still and the players and dealers alike gathered around Bemis to watch him play poker with a 'Chinaman,'" Bailey recalled. "The Chinaman was a leader among his race in the camp, and he and Bemis had met in many a friendly game. Sometimes luck was with one and then with the other." Still, poker is not an especially friendly game, and in the mining camps of the Idaho high country there were better ways to enjoy friendship and hang on to one's grubstake. A big crowd of gawkers watched. "It was not the game which attracted, but the unusual stakes for which it was being played," Bailey noted.

The Chinese gambler, Bailey tells us, had lost every hand to Bemis. They were playing for gold dust, but the Chinese man's gold dust had run out along with his luck. "But he was still a good sport and was willing to go the limit. He had but one possession left. This was a beautiful Chinese slave girl, who was 18 years of age and had been brought from China to San Francisco and then passed from one tong to another until she had finally come into the possession of this rich Chinese merchant in Warrens."

Bancroft also says that Polly came to Warrens as one of a "bevy of Chinese dancing girls" who were brought from San Francisco at the behest of the owner of a large dance hall in Warrens, next to Charlie Bemis's place. Bancroft is rather decorous in his description of Polly's career in Warrens. He describes her as "Polly with the pink cheeks and shy, modest ways."

Bancroft does not identify the owner of the dance hall but recalls that the proprietor, whom he describes as "shrewd and progressive," imported a number of Chinese dancing girls from San Francisco. Dancing girls or sing-song girls, to use another popular expression of the time, were invariably prostitutes.

Bailey tells us:

> With all eyes focused on them, neither man would back down, and when the "Chinaman" offered his last and most cherished possession—the slave girl—

against the table stakes, Bemis was equal to the occasion, and not only put up the money in sight but went to the safe of the gambling house, withdrew all the money he had in gold dust, and threw this into the pot.

Cards were dealt. Carefully the men looked over their hands. Cards were discarded and others drawn. It was a tense and dramatic moment.

As old-timers told Bailey, "a pin could have been heard to hit the floor had it fallen. The intake of breath by the two men in the intense silence sounded like the exhaust from a steam engine."

Bemis won the hand. In the words of Bailey, "the luck of Bemis was with him, and the slave girl as well as a small fortune in gold was his." Neither Bailey nor any of the old-timers present seems to have thought some mention of the winning hand might be in order, although Charles Kelly, a popular historian of Utah who also chronicled the story, claims that Bemis beat the Chinese merchant's three aces with four of a kind. In 1954, more than twenty years after Polly Bemis died, Ladd Hamilton, a columnist for the *Lewiston Tribune,* wrote an account of the poker game for *Saga* magazine titled "How Mr. Bemis Won the Chinese Slave Girl." In Hamilton's lively version of the poker game the hands were three queens and a pair of treys for Bemis, over three jacks held by the Chinese gambler.

Bailey assured his readers that even half a century later the famous game was still a popular topic of conversation in the Idaho backcountry. William E. Warden, a rural mail carrier along the 100-mile route between Mount Idaho and Warrens in the late nineteenth century, confirmed the story of the poker game in an interview with the *Lewiston Tribune* published on September 25, 1941: "Charley won the beautiful Chinese girl, Polly, in a poker game one night, married her and they lived happily for years." A. W. Talkington, a veteran of the Warrens mining camp who started there in the 1870s, related the story of the poker bride to Sister M. Alfreda Elsensohn, another lively chronicler of Idaho's history. From this point on, Charlie and Polly Bemis were together.

"She lived with him at his camp in Warren, did his cooking, mended his clothes and became very useful to Bemis, who had never married," Kelly, who almost single-handedly revived the story of Butch Cassidy and the Sundance Kid, noted. He added that Bemis was forty-eight at the time, so his account presents a slight problem with chronology, as it would mean that these events were taking place in 1896.

Old-timers from the pioneer days and chroniclers of the boom times like Charles Kelly were not the only ones who related the story of the poker bride. One of the first to take a serious look at the story of Charlie Bemis and his Chinese bride was Fern Coble Trull, who completed "The History of the Chinese in Idaho from 1864 to 1910" as a master's thesis in history at the University of Oregon in 1946. While acknowledging that the story of Polly and Charlie was "clouded with romantic rumors," Trull said that many old-timers in the country believed Charlie had won Polly in a poker game. She also quoted John Routson of Big Creek, Idaho—a mail carrier, like William E. Warden—as confirming the story of the poker bride. Another academic, Melvin Wikoff, took a look at the story of Polly Bemis in his master's thesis at Texas A & I University in 1972. "Much of her early life has been lost in the shadows of history. Time has erased any sordid facts and left a highly romanticized heroine dear to the heart of Idahonians," Wikoff noted. He seems to be referring to the tendency to downplay Polly's early days as a concubine.

Considering the reports of early pioneers, Wikoff, a native of Idaho whose family lived around Grangeville, concluded that "Bemis actually won Polly in a poker game, but did not marry her until years later."

Wikoff quoted at length the personal reminiscences of Mrs. John D. Long that had been reprinted in the *Idaho County Free Press* in 1966, confirming that Bemis took Polly from her Chinese master in a card game. Wikoff noted that the federal census of 1880 showed Polly as a twenty-seven-year-old housekeeper living with Charles Bemis, a thirty-two-year-old saloon keeper in Warrens. This was fourteen years before the couple were legally married. Mrs. Long, who moved to Warrens in 1889 and was a close friend of the Chinese woman, said that Polly lived in a house located next to Bemis's cabin and that she kept boarders and washed, ironed, mended clothing, and cooked for the miners. A number of other veterans of the mining camp had similar recollections of Polly's life, and many frequently commented on the romantic nature of the whole story.

But the romance of the poker game was not the final chapter in the saga of Charlie and Polly. A decade after the census of 1880 showed them living together, probably as common-law husband and wife, an event more dramatic than the poker game took place, propelling the couple into marriage and finally to their long hideout deep in the canyon of the Salmon River.

The Salmon River and the Bemis Ranch, early twentieth century.
Idaho State Historical Society - 79-98.109a.

Eight

––––◆––––

THE SHOOTING AFFRAY IN WARRENS

The story [of Polly Bemis] is clouded with romantic rumors . . . filled
with the romance of the old wild west thriller.
"The History of the Chinese in Idaho from 1864 to 1910"
—Fern Coble Trull

The end of the road was not a world where it was always easy to find someone to trust or prudent to trust just anyone. Charlie Bemis was trustwor-
thy, the mining engineer George Bancroft, who knew the old gambler at
the end of his life, recalled. His reputation may well have derived from
that of his father, Alfred, who was prominent in the mining camp. When
Alfred Bemis died of tuberculosis in 1876, the *Idaho Tri-Weekly Statesman* described him as "an old pioneer of Warren's camp . . . formerly of
the firm of Sanderson & Bemis, bankers and miners."

"His [Charlie's] great reputation for square dealing brought him certain responsibilities which were not entirely pleasing," Bancroft remembered. "It was and is the habit of miners and cowboys and timber-jacks
to safeguard their 'pile' by giving some of it to a trusted friend before
starting out to 'have a good time.' So Bemis procured a big wooden safe
in which to keep his gold dust and that of his depositors."

Bemis was, in effect, a kind of bank for the local miners. According
to Bancroft:

For instance, a miner would come in from the diggings with six buck skin
bags full of gold dust and nuggets. He would go to Bemis and give him four of

the sacks and say, "I am going to have a little celebration, Charlie, and I may get so enthusiastic that I may want to spend all this dust, but don't you give it to me till you are sure I am absolutely sober again."

So Charles Bemis would put that "pile" in the big wooden safe and keep it until there was no doubt that the "morning after" had really arrived, when he would deliver it back to the grateful owner.

The social significance of Charles A. Bemis in a mining camp like Warrens largely derived from this position as a saloon keeper (and gambler). The saloon, a public gathering place as well as community watering hole where food and drink were served, often twenty-four hours a day, was the heart of life in such a world. It was the town hall, the church, and the center of business life, too.

Saloon keepers were important figures in these communities, for many reasons. "At the pinnacle of the business, social, and recreational structure of the mining camps were the saloon owners," the mining historian William S. Greever has noted. "By adding water, burnt sugar, and a chemical, they could make either bourbon or cognac from their kegs of alcohol in about five minutes. They were the community's bankers, safekeepers of valuables, leaders in every charitable enterprise, arbitrators in disputes, trusted advisors, and friends of the needy. They generally kept their establishments open twenty-four hours a day."

According to Bancroft, a half-breed Indian, whom he does not name, who had found gold prospecting on the Crooked River came into Bemis's saloon one day and asked the gambler to hold his "pile" until he was sober because he intended to take the money and return to his native California and buy a farm. Bemis promised the man that he would put the gold in his safe.

But the next night, about midnight, the half-breed returned and demanded his gold dust.

"He was very drunk and Bemis told him to go and sober up," Bancroft recalled. The man returned later and again demanded his gold but Bemis told him he could not have it until the next morning. "Bemis was used to all sorts of drunken threats and entreaties, having handled many similar commissions before, so he put the half-breed out on the street and told him not to drink any more that night and he would return the 'dust' when he [Bemis] got up about 10 A.M."

Early the next morning, about six o'clock, according to Bancroft's account, the half-breed climbed through an open window into Bemis's bedroom and demanded his gold. Bemis again rebuffed the man:

> The half-breed sat down on a chair and lit a cigarette saying "If you don't give me my 'dust' before I finish this cigarette, I shoot your eye out."
>
> When the cigarette was finished the half-breed shot at Bemis' right eye. He missed the eye by a hair, the ball entered the face under the eye and plowed through the lower part of the head to the back of the neck. Polly heard the shot and came running over. She aroused the town marshal and the doctor. Bemis could not speak but he could write and he thus informed the town marshal that the half-breed did the shooting. The town marshal thought it was a waste of public funds to arrest and try a half-breed, so he rode after the rascal on a fast horse and shot him down at long range with a rifle.

That was one version of the story.

The *Idaho County Free Press* said that the shooting of Charlie Bemis in Warrens took place at seven o'clock on the evening of September 16, 1890. He was hit once in the head at close range with a pistol. William Hutton, an occasional mail courier, volunteered to go for help because there was no doctor in the mining camp. Riding hard all night across nearly 100 miles of rough terrain, Hutton reached the Idaho County seat of Grangeville after twelve hours, hoping to bring Dr. Samuel E. Bibby back to Warrens.

Three days later, the *Idaho County Free Press* published an account of the incident as its lead article, under the headline "Shooting Affray in Warrens." In addition to seeking help, Hutton had brought the news to the *Free Press* and was the source of its dispatch.

"The shooting was done by one Johnny Cox, a well-known hard case from Lewiston who only recently shot a man to death somewhere in the Palouse country," the newspaper told its readers, assuming some familiarity on their part with the shooter. Hutton had told the *Free Press* that the bullet entered through Bemis's cheek and came out at the back of his head. When Hutton left Warrens to ride for help, it was unclear if Bemis would live. Cox had not yet been arrested, according to the newspaper's brief account. The newspaper, which came out once a week on Friday (and cost three dollars for an annual subscription), followed up the story in the next issue on September 26.

By then, Dr. Bibby had returned from Warrens and told the newspaper that Bemis's wound would probably be fatal sooner or later. The bullet, on entry, had struck Bemis's cheekbone and split. Bibby said he had been able to extract only half the bullet and fourteen pieces of bone. "The other part of the bullet is still in the head and in all likelihood will induce blood poisoning, unless the system is strong enough to expel the remaining fraction of the ball," the newspaper quoted him as saying.

Bibby seemed to be Charlie Bemis's last, best hope. Educated at Edinburgh in Scotland, at what was then one of the greatest medical schools in the world, Bibby was a highly skilled surgeon who had come west for reasons of health in the late 1870s and served as a U.S. Army surgeon at Fort Lapwai in Idaho. He comes off as an indifferent quack in many versions of the shooting of Charlie Bemis, although *The Illustrated History of Idaho* hailed him as a distinguished physician—"a man of sterling integrity and one devoted to his profession and the interests and welfare of those to whom he ministered." It is unclear how much actual doctoring Bibby did for Bemis, because subsequent accounts of the shooting incident were dismissive, commenting only that Bibby demanded $500 for his services and returned to Grangeville.

Bibby, who was by most accounts a prominent and popular member of the Grangeville community, died in 1905 at age fifty-eight. But his reputation was tarnished by chroniclers of the "shooting affray" at Warrens—including Sister M. Alfreda Elsensohn, who depicts him as an incompetent moneygrubber—perhaps by way of introducing Polly Bemis into the story as the heroine.

According to Bancroft's account, the doctor said Bemis would die, but Polly refused to give up:

> The doctor said Bemis was fatally shot. There was no good of doing anything, just let him die peacefully, but Polly didn't think so. She knew something of Chinese cures. So she bathed the wound and put extract of herbs in it to stop the bleeding. For two weeks, day nor night, she never left his side, then the fever went down and he began to get better.

According to Bancroft, Polly then found the remains of the bullet embedded in the back of Bemis's neck: "Bemis was so cross at the doctor for refusing to do anything to try to save his life that he would not have him come near the room, so Polly, the dancing girl, got a razor and cut out the bullet."

The *Idaho County Free Press* added some new details about the shooting in subsequent issues. "From all accounts the shooting was entirely in self-defense and so Cox was not arrested," it reported on September 26. But contrary to this (and to Bancroft's story that Cox was shot dead from his saddle), the next week's edition of the *Free Press* said Johnny Cox had been arrested. The headlines read: "Cox in Jail" and "The Perpetrator of the Shooting in Warrens Captured in Pocatello."

Under those headlines, readers learned that two lawmen—H. W. Cone accompanied by James McGrane—had arrived in Grangeville with Johnny Cox under arrest. The newspaper reported that Cox had fled Warrens after the shooting, traveling toward Weiser, before selling his horse at Salmon Meadows, where he was using a false name. He then took the stagecoach to Weiser. The authorities guessed, correctly, that from there Cox had taken a train headed east. The sheriff knew that it was payday in Pocatello and that Cox, a professional gambler, would go there for the pickings. Cone arrested Cox in Pocatello on September 25 without incident.

Not long after this, the editor of the *Free Press* made a trip up to Warrens, saw the victim, and reported in detail: "We saw Bemis and found him sitting up and dressed and able to talk and smoke, but looking ghastly with that horrible bullet hole through his face. The wound is discharging pus freely, and it seems absolutely certain that blood poison and death will speedily result."

The circumstances surrounding the shooting changed in this account: "The shooting was cold blooded and premeditated, and the camp raised $300 in twenty minutes by voluntary subscription for the purpose of pursuing and arresting the heartless scoundrel who fired the dastardly shot."

The editor of the *Free Press* then added this detail: "Bemis is being attended by Mr. Troll, who combines in himself the happy faculties of doctor and nurse." Where this mysterious Mr. Troll came from is never explained. Perhaps the *Free Press* had formed its own opinion of Dr. Bibby?

By early November Bemis appears to have been recuperating, for the *Free Press* reported that a grand ball, the largest in recent years, had been held at his hall in late October and an "elegant supper" had been served. No mention of Polly Bemis occurs in any of these stories, although she was living with Bemis at the time, according to the federal census. This silence in the historical record may be attributed to the status of the Chinese in the West, and to her rather unusual position in the community as a former concubine or dance-hall hostess and the apparent common-law wife of a white man. Miscegenation, particularly that involving a white man and a Chinese woman, was almost unheard of at the time, and the *Free Press* may well have been treating the subject decorously.

Sister M. Alfreda Elsensohn picks up the tale in her two-volume *Pioneer Days in Idaho County*. Much of her account is derived from the *Free Press*. She says that Bibby, whom she describes as a 350-pound X-ray surgeon (this is problematic, as the X-ray had not been discovered yet), came from Grangeville in a buckboard and declared, "Nothing can be done. He is too far gone."

Elsensohn, who grew up in Grangeville in the early twentieth century and certainly knew some of the players in this drama, added: "The trip to Warren by way of Florence must have been a rugged one for the good doctor, as well as for his team of thorough-breds and the old beat-up buckboard that he always rode in. Perhaps he was thinking of the road out of Slate Creek when he presented his bill for $500 for services for the well-to-do saloon keeper."

Here her tale takes a dramatic twist: "The opinion of the doctor was accepted by the Warren community but not by Polly. Stepping out of her character as a slave, she took command and went to work to save the life of the man Bemis. A Mr. Troll helped some but Polly went to work with her Chinese herbs and remedies for the man she had learned to respect and even to love. She removed the bullet from his neck with the help of a razor, cleaned out the festered wound with her crochet hook sterilized no doubt with whiskey, and nursed him back to health. After a month he was able to sit up and smoke but it took much longer for complete recovery." Elsensohn does not say where she obtained this information.

Elsensohn, an unusual chronicler of Wild West tales, also based her first account of the shooting of Charlie Bemis on a letter sent to her by Peter Klinkhammer, one of the two prospectors who settled across the Salmon River from Charlie and Polly in the early 1900s. Klinkhammer and his partner, Charles Shepp, probably knew Bemis and his wife better than anyone else. They were their closest neighbors and cared for them in the last years of their lives. But they did not enter Charlie and Polly's world until long after the shooting.

According to Klinkhammer's account, Bibby did not enjoy the rough trip from Grangeville; because he was "a large man the trip was probably hard on him and he was not in a good humor. He took a look at Bemis, pronounced the case hopeless and denounced all connected with the accident. He collected $500 for his trouble and went back to Grangeville." Bibby died in 1905, after Shepp and Klinkhammer had settled in the Salmon River country, so it is probable that they knew him.

Klinkhammer told Elsensohn that Polly saved Bemis's life. "Polly took the case over. I think Polly did a good deal of nursing whenever there was sickness in the camp. She probably saved more than one life," Klinkhammer recalled. He also provided more detail about the shooting:

> C. A. Bemis did not lose sight in his injured eye. The bullet entered below the eyeball. It did disfigure Bemis and finally came out. The real story of the shooting is that there was a poker game in the evening and Cox lost money. He went to see Bemis the next morning after he opened up for business and told him that he wanted his money back. He told him he would give Bemis time to think while he rolled a cigarette. If he did not give the money back by that time he would shoot his right eye out. Bemis did not return the money and so the shot was fired.

That was Klinkhammer's version of the story as Elsensohn reported it.

On August 13, 1894, almost four years after the shooting in Warrens, Charlie Bemis and Miss Polly Nathoy (as she was called) were married at the Bemis residence in Warrens (as the justice of the peace, A. D. Smead, called it). W. J. Kelly and George L. Patterson were listed as legal witnesses to the marriage. Polly had been living in Warrens for twenty-two years at this point. The only other official document pertaining to her was a certificate of residence issued by the collector of internal revenue for the district of Montana on August 10, 1896. These were documents that Chinese residents were required to obtain. Polly Bemis's occupation was listed as "laborer." She said she was forty-seven at the time she received this certificate.

It is possible that romance was the only motivation, but Elsensohn writes that Bemis married Polly to keep her from being deported to

China (this would have been in the decade following the Chinese Exclusion Act). Whether the mere fact of marriage would have prevented
this was never tested. Bemis and his bride were then living in the remote Salmon River country, far from the long arm of the law.

Coming on the heels of the popular outcry against the Chinese, the
Chinese Exclusion Act of 1882 barred the entry of Chinese from the
United States for ten years. This prohibition was later extended. It began
what one chronicler of the Chinese experience, Corrine K. Hoexter,
called "a long nightmare for the Chinese immigrant."

The late nineteenth century was an especially difficult and dangerous
time for the Chinese in the American West. The Chinese government
continually protested against the treatment of its citizens across the West,
often demanding reparations when they were abused or killed. In Los
Angeles in 1871, a dispute between two tongs over possession of a slave
girl resulted in the accidental shooting of a white police officer and another white man that led to mob violence against the Chinese. Much of
Chinatown in Los Angeles was burned during the melee. The historian
Iris Chang believes that at least two dozen Chinese—including a prominent doctor and a twelve-year-old boy—were lynched by a mob.

Anti-Chinese rallies—fanned by American labor organizations that
were fiercely racist—were frequent in the American West, and these led
to further violence against the Chinese. In Tacoma, Washington, in
1885, a mob dragged Chinese residents from their homes and herded
some 600 Chinese to the railroad station, where they were kept without shelter, in the rain, overnight. At least two men died of exposure
and the wife of a merchant went insane as a result of this treatment,
according to Chang, who notes that the Chinese were rescued by the
railroad and taken to Portland, Oregon, for safety. There were anti-
Chinese riots in Seattle and Denver, too, at this time. In many communities, large and small, across the West the Chinese were actually expelled,
physically driven out of town, their possessions destroyed or damaged
and their homes and businesses burned.

The Snake River Massacre of 1887—near the Washington, Oregon,
and Idaho borders—was one of the worst incidents. At least thirty-two
Chinese miners were killed in an ambush by whites who believed that
the Chinese had a cache of gold. Despite vehement protests by the
Chinese government and demands for reparation, no one was ever suc-

cessfully prosecuted for those murders. According to the historian David Stratton, the increasing anti-Chinese racism of the time contributed to this crime. Stratton quotes a contemporary white rancher, commenting on the acquittal of three men who stood trial for the killings: "I guess if they had killed . . . white men something would have been done about it, but none of the jury knew the Chinamen or care much about it, so they turned the men loose."

Casual violence against the Chinese was also common—cowboys might lasso a Chinese laundryman as a supposed joke, or schoolchildren might stone a Chinese coolie in the street—but the major incidents of violence against the Chinese were some of the worst in American history.

Two years before the Snake River Massacre, more than forty Chinese were murdered by white coal miners at Rock Springs in what was then still the Territory of Wyoming. The Chinese government expressed outrage about this incident and actually sent investigators. The precise death toll was never determined.

In this incident, the white miners were enraged about attempts to break a strike using Chinese laborers. President Grover Cleveland sent federal troops to quell the disturbance when the authorities in Wyoming seemed helpless—the first time in United States history that such a measure was required. Although other groups, such as Mormons and Scandanavian miners, were also being used to break the strike, only the Chinese were attacked. As in the incident on the Snake River, no one was ever prosecuted for the murders. Writing nearly a century after the killings in Rock Springs, a modern Chinese chronicler, Yen Tzu-kuei, observed that no one in the town remembered the incident.

General prohibitions against the immigration of Chinese into the United States continued until 1943, when limited immigration was allowed. Large-scale immigration of the Chinese was not permitted until 1965. No other group of foreigners was ever legislated against in such a manner. Chinese residents of the United States who had arrived prior to the act of 1882 were allowed to leave and return, but they were registered by the government and reentry to the United States was often made very difficult. The naturalization of Chinese as citizens was forbidden. The act was racially motivated and basically barred most Chinese from entering the United States, essentially freezing the Chinese population for seven decades. According to the observations of local historians and people who actually knew Charlie Bemis and Polly, such legal prohibitions against the Chinese appear to be the reason that Bemis married her in 1894. They also appear to be the reason why Polly registered with the federal government in 1896.

Numerous printed accounts of Polly's life state emphatically that she was born on September 11, 1853, and Polly is often quoted as the source of that precise date. But China did not use the Western calendar in the mid-nineteenth century, and when Polly filled out her formal certificate of residence she did not put down a birth date but simply wrote her age—forty-seven—on the form. That was on August 10, 1896. (Actually, someone else must have filled out the form, because all indications are that Polly was illiterate.) She would have been forty-two that year if she had been born on September 11, 1853—more confusion. How an illiterate Chinese woman, brought to this country as a sex slave while still a teenager, would recall the precise day of her birth is a fair question. It is improbable that Polly entered the United States legally (she said herself that she had been smuggled into the country), and therefore that she had no formal travel documents to substantiate this date of birth. Until she married and later obtained work papers, she very probably lived without any formal documentation, as did the vast majority of Chinese laborers in the West. She lived all that time in rural Idaho, which was not a state until 1890 and where there was little in the way of formal law and order or government interference until the end of the nineteenth century.

It is interesting to consider the accounts of Polly Bemis written by people who knew her and her husband. The old tramp printer Robert G. Bailey, who knew Bemis and his wife for many years and wrote a long and detailed account of their lives in 1935, makes no mention of the shooting incident. That seems odd, because Bailey would have met them in the decade after the shooting and their later marriage. It would seem a fairly significant event to mention in writing about their lives.

The mining engineer George Bancroft is one of the frequently cited sources for how Bemis and Polly became involved with each other. According to Bancroft, "Polly was always industrious and noting the untidiness of her neighbor's bedroom she used to slip over during the early afternoon and tidy up Bemis' room. This of course pleased Bemis and he took a personal interest in the little dancing girl."

In time, Charlie Bemis became China Polly's protector, Bancroft said. She would have needed one.

Bancroft also noted, "'Chinamen' would not buy much whiskey but they are liberal with their women folks. . . . The Chinese girls were a great hit. Not only did the 'Chinamen' loosen up and spend much money with the girls but some of the white miners took a great fancy to the little orientals." This was a problem, Bancroft recalled, for the interest that white miners took in the Chinese girls caused racial problems in the camp and the girls themselves were physically abused: "When things got too rough in the dance hall she [Polly] used to fly out the back door and into Bemis' back door or if unable to do this she used to call Bemis who never failed her. His quiet, sober, stern personality together with his reputation for being able to keep a can rolling with his six shooter saved Polly from several very threatening situations."

Bancroft also tells us something about Polly's other skills. "She had been taught the art of goldsmithing and she used to beg nuggets from her friends and fashion them into hammers and picks and other trinkets, which in turn she sold for goodly sums. So what with the goldsmithing, the tips she got from Bemis and the money she got from women's time-honored methods, she prospered greatly." Bancroft's use of the phrase "women's time-honored methods" is the only hint that Polly might have been doing more than dancing to cheer the lonely prospectors at the end of the road in Warrens. Bancroft hints in other places in his account that Polly might have had a fuller dance card prior to marrying Bemis:

> From the time that Polly married Bemis she became strictly a one-man-dog so far as her sexual relations were concerned, but her heart was too big and her sympathies too broad for her to confine her interests solely to her little farm. Every time a wandering trapper or prospector came to the Bemis farm he was not only sure of a hospitable welcome on the part of Bemis but he was also sure to be loaded down with pies and cakes to be delivered to Polly's old friends.

Bancroft provides a somewhat confusing chronology of Polly and Charlie's years together. According to Bancroft, who often visited the couple, Polly did not leave the canyon (which Bancroft spells canon) for fifty-two years. Bemis died in 1922, so this would mean Polly went to live in the canyon in 1870—but that is before she entered the United States.

Bancroft also says that the Salmon River was not successfully navigated until 1918, but this was not true. A celebrated Idaho "river rat" and explorer, Captain Harry Guleke, was making trips down the Salmon as early as 1896, and he may not have been the first but simply the best known. Bancroft was writing from memory, and this procedure may explain his errors or lapses. But he did make a point of composing a single essay of about 2,000 words on "China Polly," as he called her.

Sister M. Alfreda Elsensohn wrote a great deal about Polly and Charlie, although her versions of their stories changed somewhat. According to Elsensohn, Polly worked first in Warrens as a "dance hall hostess" in a saloon owned by Hong King, whom she described as Polly's "Chinese master." In her version of the shooting, the incident resulted from a dispute over $150 lost in a poker game between Bemis and Johnny Cox. Cox wanted his money back.

In 1946—before almost anything was published about the "poker bride," including the accounts by Elsensohn—Fern Coble Trull, a schoolteacher and amateur historian, completed a master's thesis for the history department at the University of Oregon. She, too, picked up the tale of the "poker bride": "Perhaps the most famous Chinese woman in Idaho history is Polly Bemis, the Chinese slave girl who married a white man and lived in central Idaho for sixty-two years, loved and respected by all. The story is clouded with romantic rumors, but there are two schools of thought regarding Polly, and both of them very interesting."

According to Trull, Polly, "a very beautiful Chinese girl, came to Warrens, Idaho, about 1870, when she was eighteen years old. That all parties agree is true, but from there on the stories do not agree." In fact, Polly was always precise about her date of arrival in Warrens—July 8, 1872. So there is disagreement on this point, too.

Trull presents the reminiscences of the printer Robert G. Bailey. But, like Elsensohn, Trull was a native of Idaho and had grown up there at a time when there were many other survivors of the Gold Rush days with whom she might have spoken. Trull tells us:

> The most popular version, filled with the romance of the old wild west thriller, is that Charles Bemis of New England, who came west to mine and to gamble, came to Warrens about 1870. One evening Bemis began to play poker in a friendly way with a very prominent Chinese of Warrens. The two had played often together, but that night Bemis "had the luck." The Chinese had lost everything he owned but one possession—the Chinese slave girl.

Here, Trull quotes Bailey's account of the fabled poker game:

With all eyes focused on them, neither man would back down, and when the Chinese offered his last and most cherished possession—the slave girl—against the table stakes, Bemis was equal to the occasion, and not only put up the money in sight but went to the safe of the gambling house, withdrew all the money he had in gold dust and threw this into the post.

The cards were dealt and the play began. It was a very dramatic moment and all the house gathered to watch the final play. Bemis won the girl and the money, married the girl and lived in Warrens until 1893 when the gold camp died.

Trull says that Dr. H. L. Talkington, a retired professor of history at Lewiston Normal School in Lewiston, Idaho, believed this version of the story. She also says that many other old hands from Idaho at the time also believed it. "Mr. John Routson of Big Creek, Idaho, affirmed the story. He packed mail in and out of Warrens but he, too, was not in Warrens until the early 1900s."

But the other version appears to be grounded in interviews with old hands from Warrens who remembered the former days and knew Charlie and Polly. Trull claims to have painstakingly interviewed more than 100 old-timers and pioneers who had firsthand knowledge of the Chinese in Idaho. These sources are quoted by name, and they corroborate the story of the "poker bride."

In this version of the story, Charles A. Bemis was the son of a noted surgeon and doctor who was a friend of Governor Shoup of Idaho. (Bemis's grandfather was a doctor in East Hartford, Connecticut.)

"Charles was a tough character when young. In a fight with another gambler, Johnny Cox, a half-breed, Bemis was shot in the neck. He needed a nurse badly, but there was none available in Warrens." Here Trull introduces an imaginative variation on the story much beloved in Idaho: "In that camp was a Chinese contractor of Chinese labor who had a young, beautiful daughter of about eighteen years. She was hired to nurse Charles and they fell in love and were married. Rumor has it that the fathers of the couple disowned them. Be that as it may, all authorities agree that Bemis and his wife, now called Polly Bemis, moved up to the Salmon River on a little creek now named Polly Creek." Trull notes that her authorities on the saga of the "poker bride" disagree at this point.

Presley T. Lomax, an old pioneer interviewed by Trull, claimed that Bemis was an invalid as a result of the shooting, and that Polly cared for him. Another old-timer, Will Shoup, confirmed that story. "He was confounded lazy and let Polly do all the work. He fiddled all day long while Polly hoed in the garden," Shoup told Trull. Bailey added a little detail of life on the Salmon River: Bemis "raised a few vegetables. . . . He also rocked gold from the sands of the Salmon River and had a fairly good herd of cattle on the surrounding hills."

Estimates of the size of Bemis's spread vary widely. Elsensohn says that it covered fifteen acres but much of the land was forested. Trull says that Bemis had three or four acres of tillable soil at the ranch, situated on the trail between Warrens and Lewiston. She also says that Bemis and his wife were largely self-sufficient: "Polly raised wheat, ground it into flour and made her own bread. Her garden was a paradise of flowers and shrubs, many of them from China." How those shrubs might have traveled from China Trull does not say. "They raised their own food and bought only a few necessities they could not raise. Produce from their garden—'Polly's garden'—was taken into Warrens ten miles away and sold or traded for their necessities, which were packed out to the farm by pack animals. However, some articles could not be purchased at Warrens and so word would be sent up the river by some person going to Salmon that Charlie and Polly needed coal oil especially."

George Bancroft, the mining engineer who visited the Bemis ranch, recalled in his memoir that after Bemis recovered from the shooting he decided to propose marriage to Polly. The pair then decided "to homestead at a little patch of farmable ground down in the deep canyon of the Salmon and make that their home." Bancroft noted, for readers unfamiliar with that terrain, "It must be understood that there is a vast difference between the climate of the highlands and the canon bottoms in central Idaho." He also noted that the high country was snowbound for six months of the year, but along the banks of the Salmon the snow rarely covered the ground.

And so it was that here, on a slim sward of fifteen tillable acres, on the bottom of a canyon nearly 300 miles long and 6,000 feet deep, the Connecticut Yankee gambler who had cheated death and his unusual bride, a former Chinese concubine smuggled into the country as a sex slave, settled down to homestead. Their curious lives together and their appealing story would become a staple for amateur historians, newspaper feature writers, and the latter-day heirs of the dime novel tradition in the American West. And virtually every traveler who went down the "River of No Return" and left any account of the trip felt compelled to add something to the mystery and romance of Charlie and Polly Bemis.

Sister M. Alfreda Elsensohn and Peter Klinkhammer at St. Gertrude's Convent Museum, Cottonwood, Idaho, January 30, 1964.
Idaho State Historical Society – 77-144.15.

Nine

SAVING POLLY

The real people of the West are infrequently cowboys and never myths.
—WALLACE STEGNER, IN *THE SOUND OF MOUNTAIN WATER:*
THE CHANGING AMERICAN WEST

On the afternoon of Thursday, July 21, 1921, a strangely shaped boat that resembled a floating window box or planter appeared on the Salmon River and pulled ashore at the remote ranch where Polly and Charlie Bemis had been living for nearly three decades. Polly Bemis loved visitors. She would bake and cook for them. She put on her neatest dress if there were callers. She chattered engagingly in curiously broken English, unimproved after half a century in the American West. She was not camera-shy and enjoyed having her photograph taken; she beamed happily in photographs taken of her on such occasions. She liked to joke, and she liked to boast, too, about her wilderness skills, acquired in the hard school of life at the end of the road.

But the travelers on the "River of No Return" on this midsummer day were not the usual sports or backcountry dwellers who called on Polly. No single encounter with the outside world would have greater effect on the legacy of the "poker bride." If the pilot of this vessel, Captain Harry Guleke, had not pulled his rough boat—one of the party called the vessel, which was thirty-two feet long and eight feet wide, an "unlovely, but capable little scow"—ashore that afternoon, much of what is now known about the mysterious life of Polly Bemis would probably have been lost.

It was sweltering—temperatures had soared well over 100 degrees that summer—and the travelers aboard the boat were exhausted. They had come down the river from Salmon City headed to Riggins, a trip of two weeks.

A fabled backcountry character and the undisputed king of the river rats, Guleke was thought to be the first person to successfully run the forbidding stretch of wild white water that had forced Lewis and Clark and the Corps of Discovery to make a detour. He specialized in taking rich people down the river for an adventure, and his star passenger on this trip was a newspaper heiress who was looking for excitement. Her name was Eleanor Medill Patterson, but everyone called her Cissy. At the time she went down the Salmon River, she was still calling herself Countess Eleanor Gizycka because as a very young woman she had briefly been married to a Polish count.

Cissy Patterson told everyone that no woman had ever made this trip before—this was not true, but only a few men had ever done it. It was a grueling odyssey, even with a steady hand like Guleke on the sweep, an eighteen-foot oar with a six-foot blade that steered the bizarre vessel he had invented. No one had ever returned upriver; that part of the story was true. Most of the outhouses in hardscrabble Riggins, the village at the end of the trip, were made out of lumber that had come downriver as a piece of one of these strangely designed boats. Guleke took Cissy Patterson and her party down the Salmon, and along the way she met the "poker bride" and left behind her one of the few firsthand accounts of Polly Bemis, vital fragments of the romantic life of this isolated Chinese sojourner.

Guleke, who had pioneered navigation on the river, had promised the travelers many unusual things during their trip. He knew the river, he knew the country, and he knew, too, the fabulous eccentrics who lived in those wild places—survivors of the days of the great gold strikes, remote prospectors living in mining shacks a week's ride from a dirt road, hermits who rode into end-of-the-line mining camps like Warrens, Elk City, and Florence once a year or came out only to vote. Men still disappeared into the Clearwater Mountains in those days. But Polly Bemis was the rarest figure of all. There were few women in this country, even in the early twentieth century, and possibly not another Chinese woman with the mysterious past of Polly Bemis. She would spend some sixty years of her life in the Idaho backcountry and more than half of that time living almost like a hermit in a canyon bottom.

By 1921 Polly Bemis was a seldom seen but already fabled figure in the Idaho backcountry, like an exquisite bird. No one was more alluring than Polly, a living reminder of a vanished time that seemed almost mythical. Town was far away then. She did not go to Grangeville, the Idaho County seat. She did not even go to Warrens, the old mining boom town where she had first settled. She lived in a cabin on a bank of the Salmon hard by Polly Creek, named after her. Charlie Bemis was equally legendary. They were survivors of the Gold Rush who had retreated to this little ranch in the mid-1890s. Polly had married Charlie in the summer of 1894 after living with him for years. When Guleke's party pulled ashore on that afternoon, Polly Bemis had been in Idaho for nearly half a century.

Guleke knew Charlie and Polly, as he knew all the characters of the backcountry, survivors of the old West. He was their friend and their helper. His regular passages down this wild stretch of water allowed Charlie and Polly and their remote neighbors to exist or in any case to live a little more comfortably. He brought the outside world to the wilderness. He delivered packages. He brought the mail. He stopped and enjoyed a piece of Polly's pie. He brought Polly a pair of boots (she wore a child's size). He brought bolts of gingham for making dresses. He brought any necessity that could be obtained only from the outside world. As remote as the banks of the Salmon were in 1921, and as few as the year-round residents were, there were a few scattered recluses living here, still scratching at the ground at some forgotten, long-unworked mining claim, looking for gold or just getting by with a few cattle, some chickens, a big lush garden, and a half-wild orchard. This was pretty much what the captain and his party found that summer day when they stopped at the Bemis ranch.

A legendary eccentric in both newspaper and society circles, Cissy Patterson had married her Polish count when she was only nineteen. At the end of her wild life, *Collier's* magazine described her as "possibly the most powerful woman in America." That was an exaggeration, but Cissy Patterson liked exaggeration. She was, by various accounts, a magnificent horsewoman, a superb swimmer, an expert big-game hunter, and a subject of gossip in Europe's two most romantic capitals, Vienna and Saint Petersburg.

After her early marriage failed, it required the intervention of Czar Nicholas of Russia (responding to a handwritten note from President William Howard Taft) to get Patterson's one-year-old daughter returned to her. Patterson was the most exotic member of a family of prominent American journalists connected with the *Chicago Tribune*. Her grandfather was Joseph Medill, founder of the *Chicago Tribune*. Her father had married Medill's daughter. Her brother, Joseph Medill Patterson, founded the *New York Daily News*. Cissy Patterson had her own colorful career in journalism, eventually owning and merging two major newspapers in the nation's capital—the *Washington Herald* and the *Washington Times*. It was at her vacation ranch in Wyoming, near the Grand Tetons, that she first heard about the Salmon River and decided to have an adventure.

Her guide on the river, Harry Guleke, was more a captain than she was a countess. Whether he had ever seen the ocean cannot be determined: his skills were limited to the torrent of one of the wildest cataracts in North America, but that was water enough. Guleke was said to be the finest river runner in the American West, on a par with the fabled John Wesley Powell, the one-armed Civil War veteran and amateur geographer and explorer who had descended the waters into the Grand Canyon in the 1860s in a rowboat. If one was going to try to navigate the "River of No Return" without dying, Harry Guleke would be the man to take along. When he died in 1944, newspapers described him as "the first white man to have made the complete trip down the turbulent Salmon 'river of no return' in 1896."

And so it was that—almost two weeks out of Salmon City, on a cloudless July afternoon, tired from sleeping rough, badly in need of a bath, sunburned, mosquito-bitten, and growing more than a little bored with her adventure—Cissy Patterson met Polly Bemis, the legendary Chinese slave girl. Guleke was in the business of making sure his "sports" on the river had a good time, whether they wanted to fish or hunt or experience whatever sort of thrill appealed to them. It is likely that he understood how a romantic figure like Polly Bemis would appeal to an eccentric with the pedigree of Cissy Patterson. His judgment was correct, and the encounter with Polly Bemis was the only meeting with a living person during two weeks on the river that Cissy Patterson chose to include at any length in her account of the adventure, which appeared two years later in *Field and Stream* magazine.

In *Field and Stream*, Patterson picked up the story of Polly Bemis, or one version of the story: "Fifty-one years ago Bemis was shot in a bar room at Warrens, a mining town, and left for dead. Polly, the little Chinese slave-girl, nursed him back to life and in a year or so he married her."

The dates in her account are not correct, but Patterson met Polly Bemis and talked with her at length, and this fact distinguishes her from various other chroniclers—speculators, amateur historians, Idaho history buffs, academics, and pulp magazine writers who would attach themselves to Polly's tale. Some members of the party photographed Polly, too. Patterson wrote:

> She stands not much over four feet, neat as a pin, wrinkled as a walnut, and at sixty-seven she is full of dash and charm. She rolls from side to side when she walks—the strangest simian kind of gait.
>
> Polly told me—for we took to each other at once—part of her story, *sotto voce*, darting her wise old eyes about to see if the others were listening.

The old lady had told the story before. She had other visitors over the years.

> "My folluks in Hong-Kong had no grub," she said. "Dey sellee me . . . Slave girl. Old woman she shmuggle me into Portland. I cost $2,500. Don't looka it now, hmm?" She chuckled. "Old Chinee-man he took me along to Warrens in a pack train. I never seen a railroad."

"Fifty years in America have not broken Polly of her pidgin English, nor her low, gutteral voice," commented Patterson. "Presumably, if a child once learns Chinese its vocal cords grow that way." She also noted: "The captain told me that Polly always went hunting with her husband in the old days for she could see game when he couldn't; and she used to run up and down and whisk around the hills like a squirrel in a pine-tree."

Charlie Bemis, who would die in 1922, was already an invalid by the time Patterson stopped at the ranch, and she did not meet him. She also appears not to have met either of the couple's neighbors, Peter Klinkhammer or Charles Shepp. In the typically taciturn way of this country, Shepp and Klinkhammer did not stop their routine chores and bother to row across the river to visit. Patterson writes:

> I asked Polly where Mr. Bemis was, and she said, "Abed. He bin abed most two year now. He pretty closs, too. I gotta pack grub all time—all time."
>
> "You'd better get yourself another husband," I said, to see how she'd take it. "Hee! hee!" she laughed, coy and amused. "Yas, I tink so, too."

Guleke told Cissy Patterson that there were two or three old bachelors living in the backcountry nearby who would fight at the drop of a hat for Polly.

"Well—there must come an end to every romance," mused Cissy.

When Patterson and her party left the Bemis ranch, Polly Bemis warned them about rattlesnakes. They were camped in a field between her cabin and the river. And in the morning, without so much as a goodbye, the party went down the Salmon: they were only one day out of Riggins, and the adventure had worn thin.

Photographs taken of Polly Bemis that day show her as spry, elfin, alert, and smiling. She had a sharp sense of humor and teased her neighbors when her chickens proved to be more productive than theirs at laying eggs or when she caught more fish than they did. Most photographs taken of her—chiefly in the last decade or so of her life—show her neatly turned out in a gingham or checked dress and wearing a long apron with a large pocket in front. She was almost always smiling. She often was photographed with her dog, Teddy, or with an old horse that towered over her. Some photographs show her with her chickens or standing in her garden with a battered man's hat on her sun-browned, weathered face. By the time anyone got around to photographing Polly Bemis, she was no longer the beautiful Chinese courtesan or exotic slave girl of the story, but a sturdy old woman with her hair tucked up in a neat bun and often wrapped with a bandanna. She appears to have put on her best dress to be photographed with Cissy Patterson and Patterson's party.

Despite her boast, Patterson was not the first to make this trip, of course, or the first to write about it. "Notwithstanding the inaccessibility of the Salmon River Canyon, there are dotted down through it at many points a few quaint people," the travel writer Lee Charles Miller observed in *Outing* magazine in 1922. Miller made his own trip into the backcountry in 1920, before Cissy Patterson organized her expedition. His article—"The Boat That Never Came Back," a reference to the one-way travel on the river—mentioned some of the backcountry old-timers still living, remnants of the Gold Rush days.

Along with a grizzled old Scot, John McKay, Miller described "Polly Bemis, the quaint little Chinese woman who came to Warren, Idaho, in '72, married a miner, who was a saloon keeper, and when Warren died as a mining camp, moved to the Salmon River, where they have mined and farmed for twenty-seven years, and where Polly (and her now invalid husband) still lives, her intrepid spirit undaunted by her lonely life."

———

Cissy Patterson's account of her trip down the "River of No Return" appeared in the May and June 1923 issues of *Field and Stream*. The white-water rafting business did not suffer: Harry Guleke had more high-rolling passengers bent on excitement after that. Celebrity adventurers would eventually include the founders of the Mayo Clinic and the western novelist Zane Grey. But the real significance of the trip (and the magazine article it inspired) was that much of what would be known about Polly Bemis came from her encounter with Patterson.

Nearly a quarter of a century after that meeting, the person who would have the greatest impact on the accounts of the "little Chinese slave girl" picked up where Cissy Patterson had left off. That chronicler was an elderly Benedictine nun at a convent in Cottonwood, Idaho, Sister M. Alfreda Elsensohn. She never met Polly Bemis, but no one did more to save the story of the woman she called "Idaho's most romantic character." Without her there would probably be no memory of Polly Bemis.

Elsensohn discovered Polly when she began to compile what would become *Pioneer Days in Idaho County*, an 1,100-page, two-volume grab bag of pioneers' recollections. She included the first sources of her own fascination with the Chinese in Idaho. Eventually she would produce a 121-page paperback book, *Idaho Chinese Lore*, a rambling account of the migration of Chinese miners and laborers into the Idaho Territory in the nineteenth century. A sort of scrapbook, *Idaho Chinese Lore* was a crazy salad of facts, anecdotes, half-remembered pioneer tales, and yellowed newspaper snippings, reminding anyone who cared that there had once been Chinese by the thousands in Idaho. Elsensohn's research, however informal, was all that anyone bothered to do when some sort of primary materials were available. When she began, there were still many old-timers alive who remembered the days of the "Chinamen," and it was to them that she first turned.

By then, the Chinese were long gone. They were fading figures even in the minds of the pioneers, who in the early twentieth century retained only distant recollections of the Chinese sojourners living in tiny windowless shacks on the outskirts of towns, stealing an occasional chicken or scavenging coal for winter fuel in the railroad yards, coming with baskets of vegetables suspended on long poles draped over their bent shoulders, sunning themselves by their mining claims, speaking their own strange singsong language and broken English. They left little behind them: some terraced gardens on hillsides, a practice they had brought from China, where every foot of ground was precious; some bits of pottery; opium tins and pipes; coins; and other fragments of an ancient culture that was always alluring to westerners.

Edith Elsensohn, who entered Saint Gertrude's Convent in Cottonwood in 1915 and took the name Sister Alfreda, had been a girl in Idaho when Idaho still knew the Chinese. "The Chinese were rather numerous and were an endless source of interest and wonder to my childish mind," she recalled. "Idaho County has boasted many interesting characters but none more fascinating than Polly Bemis, a Chinese, who came to Warrens when she was a comely miss of eighteen."

Elsensohn was an unlikely chronicler of the Chinese in the American West. She was not Chinese; she did not speak or read Chinese; she had limited contact with anyone who was Chinese—but she became Polly's Boswell.

Mount Idaho was where Elsensohn's fascination with the Chinese began, for it was here that, as a small child, she observed the Chinese closely. "The author recalls how, as a child, she and her friends were warned not to go near the 'bad Chinamen,' some distance below town, probably because parents did not want their children straying so far from home. Those 'Chinamen' across the street were, in contrast, referred to as 'good Chinamen.'" The Chinese community was on the decline by the time Elsensohn was a child. About twenty-five to thirty Chinese, mostly older men—cooks, laundrymen, shopkeepers, and packers—still lived in Mount Idaho at the turn of the twentieth century.

Elsensohn writes: "More than one piece of their Chinese candy was bestowed upon me gratuitously in the store kept by the 'good Chinamen,' where my mother frequently sent me to make purchases."

Most of the Chinese whom Elsensohn remembered—Ah Bing, a longtime cook at the Mount Idaho Hotel, the laundryman Hop Lee, or Old Sleepy Can, who owned a string of packhorses—were "good Chinamen." She remembered Gue Owen, "the Christian Chinaman" who lived at Grangeville and who one day cut off his queue and joined the Methodist church to which the family he worked for as a domestic belonged. And when he returned to China, this church gave him a farewell reception and presented him with a fine picture, a token of goodwill. Gue Owen was not expecting such a send-off. "They gave me a reception and made me a nice present and I could not say anything, but just sat there and cried," the old man recounted.

But there were other members of the "celestial" community who were not so upstanding. "There was Gaul, a gardener and woodcutter. This individual would indulge in opium in excess for some weeks and then appear again, pale from the spree, and return to work. Lie Dick was so called because of the big, big lies he would tell. He died at the county poor farm," Elsensohn tells her readers.

Elsensohn rescued bits of Chinese lore from unlikely places. For example, she found the daybook of L. P. Brown's hotel and mill. Brown was the founder of Mount Idaho, and Elsensohn knew his family. His journal noted that Ah Bing paid fifty cents to send a watch to Lewiston for repair, Ye Sing paid a dollar for grazing three horses in a field, Ah Hoe paid a dollar for lumber to build a coffin, and a small boy named Ah Chewey paid $2.50 to take the stage from Cottonwood to Mount Idaho. The journal also noted that the stagecoach fare from Mount Idaho to Lewiston was eight dollars one-way or twelve dollars round-trip, for both white and Chinese travelers. And Elsensohn reported, "Neil Smith said that the last two Chinamen left Mount Idaho with a bundle tied on a stick and without saying goodbye to anyone or saying where they were going."

Elsensohn saved a newspaper clipping from the *Lewiston Tribune,* a story written in 1942 by Grace Kettenbach Pfafflin about Chinese market gardeners in the late nineteenth century selling produce, one of the few livelihoods they were allowed. "The Chinese peddle vegetables, especially the luscious Chinese radishes. Several packhorses loaded with vegetables were brought in each week during the vegetable season from the Harpster gardens," Elsensohn recalled.

She reported pioneers' tales of seeing the Chinese use an abacus to do business accounts. She remembered when there was a joss house—a Chinese temple. She displayed a sense of humor in recounting her tales of the "celestials" in Idaho, too. "It was customary in the early years of the Chinese colony to engage a brass band or an orchestra to furnish the music for funerals and this was always dance tunes or peppy marches. Referring to the practice of placing food on the grave, a white bystander once asked, 'When do you suppose your friend will come back to eat all that food?'" Elsensohn was nobody's fool. She noted: "The 'Chinaman' retorted, 'When will your friends come back to smell your flowers?'"

Elsensohn remembered when an old Chinese laundryman, Kwong Wong, standing at the corner of Sixth and Main in Lewiston, saw a car for the first time: "No horsee, no pullee, allee same go like helle." She remembered a fire in Lewiston in 1902, when a vast cache of fireworks exploded. She remembered the houseboys, cooks, and laundrymen who had died or gone home to China. She remembered when the first "Chinamen" came to the Oro Fino. She recalled the unsolved murder of Ah Fong, who had lived on Shanghai Summit until his death in 1932. She remembered when the "Chinamen" smoked opium and the Chinese women were all whores. She remembered times when there were three whites and 300 "Chinamen" at Pierce City. She remembered old Chinny Lee, as small children called him, who showed Idaho mothers how to treat poison ivy with herbal remedies. She remembered Ah Bing, who came to Mount Idaho at the age of sixteen and wound up cooking at the Mount Idaho Hotel for almost thirty-five years: "During this period he made two trips to China, buying a wife each time." Elsensohn recalled that, at the end of his life, Ah Bing came to the funeral of Mrs. L. P. Brown in Mount Idaho, "shook hands with the members of the family and said, 'My friends all gone, now pretty soon I die. Go China.'" And the next day he left for his homeland.

She recalled the first Chinese baby born at Mount Idaho—June 18, 1886. The *Idaho County Free Press* noted: "There was 'tall doins' in Chinatown at Mount Idaho last Friday night, the occasion being the naming of the Chinese baby recently born over there. A press rounder took in the celebration and the celestials did the honors in aristocratic style. The youngster is the object of much attention on the part of Caucasians and Celestials." And a few weeks later, the *Idaho County Free Press* continued to report on the Chinese baby: "Chinese babies are a rarity in this county. The little waif at Mount Idaho is the subject of much solicitude on the part of the Chinese and curiosity as applied to the white residents of the burg. A little pocket suspended from its neck was literally filled with packages of gold dust, present money, etc., donated by visitors. We learn that the 60th day after birth the head is again shaved with the exception of a small spot from which the queue grows."

Elsensohn's history of the Chinese, the reminiscences of old-timers and sometimes those of the children of pioneers, contained the memories of whites who watched the Chinese with a mixture of bemusement and distrust. They thought "Chinamen" would steal, given half a chance. A "Chinaman" would lace his gold dust with lead filings. "Chinamen" were crafty.

But pioneers in Idaho found Chinese festivals, including the Chinese New Year—usually in early February—great fun. The *Idaho County Free Press* of February 4, 1888, reported that 40,000 firecrackers were exploded. "The celebration of their New Year's Day was a time for great hilarity on their part which echoed across the street to our home," Elsensohn recalled.

Elsensohn understood anti-Chinese sentiment, too, making no objections to it but merely reporting the facts, largely gleaned from old newspapers. The same year that the *Free Press* reported on a lively Chinese New Year's celebration, it also reported that a steam laundry had been started in Lewiston, noting, "The Chinese must go." But by 1902, the same newspaper was saying that Grangeville needed a steam laundry: "At present all washing is done by 'Chinamen.'"

She remembered Butt Cut, whose real name was Ah Foo. (Elsensohn says that all "Chinamen" in Idaho had nicknames, often because their own names were hard to pronounce). Butt Cut is a short cut of wood in a sawmill, and this Chinese man was short. He was a celebrated character around the town of Cottonwood, where he performed various tasks, including cutting wood and shoveling snow in the winter. He was kind to children. He was known to steal an occasional chicken. He liked practical jokes. His English was incomprehensible.

Elsensohn recalled that the Chinese loved children, and she repeated countless stories of Chinese miners and laundrymen giving children little presents. Children, alas, did not always return the kindness: "One of the favorite pranks of Silver City's youngsters [was] to dig holes in the Chinamen's paths, camouflage the opening and hide nearby to see the fun when an unwary 'Chink' fell in. If the victim recovered from the fall and gave chase yelling at the top of his lungs, it added to the sport. In most cases food left on the grave of the deceased was stealthily eaten by the young white 'heathens' when the Chinese were out of sight."

To the children of Mount Idaho, the Chinese were mysterious and dangerous, too: "In 1941, Mrs. Aletha McGree of Grangeville recalled Old Ho, one of the Chinese who lived below town, who always walked with his hands behind his back. She was deathly afraid of him as a child because it was rumored that he had killed another 'Chinaman,' so she crawled under the sidewalk whenever she saw him approaching."

In its heyday, Lewiston had one of the largest concentrations of Chinese in the Northwest, so there was no shortage of opportunities for this sort of cruel entertainment: "Around 1900 and later older boys liked to find means to annoy the 'Chinamen.' People who lived on the hill [Lewiston is built on a hill] built a wooden stairway up the hill. One day a big rock was rolled down the hill into the window of a Chinese business house. Chinese swarmed out armed with cleavers, knives, or some other weapon. No one was in sight except a small boy. . . . When he saw the angry Chinese he ran as fast as he could up the steps and home." Elsensohn also recalled that "another source of annoyance was to close up the stovepipe so as to smoke the Chinamen out."

Pranks could go awry, too. When cowboys lassoed an old miner—Sam Lee—off the back of his donkey near China Flat in lower Idaho, the fall killed the old man. Such crimes largely went unpunished. Elsensohn recalled a case before a justice of the peace in Nampa in the 1890s involving the murder of a Chinese man. "There is nothing in the law book that says it is murder to kill a 'Chinaman,'" said the justice of the peace. "Case dismissed" was the ruling.

———

Pioneer Days in Idaho County was Elsensohn's debut as historian. It led to her next project, the little volume *Idaho Chinese Lore,* which had a separate chapter on "Polly Bemis, Legendary Heroine." Eventually, Elsensohn would write *Idaho's Most Romantic Character: Polly Bemis,* in 1979. Although not the first mentions of Polly Bemis in print, these books represented a significant attempt to save her story.

"Perhaps no one person in Idaho County has evoked more interest than the Chinese woman Polly Bemis," Elsensohn told her readers. "She seems to have attained national fame. Requests for pictures or information about her have come from New York City, Denver, Tacoma, Spokane, Ashley Falls, Massachusetts; from Oregon, from Pocatello."

Elsensohn reports that Polly's real name was Lalu Nathoy (a supposed fact often repeated by other writers). She does not explain how she knows this. She also reports that Polly could neither read nor write and appeared to have forgotten her native language. According to Elsensohn, Polly was said to have a good head for figures and math: she could count and make change, and she might have acquired these skills in a gambling house or saloon. She was said to have a phenomenal memory; she remembered the dates of births and deaths. However, on the one occasion when she was known to write her name in Chinese, an examination suggested that she might have been trained to write it. The signature is illegible and cannot be translated.

"When school came to Warren, Polly remarked, 'I can't go to school. I got to make money. God gave me that much,' she said pointing to her head. 'I learn right along,'" Elsensohn wrote, quoting old-timers who had known Polly.

Elsewhere, Elsensohn noted: "When they first came to the ranch Charlie started to teach her but after a while he discontinued his lessons. She could add and play cards and was able to make change for prospectors who came to buy food."

Like others who actually knew Polly, Elsensohn recalled that she had an amazing memory for facts and names and dates: "She knew the name of every child born in Warren and the date of its birth. She also remembered every death and when it occurred."

Polly Bemis was famously generous. "People had felt free to call on Polly for anyone sick in Warren," Elsensohn noted in *Idaho's Most Romantic Character: Polly Bemis.* "Several writers including R. G. Bailey pictured her in nursing garb and called her 'The Angel of the Salmon River.' She was official nurse for anyone who became ill or was injured whether they could pay or not."

She recalled Bailey's tribute to Polly and Charlie: "I visited several times with this couple, and never have I been more courteously entertained. They were hospitality itself, and would take no remuneration for their trouble."

"Everyone has a good word for her," Bailey adds in *River of No Return.* "By her kindly acts to visitors and her loyalty and devotion to her husband, she has endeared herself to every one who knows her personally or has heard her dramatic story. She has a yellow skin but a white heart encased in a sheathing of gold."

Polly's celebrated kindnesses outlived her. When a National Geographic Society expedition came down the Salmon River in the 1930s, after her death, its account noted: "For many years the generous hospitality of Polly and her husband was a byword among the mountain people. Her death removed the Salmon's most romantic figure."

Elsensohn, like other sources, reports that Polly was born on September 11, 1853, in China, on the frontier near one of the upper rivers. How she established the date she does not tell her readers; and, as noted in Chapter 8, China did not use the Western calendar at that time. But

Elsensohn does elaborate on the story that Polly Bemis told Cissy Patterson in 1921: "Her parents were poor and suffered from drought to their crops and from the ravages of brigands. One year these outlaws raided the country and took all the crops. To prevent starvation for the rest of the family in that year of famine her father sold her to one of the leaders of the plundering band in exchange for seed to plant another crop."

Elsensohn changed her mind as to whether Polly had, in fact, been won in a poker game. In 1970, Elsensohn was "certain that she was not a poker bride," but a few sentences later she included a detailed account of the celebrated poker game. She remained ambivalent, admitting that "there are many variations in accounts of Polly." Like several old-timers, many of whom she interviewed, Elsensohn was decorous in dealing with Polly's days as a probable concubine, although she referred to Polly as a slave.

Elsensohn was not the only chronicler of Polly Bemis's story who would soften and sanitize it. Reading the reminiscences of various old-timers reveals that Polly Bemis had many good friends who deftly dodged the precise nature of her arrival in the West. The mining engineer George Bancroft, affectionate as he was in his recollections, did hint at her life as a prostitute of sorts, or at the very least a "sing-song girl," but others were more decorous. Victorian sensibilities carried over from the late nineteenth century into the twentieth century, and some old-timers who remembered Polly or had some knowledge of her plainly felt protective toward her. They began to clean up her story. This bowdlerization of Polly's life story became pervasive, although it failed to explain what an illiterate Chinese peasant girl was doing in an Idaho mining camp in 1872. It was a tale straight out of Bret Harte.

Although one historian of Chinese prostitutes in the nineteenth-century West, Benson Tong, believes that Polly Bemis was a prostitute, the probability that she was ever a soiled dove or worked in the infamous cribs is fairly low. If she had, venereal disease alone—not to mention violence—would probably have shortened her life. But there were many levels of sexual slavery—bondage of a sort—for Chinese women, and being a concubine was merely one. Polly's sale to a single private owner may have saved her from that route and early death. Still, her early years in Warrens remain murky, to say the least. She said, for instance, that she arrived on July 8, 1872, but she does not appear in any public record until she shows up in the 1880 census, where she is listed as living with Charles Bemis. She is said to be twenty-seven (that would make the birth date of 1853 correct). On her certificate of residence—granted August 10, 1896—she said he was forty-seven, and this would have made 1849 or 1850 the year of her birth. In the census record, her place of birth was said to be Peking. She was said to be a housekeeper. And to add mystery to the tale, she was said to be "widowed." No newspaper account of Warrens or of Charlie Bemis—not even any account of the celebrated shooting affray—makes mention of Polly. Recollections of old-timers indicate that she was keeping some sort of boardinghouse and cooking and doing laundry then, too. From the distance of the twenty-first century, it is important to remember that the Chinese were nearly invisible in the American West.

"The life of an Idaho Chinese woman typifies the experiences of many," the historian Priscilla Wegars has observed. "Traded by her father for two bags of seed grain during a famine year, Polly was resold as a slave girl and later auctioned in San Francisco for $2,500. She arrived at the mining camp of Warrens, now Warren, in 1872, the property of one Hong King, who had bought her as a hostess for his gambling hall and saloon. There is no evidence to suggest that she was a prostitute in the commonly-accepted sense; although she was Hong King's concubine, he seems to have kept her for his exclusive use."

Although some of the story of "China Polly" is conjecture, her basic story, pieced together from people who actually knew her, is plausible. San Francisco was the chief port of entry from China, and it was in the infamous barracoons of Chinatown that a peasant girl like Polly would have literally been auctioned. A procurer (the old woman Polly remembered at the end of her life) would have then taken her to her new owner. Polly Bemis said she was sold for a great deal of money, and having been sold for a great deal of money she would have been worth too much to be sent to the cribs or to work as a common prostitute. Polly had several recollections at the end of her life that hint at her early days in the West but those memories leave the reader to fill in the blanks. The original marriage certificate—giving her name as Polly Nathoy—is in Saint Gertrude's museum.

Some of Elsensohn's early information is derived from the account of Polly Bemis, written by Cissy Patterson, that appeared in *Field and Stream*. Some of it is derived from Robert Gresham Bailey's account in *River of No Return*. Elsensohn knew Bailey and consulted with him on her project. Also, some pioneers recalled the last decade of Polly's life, after the death of her husband, when she made a couple of trips into the outside world. Much of Elsensohn's information came from Peter Klinkhammer, a fellow German-American, the child of immigrants, originally from Minnesota, and—most important—a Roman Catholic. Whether for religious or sentimental reasons, Klinkhammer had a long friendship with the Benedictine convent at Cottonwood.

It was from her friendships with old-timers in Grangeville that Elsensohn obtained some of the liveliest memories of Polly Bemis. One of those stories came from Ralph D. Long: "Bemis once captured a cougar (one account claims the cat was an orphaned cub) and kept it as a pet for some time evidently in the Salmon River home. The cat ate with them from a tin plate nailed to the table." Polly, who was said to have no difficulty making the cat behave, enjoyed recalling the unusual house pet long after her husband's death. Eventually, though, the cougar had to be put down. According to Long, Polly remarked, "Charlie kept um big cat but when stranger come he hump um up and spit um."

Elsensohn was not the last chronicler to be fascinated by the life of Polly Bemis. One modern collector of the story is Ruthanne Lum McCunn, who compiled considerable material in order to write a historical novel very loosely based on Polly—*Thousand Pieces of Gold,* published in 1981 and later filmed. McCunn's research supports the idea that Charlie Bemis won Polly in a poker game.

"It is unlikely that Polly got free of Hong King on her own," McCunn says. "Bringing Chinese women into the country had become so difficult that men with women already in their possession refused to sell them. It does not seem likely, then, that Hong King would have allowed Polly—who must have been drawing customers to her saloon with her beauty, wit, and charm—to buy her freedom, let alone given it to her." Polly Bemis entered the American West as a thing of value. She was worth a lot of money. It seems implausible that her "owner" would have simply allowed her to walk off.

McCunn notes that many old-timers (or their descendants) offered additional recollections about Polly's colorful life. Like so many others, Lucille Moss, whose mother had been a friend of Polly's, confirmed the story of the "poker bride." "(Mom) used to tell me the story of how Charlie won her in a gambling game, how she looked after Charlie after he was shot, her gold buttons, and how clean her house always was," Mrs. Moss wrote in a letter to McCunn in 1982.

McCunn also took into consideration that many old-timers who had known Polly tended to soften her real story. She quotes A. W. Talkington, who said: "Polly was a good woman and entitled to a good deal of consideration because of her upright conduct in rather difficult circumstances." McCunn added, "Perhaps as part of that consideration, he did not elaborate on those circumstances." McCunn also noted that the mining engineer George Bancroft claimed Polly "got money from women's time-honored methods." But McCunn points out that Bancroft "did not condemn her for it. Indeed, he described her as having 'shy, modest ways,' clearly thought highly of her, and considered himself a good friend. But he did not meet her until the early 1900s, and all the pioneers I contacted insisted that Polly had never worked as a prostitute, although they acknowledged that she may have been purchased in Hong Kong for that purpose." Bancroft obviously was fond of Bemis and his wife, but he hinted at Polly's earlier life in an essay he wrote about her, "China Polly."

A. W. Talkington, a longtime resident of Warrens, quoted at length by McCunn, insisted that Charlie Bemis "did actually take Polly away from her Chinese owner." Talkington was not the only old-timer to confirm the story of the "poker bride." McCunn quoted the daughter of Polly's old friend Bertha Long: "Polly Nathoy was brought from China to Warrens for the world's oldest profession. When taken to (Hong King's) saloon she was terrified! Charlie Bemis was present and protected her from unwanted advances." This makes a nice story, but how it would have been possible is not explained. There were also other old-timers who swore the story was a myth. (There were sufficient old-timers in those days to establish the pedigree of any story.)

Like many other chroniclers of the story, McCunn theorized that Bemis formalized his relationship with Polly because of the Geary Act of 1892, which required Chinese residents in the United States to carry a residency certificate. McCunn noted that Polly was in the country illegally and probably feared deportation. Whether marriage alone would have prevented deportation is another matter, but Polly obtained a residency certificate in 1896. By this time the couple had retreated to the banks of the Salmon River, where the probability of deportation was rather slight.

The memories of old-timers have complicated this tale, but not all chroniclers have been able to acknowledge that problem. What Polly Bemis did most successfully was survive. She survived an experience and a system that killed most of the young women who entered it, and she remains the face of nearly every Chinese woman brought into this country in those days because of that simple fact.

Chinese man mining along river.
The Bancroft Library, University of California, Berkeley, BANC PIC 1996.001:88—ALB.

Ten

LAST DAYS ON THE RIVER

The dullest diary is better than the sharpest memory.
—JOHNNY CARREY AND CORT CONLEY, *RIVER OF NO RETURN*

Polly Bemis was always lucky, as someone who was won in a poker game ought to be. After marrying Charlie Bemis and moving to the Salmon River canyon in the 1890s, she was lucky to have good neighbors. Shortly after the turn of the twentieth century, two prospectors located across the river from the Bemis ranch at the mouth of Crooked Creek. These homesteaders were Charles Shepp and Peter Klinkhammer—and if Sister M. Alfreda Elsensohn saved the memory of the "poker bride," they saved Polly Bemis herself. Without their friendship and kindness, Polly Bemis would not have been able to remain in the backcountry after Charlie died.

Shepp was an Iowan who had drifted off the midwestern plains, worked around the Pacific Northwest, and tried his hand—unsuccessfully—at gold mining in Alaska at the time of the Klondike strike. He settled on the Salmon River in the early 1900s during one of the periodic booms that were largely illusory or at best short-lived. Klinkhammer, twenty years his junior, soon joined him. Although accounts always mention that they were prospectors, and although both men—especially Shepp—had experience digging for gold, they really were homesteaders, self-sufficient hermits who were seeking privacy.

For thirty years, Shepp and Klinkhammer were the best of neighbors, kind, generous, resourceful, and discreet. Much of what is known about them—and about the life of Charlie and Polly Bemis on the river—is contained in a ranch diary they kept from the early 1900s until Klinkhammer's death in 1970. The modern chroniclers of the Salmon River country, Johnny Carrey and Cort Conley, whose history-guidebook of 1971 was also called *River of No Return,* quote freely from the Shepp ranch diary, observing, "The dullest diary is better than the sharpest memory." And so it was with Shepp and Klinkhammer's diary, a record of life in a remote, hard country that offers many glimpses into the world of Polly Bemis.

Shepp was the first diarist; his spidery handwriting was quite legible. He died in 1936, and Peter Klinkhammer took over after that. Klinkhammer and Shepp were not prose stylists. The diary entries are blunt, specific, simple statements of fact, like a ship's log. For instance, the weather of the day, vital to someone surviving in the wilderness, was always noted.

Largely a collection of brief notations about day-to-day chores and the challenges of living on a remote ranch, the diary reports on deer shot and cattle and horses fed. It makes note of cold days and heavy rains. The diarist saws wood, plants tomatoes, carrots, radishes, and onions. There is hay to be cut, there are horses to be cared for, and a barn roof is in need of fixing, too. The garden—the crucial supply of foodstuffs and an occasional source of revenue when miners and travelers on the river needed vegetables—requires watering.

Many little kindnesses were exchanged on the banks of the Salmon River. The neighbors crossed the river to share meals. Someone occasionally made cider. Shepp and Klinkhammer once gave Charlie and Polly a pumpkin. Holidays were observed, too. They spent Thanksgiving together in 1910. Bemis and Polly came for dinner; Polly brought over eggs—she always had chickens. Shepp and Klinkhammer gave her a jar of blackberries and a pumpkin. The diary reported that there was "snow all day. The first of the season. Snowing hard at 8 p.m."

The ranch diary makes note of the neighbors as early as September 22, 1909—a Wednesday—when Shepp reports that he got forty-five pounds of vegetables from Bemis. According to Cort Conley and Johnny Carrey, the 136-acre Shepp ranch, as it is still called, had gardens that grew potatoes, corn, beans, beets, carrots, parsnips, turnips, asparagas, rutabagas, popcorn, watermelons, squash, tobacco, gooseberries, raspberries, blackberries, strawberries, currants, grapes, and hops. The orchard provided a dozen varieties of apples, six kinds of cherries, peaches, plums, pears, apricots, walnuts, and chestnuts. Charlie and Polly Bemis had a similar orchard and garden. Travelers on the river, such as Captain Harry Guleke, along with assorted miners, bought fruits and vegetables grown on the Bemis ranch.

Shepp liked to bake. He listened to the radio. He was an amateur radio buff and he tinkered with crystal sets. The diary often reports on distant radio stations that were picked up. Shepp and Klinkhammer appear to have dabbled in photography, too, for many photographs survive of their lives at the mouth of Crooked Creek, and many of the photographs that were taken of Polly and Charlie Bemis—when they were elderly—appear to have been taken by their neighbors. In many of the photographs, a bearded Charlie Bemis looms, slightly stooped, like a gaunt giant next to his elfin, smiling wife.

The notes about Polly were largely about doing chores for her. Picking apples. Cabbages. Cutting wood. Tending to livestock. Some days there was a bit of news—a bear ate the blackberries; a big hawk killed a chicken (Shepp shot at it but missed); the horses got into the orchard. Shepp and Klinkhammer shared a meal or performed a chore for Polly and Charlie. There were always things to do. They canned peaches and gooseberries, made currant jelly, cut their hair, washed their clothing.

On Thursday, July 21, 1921, the diary noted that a boat came down the river (it was the boat carrying Cissy Patterson and her party, one of the most important encounters Polly Bemis had with the outside world). No other details were offered. Life went on at the Shepp ranch that day. Shepp worked in the garden and on a ditch. He canned four quarts of strawberries and syrup for use on cakes, and made a gallon of wine from cherries and currants and three pints of currant jelly. The diary noted that it was a fine day, cooler. The next day, Friday, July 22, Shepp went "over river" to Polly's house. He noted in the diary that the boat carrying Cissy Patterson and her party had left. It was very hot—98 degrees. The next day it was 102. There was no rain.

On August 18, 1921, Polly and Charlie Bemis had an unusual visitor. An old Chinese pioneer from Warrens came down to see them. The diary noted simply: "Ah Can at Bemis this afternoon." Only a few elderly Chinese pioneers were left in the backcountry then. Shepp crossed the river to see the old man.

The diary largely reflects the nearly three-decade relationship between friends in a remote place where one's life could depend on a good neighbor. Much of the detail records the social contact between Shepp and Klinkhammer and the old Connecticut Yankee gambler and the Chinese woman.

Not long after Shepp and Klinkhammer had settled on the river—August 17, 1910—the diary noted, "Polly & Bemis over to dinner. Polly caught 27 fish." There were other details. "Polly had watermelon." The diary invariably added, "Fine day."

The next year, on July 4, 1911, America's birthday was observed. Shepp reported in the diary, "Bemis & Polly over to dinner. Had peas, new potatoes, cherry pie and strawberry short cake and fish. . . . Fine day."

Notes attached to the 1910–1911 diaries provide more information: "Bemis did not have an income. Polly had a little money saved up from her days in Warrens. She was a sharp gambler in a crib game & used to pit her wits against the best of 'em."

In the matter of Polly's literacy, the diarist noted that she could count money and play cards. "Bemis started to teach her to read once but she got along too well & he quit. It wouldn't have taken her very long if he'd been willing to put out the effort. Polly was a fair cook. She loved to fish and was good at it. She did all the gardening. We'd see her at work and she'd bend to the earth real quick, then shove something into the big pocket of her long dress. Come three o'clock every day Polly had her gardening done and her fish bait ready & waiting in her pocket. We used to know what time it was by watching her.

"Polly used to keep three set lines on the beach across river. She checked on them first thing in the morning, at noon and at nite. Every once in a while something would come along & take line pole & all."

Polly's childhood in rural China appeared to have outfitted her with many of the skills vital to survive in the Idaho wilderness. She was a quick study, too. She said later that she learned to cook American food by simply watching someone prepare it. Her skills recalled Mark Twain's wry observations on the Chinese: "Chinamen make good house servants, being quick, obedient, patient, quick to learn and tirelessly industrious. They do not need to be taught a thing twice, as a general thing. They are imitative. If a Chinaman were to see his master break up a centre table, in a passion, and kindle a fire with it, that Chinaman would be likely to resort to the furniture for fuel forever afterward."

There is even speculation in the diary as to how Polly came to be living with Bemis in the wilderness. The diary asks at one point, "Why did Polly marry the lazy Bemis?" Peter Klinkhammer's opinion was that "it was more a marriage of convenience on the part of both": "They had known each other well for many years in Warrens where both were connected with the gambling houses. Polly would work and had a little money saved up. Bemis was lazy. Polly was ever faced with the threat of being sent back to China."

Bemis appears to have sold off some property in Warrens "and they moved to the river where Polly could work and Bemis could doze." Some years after Pete and Shepp came, Polly's money ran out. Peter paid a $400 grocery bill at Warrens.

Various chroniclers note that Polly could not read or write in either English or Chinese. The western historian Charlie Kelly recalled one of Polly's last encounters with the outside world when the explorer and physician Dr. R. G. Frazier of Utah went down the river in 1931.

"Polly was living alone and was 79 years old but still active and cheerful," Kelly noted in an account of her life that appeared in several western publications in 1970. "She had forgotten her native tongue and spoke only in Pidgin English. For many years China Polly had been the only woman on the Salmon River and was known to every placer miner who visited the area, some of whom remained and established themselves at convenient locations as Bemis had done."

Kelly recalled the legacy of Polly Bemis: "For many years Polly had provided vegetables to all the miners who passed and had become the official nurse for anyone who became sick or injured. Some came to call her the 'Angel of the Salmon River.' She never refused anyone whether they could pay or not."

Kelly made a later trip down the river, also in the company of Frazier, but by this time Polly was gone: "Polly had died in the meantime, but the cabin, although empty, was still in perfect condition. We explored it for souvenirs but the only relic Doc could find was an abandoned gasoline flatiron. In an ash heap back of the cabin I found an old, nickel plated six-shooter that had been through a fire, and that was the extent of our loot." Kelly added that he hoped no "crazy prospector" would burn down the cabin, "a fate which meets all abandoned cabins in the west." He re-marked: "When I was there in 1939 she was gone and I regretted very much not having the opportunity to meet her because she was the most interesting character who ever lived on the Salmon River. She began life as just a pawn in a poker game, but during her long lifetime China Polly became admired and respected by everyone who ever met her."

Polly was well on her way to becoming a legend. An account of how she came to be living on the banks of the Salmon River appeared in the *Deseret News* in Salt Lake City in July 1939, after the Frazier party (in-cluding Charlie Kelly) came along the river. One of the three boats used to make the trip was named the *Polly B* after her. The account was lively, a composite of various stories often told about her.

In the end, Shepp and Klinkhammer were the chief links with the outside and they provided Polly Bemis with some of her rare glimpses into a modern world that existed away from the canyon. It was a world that amazed and frightened her.

"It was in their home in the early twenties, that Polly Bemis heard her first radio," Elsensohn wrote in the first volume of her *Pioneer Days in Idaho County*: "When Polly first heard the radio at Shepp and Klink-hammer's place, she thought it was evil spirits chattering out of the box and wanted to run away."

Klinkhammer gave Elsensohn many of the materials that corrobo-rated accounts of Polly's life in Idaho, including her original mar-riage certificate and her application for residency. He also presented the museum that Elsensohn started at the convent in Cottonwood with several dresses that had belonged to Polly, some buttons she had made of coins, bits of her jewelry, and a set of old scales that Charlie Bemis had used to weigh gold.

In 1922, the Bemis cabin burned to the ground. The fire was the beginning of the end and would signal a new way of life for Polly, who was then nearing seventy. Shepp and Polly rescued the invalid Bemis, but little else was saved, and the old man died two months later. The two prospectors also saved the chickens, but Polly's dog Teddy died in the fire. The ranch diary, in a rare burst of drama, noted: "Bemis house burned. . . . Got the old man out by the skin of my teeth. Lost Teddy (Polly's dog). He got burned. Polly and I got the old man over about 4. Had hard time. Didn't save a single thing. The whole place was on fire when I got over. Everybody's feet burned." Peter Klinkhammer was away at the mining camp of Dixie on the day of the blaze. The next spring, the two prospectors built a new log house, a tiny cabin, for Polly on the Bemis ranch. That building still stands.

In its typically taciturn fashion, the diary noted the death of Charlie Bemis with no fanfare. On October 29, 1922, Shepp recorded: "Bemis passed at 3 a.m. I went up to War Eagle camp at 5 a.m. to get Schultz and Holmes. We buried the old man right after dinner. Fine day."

And two days later, on October 31:

"Polly going to Warrens . . ."

After Charlie Bemis died, Polly went out into the world for a brief glimpse at life outside the Salmon River canyon country. Her first visit, in the summer of 1923, was front-page news in the Idaho County seat of Grangeville, where J. C. Safley, the editor of the *Idaho County Free Press,* recognized a good story. Safley presented the news of Polly's arrival in town after more than half a century across the top of the front page—"Polly Awakes after Half Century Slumber in Mountains."

James Clifford Safley, who would later be a prominent journalist in the American West, was learning the trade in central Idaho, where he both owned and edited the weekly. He did most of the reporting, too. Safley interviewed Polly himself and made her arrival in the county seat the lead story of the week in the August 16 edition. The headlines told the tale: "Woman of 70 Sees Railway First Time"; "Chinese of Old Days Dumbfounded by Grangeville"; "Is in Mountains for 51 Years and Chuckles with Glee at Movie and Takes First Automobile Ride"; "Can't Read or Write."

The story recounted how Polly Bemis had lived "in the rugged mountains of Idaho County for fifty-one years, during which she had been only three places, at Warren, at her home for twenty-eight years on the Salmon River and once to Slate Creek."

The newspaper account recorded in spirited detail how Polly—
"Chinese widow of a white man"—was visiting Grangeville. She had
ridden in an automobile for the first time in her life, seen a railroad
train, and attended what the *Free Press* called "a picture show"—a
movie. In a separate editorial, "Polly Awakened," Safley reminded his
readers of the significance of this surprise visitor: "Polly is a modern
Rip Van Winkle, but instead of sleeping twenty years in the Catskills
she is awaking from a half-century slumber under the shadow of the
majestic Buffalo Hump."

Safley was amused by Polly's amazement with Grangeville, observing that the tiny county seat "to her is a veritable metropolis." The style
of the editorial was lively. Noting that Polly had never see an automobile or a train, he wrote: "The method of locomotion employed by Eve
in the Garden of Eden was hers, by her own feet and not in twenty years
had she even ridden horseback, the necessarily favorite means of transportation in the mountains."

Safley also wrote: "Grangeville, with its 1,600 people, its picture show,
its brick business blocks, its hundreds of speeding automobiles, and far
more wonderful than that the steaming steel locomotive that nightly
pulls the passenger train into this metropolis—as Polly views a typical
western town that in many parts of the country would be termed nothing more than a village—it's all marvelous, so marvelous."

Polly was literally speechless, Safley told his readers: "She cannot
explain her delight, her utter astonishment at what she has seen. She
stands aghast. She chuckles for joy. She walks in the street of Grangeville
grasping the arm of her companion, for fear she may become lost—that
she may be engulfed in the maelstrom of the mad throng. The wonders
of it all—they are to her a great, great puzzle, as much of a mystery as is
life itself and death. She cannot solve it."

The accounts of her visit in the *Free Press* made special mention of
her amazement with the railroad train. She had entered the Territory
of Idaho long before the first trains crossed the mountainous countryside: "Polly was taken to the railroad station to witness the arrival of the
evening train. When the trainmen were advised that she had never before seen a locomotive or cars, they lifted her into the engine cab, opened
the firebox, and allowed her to peer at the seething, roaring furnace. But
she was frightened, much frightened, at the steaming black monster of
the rails."

Safley wondered what "this plucky, good natured Chinese woman" would make of San Francisco, New York, or London. But the trip to tiny Grangeville had worn Polly down, and she told the newspaper she wanted to return to her cabin in the mountains: "It's home and I want to go back."

"Polly has seen the world," Safley wrote. "She is satisfied to go back to the mountains and spend the rest of her days amid the scenes she has known so long."

Her departure from town was also the lead story, under the headline "Polly Returns to Warren after Happiest Days in Fifty Years" across the top of the front page.

Polly told the *Free Press* that coming to town was expensive but that she would not rule out another visit. "Maybe I come back next year."

The newspaper described the old woman at the end of her celebrated visit: "Bedecked in a new dress, a gay hat and white shoes, and with a grip filled with new clothing, all gifts of friends, this 70-year-old Chinese woman . . . was as happy as a child after the annual visit of Santa Claus. Particularly proud was she of the new gold-rimmed spectacles with which she was fitted while here."

One trip to Grangeville proved insufficient after half a century of isolation, and the next summer Polly again came down out of the mountains. Her arrival in the outside world was still front-page news and the *Idaho County Free Press* again called her "Idaho County's Modern Rip Van Winkle." She was seventy-two that summer, and the particulars of her life in the mountains related in the *Free Press* were vivid if not entirely accurate.

Polly Bemis's latest visit to the outside world was a trip to the Idaho state capital at Boise for "her first peep at a modern city, with paved streets, tall buildings and street cars." This trip left her delighted but exhausted: "She had seen her first street car, her first high building, her second movie show, and ridden in her first elevator, all in one day."

Her first trip down out of the mountains in the summer of 1923 had taken her only as far as Grangeville to visit a dentist and obtain eyeglasses. The excitement of that had been enough for Polly: the changes in the world during the half century while she had "hibernated"—as the *Free Press* described it—in the Idaho high country had astonished her. But the visit piqued her curiosity.

Safley pulled out all the stops for her second visit, which was covered in great detail and featured on the front page of his newspaper. The headline read: "Polly Bemis Has Big Time on Visit to the State Capital." The story, largely lifted verbatim from the *Idaho Statesman* in Boise, was accompanied by a photograph of Polly: wrinkled, sun-browned, her hair up in a bun. She wore earrings and wire rim eyeglasses.

Polly's trip to Boise was with Mr. and Mrs. Jay Czizek. Czizek was a prominent mining developer and a former pioneer who had known Polly for decades. He was also the source of yet another version of her story, in which an Indian maiden named Molly, not Polly, had been won in the poker game. It is hard to decide whether Czizek was simply being decorous in recounting this tale, for he made no mention of how Polly happened to be living in an Idaho mining camp in the first place. His affection and respect for her may have had a lot to do with what he decided to remember.

"Czizek eat in my boarding house thirty-two years ago. I know him long time," Polly told an interviewer. A reporter from the *Idaho Statesman* found the unusual traveler at the Idanha Hotel, a luxurious landmark a few blocks from the state capitol in Idaho's largest city. It was the only city Polly had seen since she passed through San Francisco in 1872.

In an account headlined "Polly Bemis of Warren's Diggins Sees City's Sights for First Time," the reporter described her as a "tiny woman with iron gray hair, the brightest of eyes, dressed in a blue cotton dress, her whole appearance scrupulously neat." (The *Idaho Statesman* used an old pioneer term in referring to Warren as a "diggins"—a mining camp.) Although Chinese immigrants had accounted for the majority of the population in parts of Idaho at various times in the nineteenth century, and Boise still had a modest Chinatown in 1924, the arrival of Polly Bemis in the state capital was news. The edition of the newspaper that reported on her visit also covered the ongoing trial of Leopold and Loeb for murder in Chicago, reported that once again sections of the West were experiencing wildfires (as they were in the summer of 1872 when she rode into the country), noted that Calvin Coolidge was finishing up his first year as president and making plans to run for reelection, and reported that the novelist Joseph Conrad had died in England. But Polly's appearance in the Idaho state capital was just as newsworthy, or more so. Conrad rated one paragraph in the newspaper; Polly's visit was a major story:

> Her speech is excellent with just enough of the "pidgin English" to make it fascinating. Her memory is remarkable, particularly for dates, and her eyes twinkle as she tells jokes on herself, as when she spoke of the miners not liking the coffee she made in camp, and the way she silenced them by appearing with a butcher knife and the question, "Who no like my coffee?"

She offered the interviewer from the *Statesman* a somewhat different account of how she came to be living in the Idaho mountains for half a century. The newspaper noted:

> According to her story—she and two other young Chinese girls were enticed from their hamlet home in 1869 to Hong Kong and to America by an American woman, who told them she wanted them to work in the gold camps of America, where they could pick up gold coins—from the streets. They were taken almost directly to Florence, Idaho, and Polly tells the tragic story of their disillusionment.

But the story in the *Idaho Statesman*—reprinted in the *Free Press* a few days later—stopped short of providing any additional details of her trip from China or her arrival in the mining camp of Florence, once a celebrated boom town, or describing what her "disillusionment" might have been. Still, her account is remarkably consistent with stories of other young women who were lured from China to the American West.

Polly's world opened up after Charlie Bemis died. There was no question about that. "My husband say, 'We will never see railroad, I guess,' and then he die, then I come out to get dentist to see my teeth and I see railroad at Grangeville last summer. Now I see Boise, big city, stores, five, six stories high, streetcars run middle of street. Lots of people. I like it, but it makes me tired to look so much," she told an interviewer.

Little details about Polly creep into the newspaper account. One of her most cherished possessions, readers learn, was a blue silk dress made out of material brought from San Francisco for her thirty-five years earlier. The dress was lost in the fire in her house on the Salmon River, but she saved the buttons. They had been made by Charlie Bemis from $2.50 and five-dollar gold pieces.

Polly Bemis arrived back in the world at the height of the "roaring twenties" and the newspaper reporter in Boise was curious about what she thought of it. He asked her about "flappers"—young women with rouged, powdered faces and bobbed hair. Her response briefly revealed something of her mysterious past: "I paint like that, too, all the time, till I go to my man. Then I not have to paint any more. American girl today paint till she gets man too."

Modern styles made little impression on her: "Bobbed hair is not to Polly's liking, however. She recalls the long glossy tresses of the Chinese maidens dressed in huge pagodas atop the head and shakes her head at the shorn locks. Of modern dress she quite approves.

"Asked how she liked the movies she said, 'Some very nice—ships and big sea—and some very bad, shut eyes.'" The reporter neglected to mention which films Polly saw.

A high point of Polly's second trip into the world, the *Idaho Statesman* noted, was a special social call. Polly had not seen a Chinese woman in the thirty-five years since the other Chinese women living at Warrens died, according to the account of her visit to Boise. "She is going to pay a visit to some of the members of the local colony today," the *Idaho Statesman* told its readers:

> Another person she would like to meet is "Bob No. 2," [almost all Chinese workers in the West had English nicknames]—a Chinese man who worked for Bob Katon of Warren, who, she understands, is now living in Boise. She plans to return to Warren Tuesday.

The newspaper account of her visit explained something of her life in the high country, too: "For years Polly ran a boarding house for the miners at Warren and she is beloved by all the old timers of the camp. She knew nothing of cooking, she said, and, as no one was willing to teach her, she simply watched two American women who did cook, and then started in."

The trip to Boise to see the dentist, tall buildings, and motion pictures was her last glimpse of a world she had never known. When she came out again it was at the end of her life.

After Bemis died, Shepp and Klinkhammer became a support system for Polly, enabling her to live on alone in her cabin. She was broke. Shepp and Klinkhammer must have known that Polly could not survive without their help, but they make no mention of that fact in the diary. They did, however, strike a deal with Polly that allowed her some peace of mind.

"She owned land, but that was of little avail, for she was old, so she entered into an agreement with Charles Shepp and Peter Klinkhammer to deed them her land if they in turn would care for her until death came," Elsensohn recalled. "She was now nearly seventy years old, and she made an agreement with them that if they would watch out for her, she would deed her personal property to them. They took care of her heavy gardening and provided her with food and game."

The Bemis ranch was a tidy spot and the cultivated land there would have been attractive to an outsider. Perhaps Shepp and Klinkhammer were thinking of their own privacy when they arranged to care for Polly. They were not looking for new neighbors.

Polly's introduction to modern life continued when Shepp and Klinkhammer strung a telephone line across the river between their ranch house and her cabin. A vital link across a river that might not always be passable, the telephone was a modern device that delighted Polly.

"Several times each day Shepp and Klinkhammer called to ask how she was getting along," Elsensohn noted. "If the neighbors failed to call her, she would call them." Elsensohn also reported this conversation between Polly and the prospectors: "How many eggs you get today? Six? I got ten," she would tell her neighbors, before going off into gales of giggles. "How many fish you catch? None? You no good. You fella come over Sunday. I cook great big fish I catch today."

And since she couldn't read or write, the diary often noted, "Ordered garden seeds for Polly," and "Measured Polly for dress and ordered from Montgomery Ward."

Shepp and Klinkhammer did everything for Polly after her husband died, allowing her to spend most of her final decade at the ranch. She was spry, but her eyesight was failing, and homesteading in the wilderness was not easy for an old woman alone. In the last years on the river, her health declined slowly.

Elsensohn quoted another old-timer, Frank McGrane, Sr., who re-membered visiting Polly Bemis at the end of her life when she was ill in Grangeville.

"Charlie wouldn't have died so soon if he hadn't been lazy," she told McGrane. "He just sat around till he was no account."

Elsensohn noted: "It seems that often after their marriage Polly would find Bemis playing cribbage with friends. She would approach him and count, one, two, three, up to fifteen and then say, 'You go home and put wood in the wood box. Yes um, there's no wood in my wood box.' And Bemis would go.

"On another occasion Bemis was one day attentively watching a nest of ants and called Polly. 'Bemis,' she said, 'if you'd work um like these ants we wouldn't be poor folks.'"

Polly was plainly annoyed, albeit resigned to waiting on the old gam-bler, whose physical deterioration was probably related to the gunshot wound of long ago. Bemis was in a slow decline for several years before he died. Polly was his nurse, cook, and only companion. Elsensohn believed Bemis died of tuberculosis, a common enough ailment at the time. He does not appear to have left the canyon in many years, and in the last three or so years of his life he no longer even crossed the river to Shepp and Klinkhammer's homestead. He was plainly a burden on his wife.

Peter Klinkhammer provided Elsensohn with much information about the elderly Chinese woman who had been his neighbor. "Klink-hammer still has the passport and picture Polly obtained at the time she came from China," she noted. No such document or photograph ap-pears to have survived.

Klinkhammer also believed that the marriage of Charlie and Polly Bemis was a marriage of convenience. They had known each other a long time. But, most important, Polly Bemis was potentially subject to deportation during the "Chinese Must Go" movement. Although she had been in the United States for many years, her legal status was al-ways dubious. Her marriage to Charlie changed that threat.

On July 3, 1933, the ranch diary noted that Polly's birthday was coming up, on September 11, and that she would be eighty. But by her birthday, she was in failing health and already in a nursing home in Grangeville, two months from death. Shepp and Klinkhammer found her on the morning of August 4. Perhaps she did not answer the telephone and so they crossed the river to see how she was. They found her on the ground outside the house. The diary notation is brief, describing Polly as "nearly helpless."

"When she fell ill in 1933, at the age of eighty-one, they took her on horseback over narrow and winding trails to the War Eagle Mine where they had arranged to have an ambulance waiting for her. She showed herself very grateful for all that was done for her," Elsensohn noted, getting Polly's age wrong.

A deputy sheriff and a nurse came up to the War Eagle Mine to meet Shepp and Klinkhammer, who somehow got Polly onto the back of a saddle horse and took her up to the mine where there was a road. And so at the end of her life she rode out of the high country on the back of a horse as she had come into the territory so long ago.

In its typically brief style, the diary noted on November 6, a Monday, "Polly passed away this afternoon. Warm and cloudy."

One day later, the diary added, "Polly to be buried 10 a.m. tomorrow." And on November 8, "Polly buried a.m. at 10."

Both days, Shepp noted that he was working on a fence. Life went on.

Peter Klinkhammer was eighty-nine when he died on May 2, 1970. He was buried in Prairie View Cemetery in Grangeville. "During his life, Mr. Klinkhammer had always intended to buy a tombstone for Polly's grave. The heirs to his estate purchased a stone and thus carried out his desire to have a permanent marker on her grave," Elsensohn recalled.

The marker reads:

Polly Bemis
    September 11, 1853—November 6, 1933

In 1987, Polly's remains and headstone were moved from Grangeville back to the ranch she had shared with Charlie on the banks of the Salmon River next to Polly Creek. When a government surveying party came down the river in 1911, they had named the creek next to the Bemis ranch Polly Creek, at the suggestion of Shepp and Klinkhammer, according to Elsensohn, who noted: "They thought that Polly might be remembered longer than Bemis."

Ah Moon and Ah Loy photographed in Lewiston, Idaho, on their way back to China, 1927.
River of No Return by Robert Gresham Bailey/*The Lewiston Tribune* archives (from the collection of the author).

Epilogue

THE CARAVAN OF THE DEAD:
GHOSTS OF THE ORO FINO

And if he dies he is buried carefully, and in due time his bones are sent
back to the Flowery Kingdom to rest with his fathers.
—D. L. PHILLIPS IN "LETTERS FROM CALIFORNIA" (1876),
ILLINOIS STATE JOURNAL

In 1862, when they were seventeen, Mah Yung and Pun Loi caught gold
fever in a village in their native Pearl River delta and shipped to San
Francisco on a sailing vessel. Long years later, they chiefly remembered
that they were many, many weeks at sea. Steamships had not yet made
the China run. For nearly sixty years, Mah Yung and Pun Loi were placer
miners in the Idaho gold country, scratching at a claim at Pierce City,
the oldest mining camp in Idaho, and one of the most remote. Abraham
Lincoln was in the White House, the Civil War gripped the country,
and an emperor sat in Peking when Mah Yung and Pun Loi first went
to look for a mountain of gold.

When they left the Oro Fino two generations later to return to China,
the Flowery Kingdom—as Americans had called it—had been turned
upside down: the feudal China of their childhood was now a republic.
At the end of their lives Mah Yung and Pun Loi came down out of the
mountains, mysterious reminders of the days when thousands of their
countrymen crowded the Idaho backcountry. They were not the only

ancient "Chinamen" from the Gold Rush days to live like this in Idaho. In the 1920s and 1930s, newspapers regularly reported on elderly Chinese miners returning to China to die. And obituaries of old Chinese miners who had lived like hermits for decades in remote mining camps appeared in the press from time to time.

Mah Yung and Pun Loi never found a mountain of gold. They appear to have been indigent at the end of their long stay in Golden Mountain, for Robert Bailey noted that the Clearwater County government had paid for their upkeep for the last two years and bought the old men stagecoach tickets to Greer, a tiny railhead on the Clearwater River. There, Mah Yung and Pun Loi boarded the first train they had ever seen. Greer was a tiny flag or whistle stop; the train heading to Lewiston halted here only on demand. From the railroad siding at Greer, the road—originally a nearly impassable trail for pack animals—snaked up into the mountains to the remote mining camp at Pierce City.

The conductor George Phillips told the *Lewiston Morning Tribune* that the old men were both amazed by and terrified of the train. He turned the pair over to members of Lewiston's Chinese community, who, like Mah Yung and Pun Loi, were Cantonese-speakers from the South China coast.

"The absence of horses, one of their fellow countrymen said yesterday after he had talked with them, was noted and how the trains moved without these was more than the two aged men could understand," according to an account in the *Morning Tribune*. Mah Yung and Pun Loi had seen automobiles but never a train. "Upon arriving in this city the pioneers were escorted to the Chung Lung store at New Sixth and C streets where they will remain until either Saturday or Monday when they will be furnished tickets at the expense of Clearwater County for their return to China."

Speaking through an interpreter, Mah Yung, who still knew no English after six decades in the United States, said that the pair had arrived in San Francisco on a sailing vessel and then traveled via steamer to the Pacific Northwest, arriving first in Portland. Then they walked some 350 miles to Lewiston, the route taken by Polly Bemis. From Lewiston, where there was a substantial Chinese community and thus a support system for the thousands of Chinese laborers and miners scattered throughout the high country, Mah Yung and Pun Loi continued to trudge up into the mining country. They walked 500 miles to reach the goldfields, carrying all that they owned suspended from long bamboo poles, yoked across their shoulders. Eyewitnesses of the boom and bust days in Idaho claimed that a "Chinaman" could carry more than twice his weight on those long poles. They walked, jogged, or trotted in single file all day, often covering upwards of twenty-five miles, depending on the terrain.

"Now Mah Yung and Pun Loi are going home to spend their remaining days among their own people," the newspaper told its readers. "China has advanced wonderfully since they left its shores and their bewilderment over seeing the train move yesterday has just but started. Fast trains will convey them through rich fields and thickly settled communities on their way to Seattle or San Francisco, whichever place they sail from, and the gigantic boats and their manner of being propelled at a swift pace over the waters of the Pacific ocean will serve to further astonish. Everything has changed in the world since the two men settled at Pierce City and yet these changes are unknown to them."

There are no Chinese now in Pierce City; there are only graves, the graves of the "Chinamen" who came up into the Oro Fino long ago. Clustered in a grove of fir trees on the edge of the village, the graves are empty now. The bodies were long ago collected and shipped back to China, repatriated by a benevolent society in San Francisco, which sent its agents—the bone collectors—into the backcountry of Idaho to find the remains of Chinese miners. The only other reminder of the Chinese of long ago at Pierce City, where "celestials" once greatly outnumbered whites, is a grim historical marker on the outskirts of the village noting the lynching of five Chinese in connection with the murder of an old trader there.

Americans in the nineteenth-century West were both accustomed to the Chinese practice of taking the dead home to China and amazed by it (it was believed to be unpatriotic). "Many Californians looked upon the custom of disinterring the bodies of deceased Chinese for the purpose of sending them back to China as an expression of superstition and of contempt of America," the historian Elmer Clarence Sandmeyer has noted. In some jurisdictions, officials actually prohibited the removal of a body from a grave without a permit from the local health officer— yet more mean-spirited paperwork to bedevil the Chinese.

Newspapers across the American West routinely ran notices or brief news stories reporting on the practice or advising readers that Chinese benevolent associations were searching for the remains of Chinese. On January 1, 1870, the *Capital Chronicle* in Boise reported that "a person in the employ of the Chinese companies, the railroad, or somebody else, has a car on the switch and moves up and down the track of the Pacific railroad, gathering up the remains of the dead [Chinese men], preparatory to sending them home to the Celestial Kingdom. From the number of graves along the line, it would appear that in building the railroad the wear and tear of [Chinese men] were considerable."

Bringing the dead home to China was paramount in the minds of even the humblest immigrant and the historian Shih-Shan Henry Tsai has recalled that it was among the first things a Chinese attended to on arrival in San Francisco. "He believed that if the body was buried in a strange land, untended by his family, his soul would never stop wandering in the darkness of the other world."

William Speer, the American medical missionary to China who later operated a dispensary and mission among the Chinese in San Francisco, explained to his countrymen as early as 1870 the significance of returning the bodies of Chinese dead to China. Speer said the Chinese believed that "their spirits will haunt the survivors if proper respect for them be not shown, that the fortunes and the bodily health and comfort of their descendents depend largely upon the proper selection of the tombs of parents and kindred."

But such funereal customs rarely involved women and certainly did not involve the "hundred men's wives." The bodies of women like Polly Bemis were rarely repatriated. Having a lesser status in China, women were thought not to have souls, some chroniclers of the Chinese noted. There were exceptions, as readers of Nevada's *Reese River Reveille* on November 6, 1867, would have learned from a dispatch under the headline "A Quiet Traveler": "The overland coach which arrived from the east yesterday morning brought one remarkably quiet traveler. A dead Chinese woman was boxed and dispatched by stage all the way from Helena, Montana, to this city—about eight hundred miles. For the sake of her fellow travelers on this side of the Jordan, it is hoped she was well preserved."

A few years before this quiet traveler reached the attention of the editor of the *Reese River Reveille*, Mark Twain was learning to be a journalist in Virginia City in western Nevada. In *Roughing It,* Twain noted:

Chinamen hold their dead in great reverence—they worship their departed ancestors, in fact. Hence, in China, a man's front yard, back yard, or any other part of his premises, is made his family burying ground, in order that he may visit the graves at any and all times. Therefore that huge empire is one mighty cemetery; it is ridged and wringled from its centre to its circumference with graves—and inasmuch as every foot of ground must be made to do its utmost, in China, lest the swarming population suffer for food, the very graves are cultivated and yield a harvest, custom holding this to be no dishonor to the dead. Since the departed are held in such worshipful reverence, a "Chinaman" cannot bear that any indignity be offered the places where they sleep.

Twain was well aware of the practice of repatriating the Chinese dead, observing:

A "Chinaman" hardly believes he could enjoy the hereafter except his body lay in his beloved China; also, he desires to receive, himself, after death, that worship with which he has honored his dead that preceded him.

Therefore, if he visits a foreign country, he makes arrangements to have his bones returned to China in case he dies; if he hires to go to a foreign country on a labor contract, there is always a stipulation that his body shall be taken back to China if he dies; if the government sells a gang of Coolies to a foreigner for the usual five-year term, it is specified in the contract that their bodies shall be restored to China in case of death. On the Pacific coast the "Chinamen" all belong to one or another of several great companies or organizations, and these companies keep track of their members, register their names, and ship their bodies home when they die. Every ship that sails from San Francisco carries away a heavy freight of Chinese corpses—or did, at least, until the legislature, with an ingenious refinement of Christian cruelty, forbade the shipments, as a neat underhanded way of deterring Chinese immigration. The bill was offered, whether it passed or not. It is my impression that it passed. There was another bill—it became a law—compelling every incoming "Chinaman" to be vaccinated on the wharf and pay a duly appointed quack (no decent doctor would defile himself with such legalized robbery) ten dollars for it. As few importers of Chinese would want to go to an expense like that, the law-makers thought this would be another heavy blow to Chinese immigration.

The poet Joaquin Miller called the practice "the caravan of the dead." Half a century later the custom of hunting up the remains of long-dead Chinese workers had not waned. Notices frequently appeared in newspapers offering rewards for information leading to the recovery of the remains of Chinese miners and railroad workers. Miller wrote:

> Every five years there is a curious sort of mule caravan seen meandering up and down the mining streams of California, where Chinamen are to be found. It is a quiet train, and quite unlike those to be found there driven by Mexicans, and bearing whisky and dry goods. In this train or caravan the drivers do not shout or scream. The mules, it always seemed to me, do not even bray. This caravan travels almost always by night, and it is driven and managed almost altogether by Chinamen. These Chinamen are civil, very respectful, very quiet, very mournful both in their dress and manner. These mules, both in coming and going out of camp, are loaded with little beech-wood boxes of about three feet in length and one foot square.
>
> When the train arrives in camp these boxes are taken off the backs of the mules, stored in some Chinaman's cabin close to the train, and there they lie, so far as the world knows, undisturbed for two or three days. Then some midnight, the mules are quietly drawn up to the cabin-door, the boxes are brought out, and the mules are loaded, and the line winds away up the hill and out on the mountain to where their freight can be taken down to the sea on wheels. The only apparent difference in these boxes now is the lead label at either end, which was not there when they entered the camp.
>
> This is the caravan of the dead. No Chinaman will consent to let his bones lie in the land of the barbarian. The bones of every Chinaman, even to the beggar—if there ever was such a thing as a Chinese beggar in California—are taken back to the land of his fathers.

Four years after Mah Yung and Pun Loi came down out of the mountains, two other elderly miners—Ah Moon and Ah Loy—followed them. They too had never seen a railroad train. The railroad men found them, too, at the siding in Greer and stopped the train to collect these unusual passengers. A photograph of Ah Moon and Ah Loy appeared in the *Lewiston Tribune* showing the somber pair, then believed to be in their eighties, wearing the dark, baggy clothing associated with the Chinese in the nineteenth century. Each wore a battered hat. Ah Moon had a soft, wide-brimmed hat common in the American West; Ah Loy had an old bowler. The printer Robert Gresham Bailey, who faithfully recorded every curiosity of Idaho life for nearly half a century, made note of this, too: "Though almost within hearing of the sound of the locomotive whistles for more than a quarter of a century, the men had never seen a railroad train until they embarked on one at Greer for the homeland journey."

George Phillips was still the conductor on the train. Bailey wrote: "Conductor Phillips vouches for the story that when the train got underway, the 'Chinamen' had to be restrained by main force to keep them from leaping to the ground and again heading for tall timber."

The last Chinese residents of the mining camp of Warrens, where Polly and Charlie Bemis had lived, were Ah Sam (legally named Jung Chayo) and Ah Kan (or Can). Ah Sam died on December 15, 1933, and "the curtain was rung down and the long drama in the lives of the Chinamen who came to central Idaho in the early golden days was over," Bailey remarked. (He neglected to mention that Ah Kan was still alive.) "The deceased had come to Idaho at a time when thousands of his countrymen were there but in the end he was the last reminder, the last of the Orientals to survive." Ah Sam had become a naturalized citizen at age nineteen. He was "a well-known character in the Salmon River country, and his deeds of kindness and charity won him a warm spot in the hearts of his white friends and acquaintances."

On March 10, 1934, Ah Kan, an old packer who had come into the territory when he was only sixteen and whom the *Idaho County Free Press* referred to as "the last of the Chinese," died.

For more than twenty years the Idaho newspapers chronicled the slow surrender of the last survivors of the Chinese army that had swept into the mining country in the nineteenth century. Just who was the last Chinese living in Idaho was nearly as contentious as who had been the first Chinese to arrive in California.

On January 13, 1918, the *Idaho Statesman* had reported, "Six Go Back to China: Boise Orientals Start on Return Journey to Flowery Kingdom":

> Six Celestials turned their faces homeward Saturday for another glimpse of their land and their people before they leave this weary world. Ong Gee, Gee Gung, Louie Lang, Louie Wuo, Si Yo and one other "Chinaman" were all happy as they sat waiting in the Oregon Short Line station. Some of them were going to Hong Kong; some to Canton, but they were all going home to spend the remainder of their lives after many years in America. In the last three weeks, 25 "Chinamen" have left for the Orient.

Life was hard then for the remaining Chinese workers. A week before the six travelers left for China, the *Idaho Statesman* reported that an elderly Chinese had been caught stealing coal. Seventy-seven-year-old Charlie Ho, an Idaho resident for half a century, according to the newspaper, told the court in Boise that because he had been unable to find work for two years he was forced to steal to keep warm. Ho was arrested by Special Officer Compton while stealing from a Short Line coal car, and this was the third time he had been caught doing so.

"Tell him," Justice Anderson said through an interpreter, "that we have no wish to work a hardship upon him but that we cannot allow him to steal coal. Ask him if we let him off this time, which I understand is his third offense, if he will stop stealing."

Ho replied: "Well, I have to keep warm and eat." According to the newspaper, Ho was living at the Chinese Masonic temple but had to provide his own heat and fuel for cooking.

"The aged Celestial was told to go his way, take the coal he had already picked up and Mr. Compton said to tell him that if he were desperate for coal again to come to his office and he would give him a sack, but not to be found stealing any again."

Such stories were a fixture in the Idaho press in the 1920s and 1930s. In August 1930, an old Chinese sojourner, Doc Lee, died alone in his cabin in Idaho City. He was ninety-one and had been in Idaho for sixty-six years. The *Idaho Statesman,* reporting the death, described Lee as a "friend and philosopher of every citizen of the upper basin." A few days before he died, Doc Lee had told a visitor: "I am very tired—pretty soon maybe I take long sleep."

On March 10, 1935, the *Idaho Statesman* reported the death of another elderly Chinese miner: "Pioneer Chinese of Boise Valley Takes Long Sleep." "Ho Wah, who saw Boise grow from a rough-and-tumble frontier town to the thriving capital of a great state, shuffled off into the long sleep Saturday night at a Boise hospital. He was 85 years old." Ho Wah had come to Idaho as a youth and was for many years a cook in mining camps before moving to Boise, where he worked as a cook in restaurants. "He was one of the last of the Chinese who came to Idaho on the heels of the first gold hunters," the newspaper noted.

Two years later, an old man named Wong Wah Chong died in a rented room on Front Street in Boise. He was eighty-eight and had lived in Idaho for some sixty years.

According to the *Idaho Statesman,* "Detective James Brandon, who investigated, said Wong apparently committed suicide by taking poison. He was found in bed by friends who broke down the locked door. No marks of violence were found on his body." Wong's friends said that he had told them he was going to commit suicide because he had been ordered by the owner of the building where he rented a room to vacate his room. "They also said he had tried to give them his money 'for funeral expenses.'" Sixty dollars were found in a pocket. Wong had herded sheep and engaged in mining around Silver City and Idaho City when he was younger but had lived in Boise more recently, the newspaper noted. His only known relative was a nephew who lived in San Francisco. There is no Chinatown in Boise now. The old Hop Sing Tong building was demolished in 1972 to make way for urban renewal and its last resident, eighty-four-year-old Billy Fong, left for San Francisco.

———

The old Chinese survivors of the Gold Rush who drifted down out of the high country in the early twentieth century were not the only reminders of the wild boom and bust days. Nearly forty years after Polly Bemis arrived in Warrens, half a century after Mark Twain had described Chinese girls being smuggled into San Francisco, it was still possible to buy a Chinese slave girl in Idaho. In the decade before Polly Bemis visited Boise, the case of Chen Mory proved vividly that the romance of the "poker bride" might not have been just romance.

In January 1910, the *Idaho Daily Statesman* featured a lively front-page account of a tong war breaking out in Boise. This violent battle, involving actual hatchet men and poison daggers, was a dispute over "ownership" of a beautiful Chinese slave girl. Unlike the story of the "poker bride," cloaked in mystery and layered with the recollections of old-timers, this was an often-told tale in the pages of the *Idaho Daily Statesman* and elsewhere.

The girl's name was said variously to be Lee See and Chen Mory. In a photograph she beamed like a well-scrubbed schoolgirl and seemed the farthest thing from the "sing-song girl" of the old days. But the feud over who "owned" her extended over much of the West and, according to the *Idaho Daily Statesman,* involved rival Chinese factions in Los Angeles, San Francisco, Oakland, Denver, Salt Lake City, and Boise.

The *Statesman* reported on tong wars and disputes over the "ownership" of Chinese women right up until World War I.

Dick d'Easum, a popular columnist for the *Statesman,* later recalled the tong war of 1910 over "a little bit of a China slave girl . . . that pitched Boise's noodle society into what was probably its greatest frenzy." Dick d'Easum's columns included many accounts of gory violence among the Chinese and reflected Idaho's essentially racist view of the "Chinaman" well into the twentieth century.

Chen Mory, or Lee See, was born in China and sold while still a child to "an Oakland firm dealing in such merchandise," d'Easum recalled. Actually, she was sold often, and each time she was sold her value increased.

"She quickly became a very profitable asset," d'Easum noted. "The purchase price, cash and carry, keep until turned in on a new model, was reputed to be two thousand dollars." One newspaper account claimed she was worth $3,000.

Chen Mory, whose story was well documented in the press and in court papers, ran off with Wong Gow, a laundryman who lived in Idaho. The star-crossed couple received sympathy and support in Idaho, at least among the non-Chinese community, and Wong Gow was regarded as something of a hero in Boise. Alas, he was no Lancelot but a small-time hoodlum and jailbird wanted in California. Those facts did not deter Chen Mory's supporters.

"Religious bodies in Boise, impressed by the simple sincerity of Chen Mory, convinced themselves that it was a dastardly plot to return the girl to a life of infamy. They rose to her defense," d'Easum wrote nearly fifty years after the tong war had raged over the runaway bride. The governor of California demanded that Chen Mory and her true love be returned. But Governor James Brady of Idaho refused the extradition.

The story became more complicated when Wong Gow and Chen Mory were quickly married in a civil ceremony and Chen Mory then ran off with another Chinese man and, according to the *Idaho Statesman,* "took the train to nobody knew where."

Well into the twentieth century, Idaho's newspapers prominently featured accounts of tong wars and hatchet men. On April 6, 1917, readers of the *Pocatello Tribune* learned that "Pocatello Chinks Fear a Tong War." The headline referred to local feuding arising out of a major nationwide tong dispute among some Chinese. According to the *Tribune's* story, some fifty prominent Chinese in Pocatello were asking local authorities to ensure their safety from violent tong factions in other states.

Idaho had a history of tong violence often involving Chinese slave girls. In Boise, a long account in the *Sunday Statesman* in 1917 noted that the current problem (or for that matter any tong problem) was directly related to a scarcity of Chinese women in the city and in Idaho in general: "Looking back over the history of crime among the Chinese of Boise during the past eight years it is found that with two exceptions women were at the bottom of the trouble. Chinese women have always been scarce in the city and it was jealousy that started two of the biggest troubles among the Chinese."

———

The reporter for the *Idaho Daily Statesman* found the old man in a badly weathered clapboard shack in Idaho City as he sat sunning himself on a warm spring day in 1931. Wong Ying was, as the *Statesman* of Sunday, May 17, reported, "just a relic of Idaho's romantic Gold Rush day."

He was a big man, still strapping, tall, and broad-shouldered, with a head of white, receding hair. He did not look anything like the Chinese laborers of the nineteenth century. Wong Ying was ninety-four when reporter Horace Parker found him in the faded boom town of Idaho City, which long ago had been home to hundreds of "celestials." "Today —he earns his living tending water ditches for kindly Idaho City citizens," Parker wrote.

In the early 1930s the past was far enough away that Idaho residents were charmed by such curiosities. Wong Ying was the last eyewitness of "a great chapter in the drama of life in Idaho." Parker's account reflected the nostalgia of the 1930s, echoing Bret Harte and the dime novelists: "Gone are the western days of the luck of the roaring camp, unbroken trails, the lust of a gold-hungry populace of hardy pioneers and the salad days of Idaho's most romantic history—the song of the west in an era of glamour, color, adventure. Gone are the venturesome who plodded rutty trails, slept by the sage and felt the searing hear of a blistering desert sun and knew the smell of burning alkali dust lashed by stinging winds. All are gone—save a few—two or three, perhaps. Time and the laws of nature [have] sent the vast majority further 'west' and little remains to recall the early '60s save a few carefully written chronicles."

Wong Ying told Parker that he had come to the United States when he was eighteen years old, via San Francisco on a rickety Chinese junk that sailed in 1855. He was to spend seventy-six years in Idaho, scratching at the hard ground. The voyage from Canton took two months, good sailing time. He had come from Sun Woey, a district near Canton, he told the reporter. When the ship carrying him landed, he was met by an "old uncle"—a Chinese elder, perhaps someone from his district, who bankrolled the teenager with fifty cents. Wong Ying went to work as a cook and followed a company of Chinese workers into the interior. Like Polly Bemis, he came to Idaho City by pack train and walked much of the way from California.

"The ancient and everlasting cry, 'Gold in the hills,' sent him on a quest of success and adventure," Parker reported. The old man remembered that in the boom times there were 2,000 of his countrymen working the placer mines in Idaho City. "About 200 Chinese women followed the men to ply trades and cash in on measures not unfamiliar to the stormy days of pioneering," Parker noted, allowing his readers to fill in the blanks.

He went on: "Those were turbulent times. Murder, robbery, gunplay and licentious, boisterous freedom ruled the camp. The law was in six codes—heavy lead bullets that spat death from smoking pistols—and a man's authority rested on his ability to wheel and shoot from any position on any occasion. Through it all Wong Ying lived, worked and loved his Idaho more dearly."

There was more romance, too, Parker noted. "Gambling halls, honky-tonks and long bars sprang into being in ramshackle cabins with rough boarded floors. At night when booted miners, 'dog dirty and loaded for bear,' came in from long hours of bending and toiling over their swift-flowing sluices, the scene was transformed. Mingled with the odor of kerosene from smoky lamps, swinging high, crazily above the dance halls, was the dull drone of faro dealers and roulette croupiers. Then the shrill laugh of a coarse dance hall girl; muffled grunts of a drunken, bearded prospector; tinkling of glasses; pistol shots on the street."

Horace Parker's tale may have as much to do with dime novels and early westerns as with anything the old Chinese miner told him at Idaho City on that warm May day. Parker's "last Chinaman" overlooked Polly Bemis; Ah Sam, whom the citizens around Warren called China Sam; and the old packer Ah Kan or Can, better known as China Can. The

Six Companies did not send an agent for their bodies. They were the last "Chinamen" in the high country, as nearly as could be determined. Ah Sam was buried with the white miners and their kin on the hillside overlooking the mining camp of Warrens. Ah Kan was buried in the county cemetery in Grangeville.

The day before Polly Bemis died, the *Sunday Oregonian* in Portland stirred the ashes of her oft-told life story, referring to her as the "poker bride" in the account and at the same time raising questions about how such a strange thing might ever have happened. A few days later, the *Lewiston Tribune* reflected on her passing. News of her death was prominently featured across the front page of the newspaper, along with a photograph of the "Chinese-American pioneer" that appeared to have been taken along the banks of the Salmon River at her ranch.

The *Lewiston Tribune* flatly stated that despite any accounts to the contrary—especially accounts in a newspaper way over in Oregon—Polly Bemis was a "poker bride." Quoting a variety of old-timers, not identified by name, the *Tribune* retold the story of Polly's arrival in Idaho and her fate as a "poker bride" won by Charlie Bemis in a saloon at Warrens, in a game with a Chinese gambler: "While it has been discredited in some circles that Polly was 'the poker bride' so often referred to (some say it was an Indian girl named Molly) the story was never denied by Polly, and therefore is considered authentic."

And that was the end. They were the last of their line. No more caravans of the dead went winding up through the high country after this. No bone collectors came for Polly Bemis. The newspapers no longer printed notices seeking the remains of dead "Chinamen," for there were no more stories to be told then and soon the long-ago, exotic pioneers of Idaho became merely memories, ghosts of the Oro Fino.

Polly Bemis with horses at the Bemis Ranch.
Idaho State Historical Society – 62-44.7.

Acknowledgments

———————◆———————

You hear things in the West. One day, on the Boise-Winnemucca Stage Lines bus, a descendant of the stagecoach (the bus once traveled from Osoyoos, British Columbia, to Tijuana, Mexico—that's border to border —without striking an interstate highway), I first heard her story. I wanted to get off the main roads and this trip had been recommended to me. The bus stops in Cottonwood, Idaho, and then in nearby Grangeville, the Idaho County seat. Here I first saw the convent where Sister M. Alfreda Elsensohn lived. Here she began to save the story. And here I first heard of the Chinese slave girl who had been won in a poker game —or so the story went—a tale sprung straight out of Bret Harte, but it became on examination more plausible and more complicated.

There were pieces of the story of Polly Bemis here and there, and there were pieces, too, of the story of the "Chinamen" who had been so numerous and so important in the building of the West—for her story was part of their story. They were all gone now.

We know a lot about Polly Bemis but there is a lot that we simply do not know and will never know. She survived the sex slave trade. No mean feat. In looking for bits of her life and the lives of the Chinese in the nineteenth-century American mining country, I ranged wide from the story of Woo Loung Wah in Nevada, perhaps the last surviving "coolie" from the days of the transcontinental railroad, to the Cornwall, Connecticut, Historical Society to the files of the *San Diego Union-Tribune*.

In Nevada, where there are the remains of many nineteenth-century mining boom towns, I often walked in the cemeteries in the evening. There were graves there of "Argonauts" who had come from every corner of the world—and died there, too—Cornish miners, Italian anarchists, and a lot of Irishmen, and some ladies of dubious pedigree from

France. It was in Eureka that I first asked an old lady where the Chinese cemetery was and it was here that I heard another story. "The bone collectors came for them," she told me. Later I saw an exhibition in Folsom, California, about Chinese burial rites. And one thing, as it so often does, led to another.

At the University of Maryland, Baltimore County, I thank my colleagues Raphael Falco and Christoph Irmscher (now at Indiana University) for their unfailing generosity and fine editorial advice.

I am in debt to librarians and archivists and there was never a better one than Michael Romary, now retired from the Albin O. Kuhn Library at UMBC, who never let me down. I thank also the very patient Rachel Shapiro, Linda Mirvis, Robin Moskal, Drew Alfgren, Uta Hussong, and Gergana Kostova.

Journalists are like Masons—they tend to know someone everywhere—and my long connections with my former employee the Associated Press got me through the door at the *Lewiston Tribune*—one of the oldest newspapers in the Pacific Northwest. I thank publisher Butch Alford and I thank most especially the *Tribune's* librarian Phyllis Collins for her many kindnesses.

Many people helped me in Idaho. I am very grateful to Larry Kingsbury, Heritage Program manager at the Payette National Forest in McCall, and his colleague Gayle Dixon for reading an early draft of this book. I am also grateful to Larry for showing me what remains of boom and bust Warren, Idaho.

I thank Ellen Zazzarino at the Western History/Genealogy Department of the Denver Public Library for help with the papers of the mining engineer George Bancroft, one of the few people who actually knew Polly Bemis and wrote something down.

I owe a great deal to Kathy Hodges and Amy Vecchione and their colleagues at the Idaho State Historical Society in Boise for fielding countless questions and requests.

Special thanks for his hospitality to Lyle Wirtanen, director of the museum and archives at the Convent of St. Gertrude in Cottonwood, Idaho.

I am especially grateful to Ladd Hamilton, a veteran Idaho journalist and historian for talking with me about how the story of Polly became the story that it has become, showing me the remains of the

Chinese presence in Lewiston, Idaho, and discussing his old colleague Robert Gresham Bailey, who knew Charlie and Polly Bemis.

From the start of this project I was in debt to my former student and friend Grant Huang. His help was invaluable.

I thank Gary F. Scharnhorst at the University of New Mexico for kindly sharing his observations on Bret Harte, whose poem "The Heathen Chinee" tells us so much about what it was like to be Chinese in the American West and, sadly, so much about what many Americans thought of "celestials."

I appreciate the help of my friend Adriana Proser, John H. Foster Curator for Traditional Asian Art at the Asia Society in New York, for having a look at what may be Polly's signature.

I also thank Nathan E. Bender, head of special collections and archives at the University of Idaho Library, where the curious Shepp ranch diary is housed.

I often dipped into the files of the *Idaho County Free Press* and in Grangeville I thank Krista Green for her help there.

Thanks go to Louis Warren of the University of California-Davis for his time and advice. Doug Misner at the Utah History Research Center in Salt Lake City and Rosaline Hui, editor of the *Portland Chinese Times* in Portland, Oregon. And the crew at River Adventures who allowed me to "hitchhike" up the Salmon River one rainy day to see the Bemis ranch on the River of No Return and Polly's grave.

I am grateful to Tom Carey and Jason Baxter at the San Francisco History Center, San Francisco Public Library, for their assistance. And to Marlene Wallin of the Oregon Historical Society. Thanks also to Kathleen Maher, executive director/curator at the Barnum Museum in Bridgeport, Connecticut, Michael Maher at the Nevada Historical Society in Reno, and Arthur H. Miller at Lake Forest College for help with Cissy Patterson.

I also thank Sharon Yusba Steinberg at the Connecticut Historical Society Museum and, also in Connecticut, I thank Doris Burgdorf in South Windsor and Tom Howard in Glastonsbury, for their help with Charlie Bemis and his family.

I am grateful to Craig Warren, editor of the Ambrose Bierce Project, Penn State Erie; Steven Davenport, reference librarian, San Francisco Maritime NHP Library; Timothy Weidner, executive director, Chapman

Historical Museum, Glens Falls, New York; Robert Shindle, project archivist, University of Baltimore Libraries; Nava Hall, Mütter Museum administrator at the College of Physicians of Philadelphia; Ruth S. Flynn, esq., at the Alicia Patterson Foundation; Dr. Earl Bennett, former dean of the College of Mines and Earth Resources at the University of Idaho; John Martinson, museum specialist, Bureau of Reclamation, Boise, Idaho.

Thanks also to Gary Kurutz at the special collections branch of the California State Library in Sacramento for his delightful essay on the mysterious B. E. Lloyd, the man who wandered San Francisco at night and was so curious about "the Chinamen."

I also thank Linda Long, manuscripts librarian, Division of Special Collections and University Archives, Knight Library, University of Oregon; Wenxian Zhang, Department of Archives and Special Collections, Rollins College, Winter Park, Florida; and Zoe Ann Stoltz, reference historian, Montana Historical Society.

I also acknowledge the California History Room at California State Library, the Chinese Historical Society of America in San Francisco, the Library of Congress, the Oregon Historical Society, the Utah Historical Society, the Marriott Library at the University of Utah, the Maryland Historical Society, International Society Daughters of Utah Pioneers, Nez Perce County (Idaho) Historical Society, the California State Library/Sutro in San Francisco, California Historical Society, Montana Historical Society, Wood Memorial Library, South Windsor, Connecticut, American Heritage Center at the University of Wyoming, and the Special Collections Research Center, Syracuse University Library.

At Grove/Atlantic I thank Joan Bingham and her associate Alexander Littlefield for their patience, thoughtful editorial guidance, and good advice.

I am most grateful to my agent Eric Simonoff—formerly with Janklow & Nesbit and now with William Morris.

Thanks also to my friends for their support, including Stephen Desiderio, M.D., David Ryugo, Paul Lundberg, and Lynn Heller for sharing her undergraduate thesis with me on "The Heathen Chinee."

I owe the greatest debts to my friend and fellow journalist William Zorzi Jr., who read this book in manuscript and offered me critical advice and encouragement, and to my wife, Rebecca, for her valuable editorial suggestions.

Bibliography

Allen, Margaret Day (edited and with a foreword and additional chapters by Ladd Hamilton). *Lewiston Country: An Armchair History*. Lewiston, Idaho: Steeley Print and Binding, 1990.

Angelo, C. Aubrey. *Sketches of Travel in Oregon and Idaho*. Fairfield, Washington: Ye Galleon Press, 1988.

Arkush, R. David, and Leo O. Lee, eds. *Land Without Ghosts: Chinese Impressions of America from the Mid-Nineteenth Century to the Present*. Berkeley: University of California Press, 1989.

Armentrout-Ma, Eve. "Urban Chinese at the Sinitic Frontier: Social Organizations in United States' Chinatowns, 1849–1898." *Modern Asian Studies* 17.1, 1983, pp. 107–135.

Asbury, Herbert. *The Barbary Coast: An Informal History of the San Francisco Underworld*. Garden City, New York: Garden City Publishing Company, 1933.

Athearn, Robert G. *The Mythic West in Twentieth-Century America*. Lawrence, Kansas: University Press of Kansas, 1986.

Ayers, Colonel James J. *Gold and Sunshine: Reminiscenses of Early California*. Boston: The Gorham Press, 1922.

Bailey, Robert G. *Hell's Canyon*. Lewiston, Idaho: R. G. Bailey Printing Co., 1943.

Bailey, Robert G. *River of No Return: The Great Salmon River of Idaho*. Lewiston, Idaho: Bailey-Blake Printing Co., 1935.

Bancroft, George. "China Polly—A Reminiscence." Caroline Bancroft Archives, Denver Public Library, Western History/Genealogy Department.

Bancroft, Hubert Howe. *History of California in Seven Volumes*. San Francisco: The History Company, Publishers, 1890.

Barde, Robert Eric. *Immigration at the Golden Gate: Passenger Ships, Exclusion, and Angel Island*. Westport, Connecticut/London: Praeger Publishers, 2008.

Barnhart, Jacqueline Baker. *The Fair but Frail: Prostitution in San Francisco 1849–1900*. Reno: University of Nevada Press, 1986.

Barnum, P. T. *Struggles and Triumphs: Forty Years' Recollections*. New York: American News Company, 1871.

Barsness, Larry. *Gold Camp: Alder Gulch and Virginia City, Montana.* New York: Hastings House, 1962.

Barth, Gunther. *Bitter Strength: A History of the Chinese in the United States, 1850–1870.* Cambridge, Massachusetts: Harvard University Press, 1964.

Bates, D. B. *Incidents on Land and Water, or Four Years on the Pacific Coast.* Boston: James French and Company, 1857.

Batman, Richard. *The Outer Coast.* San Diego/New York/London: Harcourt, Brace, Jovanovich, 1985.

Beadle, J. H. *The Undeveloped West; or, Five Years in the Territories.* Philadelphia/Chicago/Cincinnati/St. Louis: National Publishing Company, 1873.

BeDunnah, Gary P. "A History of the Chinese in Nevada: 1855–1904." MA thesis. University of Nevada/Reno, 1966.

Berkove, Lawrence I. *A Prescription for Adversity: The Moral Art of Ambrose Bierce.* Columbus: Ohio State University Press, 1980.

Berkove, Lawrence I., ed. *Sagebrush Anthology: Literature from the Silver Age of the Old West.* Columbia/London: University of Missouri Press, 2006.

Berkove, Lawrence I., ed. *Skepticism and Dissent: Selected Journalism, 1891–1901, by Ambrose Bierce.* Ann Arbor, Michigan: UMI Research Press, 1986.

Bierce, Ambrose. *The Collected Works of Ambrose Bierce (vol. XII).* New York/Washington: The Neale Publishing Company, 1912.

Bierce, Ambrose. "The Haunted Valley." *Overland Monthly and Out West Magazine* 7.1, July 1871, pp. 88–95.

Bode, William Walter. *Lights and Shadows of Chinatown.* San Francisco: H. S. Crocker Company, 1896.

Bonner, Arthur. *Alas! What Brought Thee Hither? The Chinese in New York 1800–1950.* Madison/Teaneck, New Jersey: Fairleigh Dickinson University Press, 1997.

Borthwick, J. D. *The Gold Hunters: A First-Hand Picture of Life in California Mining Camps in the Early Fifties* (edited by Horace Kephart). New York: The Book League of America, 1929.

Bowles, Samuel. *Across the Continent.* New York: Hurd & Houghton, 1865.

Bowles, Samuel. *Our New West: Records of Travel Between the Mississippi River and the Pacific Ocean.* Hartford, Connecticut: Hartford Publishing Company, 1869.

Boynton, Henry W. *Bret Harte.* Freeport, New York: Books for Libraries Press, 1970.

Branch, Edgar M. *Clemens of the 'Call' —Mark Twain in San Francisco.* Berkeley/Los Angeles: University of California Press, 1969.

Briggs, L. Vernon. *California and the West 1881 and Later.* Boston: Wright & Potter Printing Company, 1931.

Brosnan, Cornelius J. *History of the State of Idaho.* New York: Charles Scribners's Sons, 1935.

Browne, J. Ross. *A Peep at Washoe.* Palo Alto, California: Lewis Osborne, 1968.

Browne, Lina Fergusson. *J. Ross Browne :His Letters, Journals and Writings*, edited with an introduction and commentary by Lina Fergusson Browne. Albuquerque: University of New Mexico Press, 1969.

Bruce, John. *Gaudy Century: The Story of San Francisco's Hundred Years of Robust Journalism*. New York: Random House, 1948.

Bryant, Edwin. *What I Saw in California*. (Introduction by Thomas D. Clark.) Lincoln/London: University of Nebraska Press, 1985.

Butler, Anne M. *Daughters of Joy, Sisters of Misery: Prostitutes in the American West 1865–1890*. Urbana and Chicago: University of Illinois Press, 1985.

Cameron, Nigel. *Barbarians and Mandarins: Thirteen Centuries of Western Travelers in China*. New York/Tokyo: Walker/Weatherhill, 1970.

Carrey, Johnny, and Cort Conley. *River of No Return*. Cambridge, Idaho: Backeddy Books, 1977.

Carter, Kate B. *The Early Chinese of Western United States*. Salt Lake City: Daughters of Utah Pioneers, 1967.

Cassel, Susie Lan, ed. *The Chinese in America: A History from Gold Mountain to the New Millennium*. Walnut Creek, California: Alta Mira Press, 2002.

Chan, Loren B. "The Chinese in Nevada: An Historical Survey." Reno: Nevada Historical Society Quarterly. Volume 25, 1982.

Chan, Sucheng, ed. *Entry Denied: Exclusion and the Chinese Community in America, 1882–1943*. Philadelphia: Temple University Press, 1991.

Chang, Iris. *The Chinese in America*. New York: Viking, 2003.

Chen, Chia-Lin. "A Gold Dream in the Blue Mountains: A Study of the Chinese Immigrants in the John Day Area, Oregon, 1870–1910." MA thesis. Portland State University, 1972.

Chen, Jack. *The Chinese of America*. San Francisco: Harper & Row, 1980.

Chesterton, G. K. *Tremendous Trifles*. New York: Dodd, Mead and Co., 1909.

Chin, Thomas W., and H. Mark Lai, Philip P. Choy., eds. *A History of the Chinese in California*. San Francisco: Chinese Historical Society of America, 1969.

Chisholm, James. *South Pass, 1868 – James Chisholm's Journal of the Wyoming Gold Rush* (introduced and edited by Lola M. Homsher). Lincoln/London: University of Nebraska Press, 1960.

"Chinese Highbinders." *Harper's Weekly*, February 13, 1886, p. 103.

Chinese in the Building of the U.S. West, consultant Samuel C. Chu, Ph.D. (Globe Book Company, a division of Simon & Schuster) Paramus, New Jersey, 1993.

Choy, Philip P., Lorraine Dong, and Marlon K. Hom, eds. *Coming Man—19th Century Perceptions of the Chinese*. Seattle/London: University of Washington Press, 1994.

Chu, Daniel, and Samuel Chu. *Passage to the Golden Gate: A History of the Chinese in America to 1910*. Garden City, New York: Zenith Books/Doubleday, 1967.

Chung, Sue Fawn, and Priscilla Wegars, eds. *Chinese American Death Rituals: Respecting the Ancestors.* Lanham/New York/Toronto/Oxford: AltaMira Press, 2005.

Cone, Mary. *Two Years in California.* Chicago: S. C. Griggs and Company, 1876.

Conlin, Joseph R. *Bacon, Beans, and Galantines: Food and Foodways on the Western Mining Frontier.* Reno/Las Vegas: University of Nevada Press, 1986.

Coolidge, Mary Roberts. *Chinese Immigration.* New York: Henry Holt and Company, 1909.

Corbett, P. Scott, and Nancy Parker Corbett. "The Chinese in Oregon, c. 1870–1880." *Oregon Historical Quarterly,* March 1977, pp. 73–85.

Cowan, Robert Ernest. *Bibliographical notes on certain of the earliests editons of The Heathen Chinee—Plain Language from Truthful James by Bret Hart.* San Francisco: John Henry Nash, 1934.

Culin, Stewart. *The Gambling Games of the Chinese in America.* Las Vegas: Gamblers Book Club, 1972.

Dam, Henry J. W. "A Morning with Bret Harte." *The Gold Rush Storyteller.* Star Rover House, 1986.

Dana, Richard Henry. *Two Years Before the Mast: a personal narrative of life at sea.* New York: Penguin Books, 1981 (edited with an introduction by Thomas Philbrick).

Daniels, Roger. *Asian America: Chinese and Japanese in the United States since 1850.* Seattle/London: University of Washington Press, 1988.

Daniels, Roger. *Coming to America: A History of Immigration and Ethnicity in American Life.* New York: HarperCollins, 1990.

DeArment, Robert K. *Knights of the Green Cloth: The Saga of Frontier Gamblers.* Norman: University of Oklahoma, 1982.

d'Easum, Dick. *Fragments of Villainy.* Boise, Idaho: Statesman Printing Company, 1959.

Defenbach, Byron. *Idaho: The Place and Its People; a History of the Gem State from Prehistoric to Present Days.* Chicago/New York: The American Historical Society, Inc., 1933.

deFord, Miriam Allen. *They Were San Franciscans.* Caldwell, Idaho: The Caxton Printers, Ltd.,1947.

De Leon, Arnoldo. *Racial Frontiers, Africans, Chinese, and Mexicans in Western America, 1848–1890.* Albuquerque: University of New Mexico Press, 2002.

Densmore, G. B. *The Chinese in California.* San Francisco: Pettit & Russ, 1880.

De Quille, Dan. *The Big Bonanza: An Authentic Account of the Discovery, History, and Working of the World-Renowned Comstock Lode of Nevada.* New York: Alfred A. Knopf, 1947.

De Russailh, Albert Benard. *Last Adventure, San Francisco in 1851.* Trans. Clarkson Crane. San Francisco: Westgate Press, 1931.

DeVoto, Bernard. *The Western Paradox—A Conservation Reader.* (Douglas Brinkley and Patricia Limerick, eds.) New Haven/London: Yale University Press, 2000.

Dickson, Hartwell. "No Prissy Is Cissy." *Collier's* 118.21. November 1946. pp. 72–78.

Dillon, Richard H. *The Hatchet Men: The Story of the Tong Wars in San Francisco's Chinatown.* New York: Coward-McCann, 1962.

Dillon, Richard. *Humbugs and Heroes: A Gallery of California Pioneers.* Oakland, California: Yosemite-DiMaggio, 1983.

Dirlik, Arif, ed. *Chinese on the American Frontier.* Lanham, Maryland: Rowman & Littlefield Publishers, 2001.

Dobie, Charles Caldwell. *San Francisco: A Pageant.* New York/London: D. Appleton-Century Company, 1936.

Dobie, Charles Caldwell. *San Francisco's Chinatown.* New York/London: D. Appleton-Century Company, 1936.

Donaldson, Thomas. *Idaho of Yesterday.* Westport, CT: Greenwood Press, 1970.

Drago, Henry Sinclair. *Notorious Ladies of the Frontier.* New York: Dodd, Mead & Company, 1969.

Dreams of the West: A History of the Chinese in Oregon, 1850–1950. Portland, Oregon: Ooligan Press, 2007.

Duckett, Margaret. "Bret Harte's Portrayal of Half-Breeds." *American Literature* 25, 1963, pp. 93–212.

Duckett, Margaret. *Mark Twain and Bret Harte.* Norman: University of Oklahoma, 1964.

Duckett, Margaret. "Plain Language from Bret Harte." *Nineteenth-Century Fiction* 11.4, March 1957, pp. 241–260.

Dunne, Finley Peter. *Mr. Dooley: Now and Forever.* Stanford, California: Academic Reprints, 1954.

Dwyer, Richard A., and Richard E. Lingenfelter, eds. *The Songs of the Gold Rush.* Berkeley: University of California Press, 1964.

Edson, Christopher Howard. "The Chinese in Eastern Oregon, 1860–1890." MA thesis. University of Oregon, 1970.

Elsensohn, Sister M. Alfreda. *Idaho Chinese Lore.* Caldwell, Idaho: The Caxton Printers, 1970.

Elsensohn, Sister M. Alfreda. *Idaho's Most Romantic Character: Polly Bemis.* Caldwell, Idaho: The Caxton Printers, 1979.

Elsensohn, Sister M. Alfreda. "Memories of Polly: Lovable Little Chinese Woman, Once a Slave Girl, Is Becoming One of Idaho County's Historic Figures." *Spokesman-Review* (Spokane, Washington) Sunday magazine, May 12, 1957.

Elsensohn, Sister M. Alfreda. *Pioneer Days in Idaho County, Volume I.* Caldwell, Idaho: The Caxton Printers, 1947.

Elsensohn, Sister M. Alfreda. *Pioneer Days in Idaho County, Volume II.* Caldwell, Idaho: The Caxton Printers, 1951.

Erickson, Edith E., and Eddy Ng. *From Sojourners to Citizen: Chinese of the Inland Empire.* Colfax, Washington: E. E. Erickson and E. Ng, 1989.

Evans, Col. Albert S. *A La California: Sketches of Life in the Golden State (1873).* San Francisco: A. L. Bancroft and Company, 1873.

Fanning, Philip Ashley. *Mark Twan and Orion Clemens: Brothers, Partners, Strangers.* Tuscaloosa, Alabama: University of Alabama Press, 2003.

Farish, Thomas Edwin. *The Gold Hunters of California.* Chicago: M. A. Donohue & Co., 1904.

Farwell, Willard B. *The Chinese at Home and Abroad.* San Francisco: A. L. Bancroft & Co., 1885.

Fenn, William Purviance. *Ah Sin and His Brethren in American Literature.* Peking: College of Chinese Studies/California College in China, 1933.

Fisher, Vardis, and Opal Laurel Holmes. *Gold Rushes and Mining Camps of the Early American West.* Caldwell, Idaho: Caxton Printers, 1968.

Fisher, Walter. *The Californians.* London: Macmillan, 1876.

Fishkin, Shelley Fisher. *Lighting Out for the Territory.* New York/Oxford: Oxford University Press, 1997.

Frazier, M. D., Russell G. Russell G. Frazier Papers, 1930–1968. Salt Lake City: Utah State Historical Society.

Frost, O. W. *Joaquin Miller.* New York: Twayne Publishers, 1967.

Fry, Kathleen Whalen. "Rendering Polly: The Romanticization, Manipulation and Decontexualization of One Chinese Woman's History in the American West." MA thesis. Washington State University, 2006.

Gerber, John. *Mark Twain.* New York: Twayne Publishers,1988.

Gibson, Otis. *The Chinese in America.* Cincinnati: Hitchcock & Walden, 1877.

Gizycka, Countess Eleanor. "Diary on the Salmon River." *Field and Stream,* May 1923, pp. 18–20, 113–115, June 1923, pp. 187–188, 276–280.

Gizycka, Felicia. "Cissy Patterson: The Countess of Flat Creek." *Teton* 10, 1977, pp. 37–48.

Goldman, Marion S. *Gold Diggers & Silver Miners: Prostitution and Social Life on the Comstock Lode.* Ann Arbor: University of Michigan Press, 1981.

Gong, Eng Ying, and Bruce Grant. *Tong War!* New York: Nicholas L. Brown. 1930.

Goodman, David Michael. *A Western Panorama 1849–1875, the Travels, Writings and Influence of J.Ross Browne on the Pacific Coast, and in Texas, Nevada, Arizona and Baja California, as the first Mining Commissioner, and Minister to China.* Glendale, California: The Arthur H. Clark Company, 1966.

Goris, Jan Albert. "A Belgian in the Gold Rush: A Memoir by Dr. J. J. F. Haine." *California Historical Society Quarterly* 37.4 (1954) pp. 311–336.

Goulder, William Armistead. *Reminiscences: Incidents in the Life of a Pioneer in Oregon and Idaho.* Moscow, Idaho: University of Idaho Press, 1989.

Greeley, Horace. *An Overland Journey from New York to San Francisco in the Summer of 1859.* Ann Arbor: University Microfilms, Inc., 1966.

Greever, William S. *The Bonanza West: The Story of Western Mining Rushes, 1848–1900*. Norman: University of Oklahoma Press, 1963.

Grenander, M. E. *Ambrose Bierce*. New York: Twayne Publishers, 1971.

Hamilton, Ladd. "How Mr. Bemis Won the Chinese Slave Girl." *Saga* 8.5, 1954, pp. 50–52.

Hansen, Gladys C., and William F. Heintz., eds. *The Chinese in California: A Brief Bibliographic History*. Portland, Oregon: Richard Abel & Company, 1970.

Harlow, Alvin F. *Bret Hart of the Old West*. New York: Julian Messner, 1943.

Harris, Neil. *Humbug: The Art of P. T. Barnum*. Boston: Little, Brown, 1973.

Harte, Bret. *The Lectures of Bret Harte*. Ed. Charles Mecker Kozlay. Folcroft, Pa: The Folcroft Press, Inc. 1909.

Harte, Bret. *Openings in the Old Trail—How I Went to the Mines*. New York: P. F. Collier & Son, 1903.

Harte, Bret. *The Luck of Roaring Camp and Other Stories*. Boston: Houghton, Mifflin and Company, 1885.

Harte, Bret, and Mark Twain. *Sketches of the Sixties: Being forgotten material now collected for the first time from The Californian 1864–67*. New York: AMS Press, 1969.

Hayes, J. W. *Looking Backward At Portland*. Portland, Oregon: Kilham Stationery & Printing Co., 1911.

Head, Franklin H. "Bret Harte's First Strenuous Revolt." *The Second Book of THE DOFOBS*. Chicago: Society of the Dofobs, 1909.

Healy, Paul F. *Cissy—A Biography of Eleanor M. "Cissy" Patterson*. Garden City, New York: Doubleday & Company, 1966.

Helmers, Cheryl. *Warren Times—A Collection of News about Warren, Idaho*. Riverside, California: Inland Printworks, 2006.

Helper, Hinton. *Dreadful California, being a true and scandalous account of the barbarous civilization, licentious morals, crude manners and depravities, inclement climate and niggling resources, together with various other offensive and calamitous details of life in the Golden State*, ed. by Lucius Beebe and Charles M. Clegg. Indianapolis/New York: Bobbs-Merrill Company, 1948.

Henderson, Daniel M. *Yankee Ships in China Seas: Adventures of Pioneer Americans in the Troubled Far East*. Freeport, New York: Books for Libraries Press, 1970.

Henriot, Christian. "From a Throne of Glory to a Seat of Ignominy: Shanghai Prostitution Revisted (1848–1949)." *Modern China* 22.2, April 1996, pp. 132–163.

Hershatter, Gail. "The Hierarchy of Shanghai Prostitution, 1870–1949." *Modern China* 15.4, October 1989, pp. 463–498.

Hesford, Walter. "Thousand Pieces of Gold: Competing Fictions in the Representation of Chinese-American Experience." *Western American Literature* 31, 1996.

Higham, John. *Strangers in the Land: Patterns of American Nativism 1860–1925*. New Brunswick/London: Rutgers University Press

Highberger, Mark. *Snake River Massacre: The Story of the 1887 Murders They Called The Crime of the Century.* Wallowa, Oregon: Bear Creek Press, 2000.

Hirata, Lucie Cheng. "Free, Indentured, Enslave: Chinese Prostitutes in Nineteenth-Century America." *Signs: Journal of Women in Culture and Society* 5.1., 1979, pp. 3–29.

Hittell, John S. *A History of the City of San Francisco and Incidentally of the State of California and a Guide Book to San Francisco.* Berkeley: Berkeley Hills Books, 2000.

Ho, Nelson Chia-Chi. *Portland's Chinatown: The History of an Urban Ethnic District.* Portland Bureau of Planning, 1978.

Hoexter, Corinne K. *From Canton to California: The Epic of Chinese Immigration.* New York: Four Winds Press, 1976.

Hoffman, William. *The Monitor: Jottings of a New York Merchant During a Trip Round the Globe.* New York: Carleton, Publishers, 1863.

Hoge, Alice Albright. *Cissy Patterson: The Life of Eleanor Medill Patterson, Publisher and Editor of the Washington Times-Herald.* New York: Random House, 1966.

Holliday, J. S. *The World Rushed In: The California Gold Rush Experience.* New York: Touchstone/Simon and Schuster, 1981.

Holt, Hamilton, ed. *The Life Stories of Undistinguished Americans—As Told By Themselves.* New York/London: Routledge, 1990.

Hom, Gloria Sun, ed. *Chinese Argonauts: An Anthology of the Chinese Contributions to the Historical Development of Santa Clara County.* Los Altos Hills, California: Foothill Community College, 1971.

Hom, Marlon. *Songs of Gold Mountain: Catonese Rhymes from San Francisco Chinatown.* Berkeley/Los Angeles/London: University of California Press, 1987.

Horan, James D. *Desperate Women.* New York: Bonanza Books, 1952.

Hoy, William. *The Chinese Six Companies: A Short General Historical Resume of its Origin, Function, and Importance in the Life of the California Chinese.* San Francisco: The Chinese Consolidated Benevolent Association, 1942.

Hunt, Michael H. *The Making of a Special Relationship: The United States and China to 1914.* New York: Columbia University Press, 1983.

Hunter, Kay. *Duet for a Lifetime: The Story of the Original Siamese Twins.* New York: Coward-McCann, 1964.

Huston, Peter. *Tongs, Gangs, and Triads: Chinese Crime in North America.* San Jose/New York/Lincoln/Shanghai: Authors Choice Press, 2001.

Irmscher, Christoph. *The Poetics of Natural History: From John Bartram to William James.* New Brunswick, New Jersey: Rutgers University Press, 1999.

Jeffrey, Julie Roy. *Frontier Women: The Trans-Mississippi West 1840–1880.* New York: Hill and Wang, 1979.

Kahn, Edgar M. *Bret Harte in California: A Character Study.* San Francisco: privately printed, 1951.

Kallenberger, W. W. *Memories of a Gold Digger.* Garden Grove, California: privately printed, 1970.

Kaplan, Fred. *The Singular Mark Twain.* New York: Doubleday, 2003.

Kelly, Charles. Charles Kelly Collection. Salt Lake City: University of Utah, J. Willard Marriott Library.

Kelly, Charles. "He Won His Wife in a Poker Game." *The Pony Express,* February, 1970.

Krauth, Leland. *Mark Twain & Company: Six Literary Relations.* Athens/London: University of Georgia Press, 2003.

Kung, S. W. *Chinese in American Life: Some Aspects of Their History, Status, Problems, and Contributions.* Seattle: University of Washington Presws, 1962.

Kunhardt, Jr., Phillip B., Phillip B. Kunhardt III, and Peter W. Kundhardt, *P. T. Barnum: America's Greatest Showman.* New York: Alfred A. Knopf, 1995.

Kwong, Peter, and Dusanka Miscevic. *Chinese America: The Untold Story of America's Oldest New Community.* New York/London: The New Press, 2005.

LaFargue, Thomas E. *China's First Hundred: Educational Mission Students in the United States, 1872–1881.* Pullman, Washington: Washington State University Press, 1987.

LaFargue, Thomas E. "Some Early Chinese Visitors to the United States." *T'ien Hsia Monthly* 2, October–November 1940, pp. 128–139.

Lauber, John. *The Making of Mark Twain: A Biography.* New York: American Heritage, 1985.

Lawson, Benjamin S. *Joaquin Miller.* Boise, Idaho: Boise State University Western Writers Series, 1980.

Layres, Augustus. *The Other Side of the Chinese Question in California.* San Francisco, 1876.

Lee, Calvin. *Chinatown, U.S.A.* Garden City, New York: Doubleday & Company, 1965.

Lee Erika. *At America's Gates: Chinese Immigration During the Exclusion Era 1882–1943.* Chapel Hill/London: University of North Carolina Press, 2005.

Lee, Rose Hum. "Social Institutions of a Rocky Mountain Chinatown." *Social Forces* 27, October 1948–May 1949.

Lee, Rose Hum. *The Chinese in the United States of America.* Hong Kong: Hong Kong University Press, 1960.

Lee, W. Storrs, ed. *California—A Literary Chronicle.* New York: Funk & Wagnalls, 1968.

Li, Yi. *Chinese Bureaucratic Culture and Its Influence on the 19th-century Steamship Operation, 1864–1885.* Lewiston, New York: The Edwin Mellen Press, 2001.

Lin, Diane Mei, and Mark and Ginger Chih. *A Place Called Chinese America.* Organization of Chinese Americans, 1982.

Ling, Huping. "Surviving on the Gold Mountain: A Review of Sources about Chinese American Women." *The History Teacher* 24. 4, August 1993.

Lloyd, B. E. *Lights and Shades in San Francisco.* Berkeley, California: Berkeley Hills Books, 1999.

Lloyd, J. D., ed. *The Gold Rush.* San Diego: Greenhaven Press, 2002.

Lockhart, Caroline. "The Wildest Boat Ride in America." *The Outing Magazine* LIX. 5, February 1912, pp. 515–525.

Loftis, Anne. *California—Where the Twain Did Meet.* New York: Macmillan, 1973.

Longstreet, Stephen. *The Wilder Shore: A History of the Gala Days in San Francisco.* Garden City, New York: Doubleday & Company, 1968.

Loomis, Rev. A. W. "The Chinese Six Companies." *Overland Monthly and Out West Magazine.* September 1868, pp. 221–227.

Loomis, Rev. A. W. "Chinese Women in California." *Overland Monthly and Out West Magazine.* April 1869, pp. 334–351.

Loomis, Rev. A. W. "How Our Chinamen Are Employed." *Overland Monthly and Out West Magazine.* March 1869, pp. 231–239.

Louie, Emma Woo. *Chinese American Names: Tradition and Transition.* Jefferson, North Carolina/London: McFarland & Company, 1998.

Lyman, George D. *The Saga of the Comstock Lode: Boom Days in Virginia City.* New York/London: Charles Scribner's Sons, 1937.

Lyman, Stanford M., ed. *The Asian in North America.* Santa Barbara, California: American Bibliographical Center-Clio Press, 1977.

Marberry, M. M. *Splendid Poseur—Joaquin Miller—American Poet.* New York: Thomas Y. Crowell Company, 1953.

Mark, Diane Mei Lin and Ginger Chih. *A place called Chinese America.* Dubuque, Iowa: Kendall Hunt Pub. Co., 1982.

Martin, Ralph G. *Cissy—The Extraordinary Life of Eleanor Medill Patterson.* New York: Simon and Schuster, 1979.

McClellan, Robert. *The Heathen Chinee: A Study of American Attitudes toward China 1890–1905.* Columbus, Ohio: Ohio State University Press, 1971.

McCollum, M. D., William. *California as I Saw It.* (edited by Dale L. Morgan.) Los Gatos, California: The Talisman Press, 1960.

McConnell, W. J. *Early History of Idaho.* Caldwell, Idaho: The Caxton Printers, 1913.

McCunn Ruthanne Lum. "Reclaiming Polly Bemis: China's Daughter, Idaho's Legendary Pioneer." *Frontiers* 24.1, 2003, pp. 76–100.

McCunn, Ruthanne Lum. *An Illustrated History of the Chinese in America.* San Francisco: Design Enterprises of San Francisco, 1979.

McLane, Governor Robert M. *Reminiscences 1827–1897.* Wilmington, Delaware: Scholarly Resources, Inc., 1972 (reprinted from 1903).

McLeod, Alexander. *Pigtails and Gold Dust.* Caldwell, Idaho: The Caxton Printers, 1947.

Meier, Gary, and Gloria Meier. *Those Naughty Ladies of the Old Northwest.* Bend, Oregon: Maverick Publications, 1990.

Menzies, Gavin. *1421: The Year China Discovered America.* New York: Perennial/ HarperCollins, 2003.

Merwin, Henry Childs. *The Life of Bret Harte with Some Accounts of the California Pioneers.* Boston/New York: Houghton Mifflin Company, 1911.

Miller, Joaquin. *The Danites in the Sierras.* Chicago: Jansen, McClurg & Company, 1881.

Miller, Lee Charles. "The Boat That Never Came Back: 200 Miles Through the Salmon River Canyon." Outing. March, 1922. 256–260, 287.

Miller, Stuart Creighton. *The Unwelcome Immigrant: The American Image of the Chinese, 1785–1882.* Berkeley/Los Angeles/London: University of California Press, 1969.

Minke, Pauline. *Chinese in the Mother Lode (1850–1870).* San Francisco: R and E Research Associates, 1974.

Moon, Krystyn R. *Yellowface: Creating the Chinese in American Popular Music and Performance, 1850s–1920s.* New Brunswick/London: Rutgers University Press, 2005.

Morgan, Ora Moss. *Gold Dust: A Compliation of the Writings of Ora Moss Morgan.* Sonora, California: privately printed, 1959.

Morrow, Patrick, D. *Bret Harte, Literary Critic.* Bowling Green, Ohio: Bowling Green State University Popular Press, 1979.

Morrow, Patrick D. *Bret Harte.* Boise, Idaho: Boise State College Western Writers Series, 1972.

Mulford, Prentiss. *California Sketches* (edited and with an introduction by Franklin Walker). San Francisco: The Book Club of California, 1935.

Murdock, Charles A. *A Backward Glance at Eighty.* San Francisco: Paul Elder and Company, 1921.

Nasatir, A. P., ed. *A French Journalist in the California Gold Rush: The Letters of Etienne Derbec.* Georgetown, California: The Talisman Press, 1964.

Nee, Victor G., and Brett De Barry. *Longtime Californ'—A Documentary Study of an American Chinatown.* New York: Pantheon Books, 1972.

Newsom, David. *David Newsom: The Western Observer 1805–1882* (introduction by E. Earl Newsom). Portland, Oregon: Oregon Historical Society, 1972.

Nissen, Axel. *Bret Harte, Prince and Pauper.* Jackson: University of Mississippi Press, 2000.

Norris, Frank. *The Third Circle.* (Introduction by Will Irwin.) New York: John Lane Company, 1909.

North, Hart H. "Chinese Highbinder Societies in California." *California Historical Society Quarterly* 27.1, 1948, pp. 19–31.

O'Meara, James. "The Chinese in the Early Days." *Overland Monthly and Out West Magazine*. May 1884, pp. 477–481.

Otero, Miguel Antonio. *My Life on the Frontier, 1864–1882*. New York: The Press of the Pioneers, 1935.

Parkinson, Jessie Heaton. *Adventuring in California, Yesterday, Today, and Day Before Yesterday*. San Francisco: Harr Wagner Publishing, 1921.

Pemberton, Thomas Edgar. *The Life of Bret Harte*. Freeport, New York: Books for Libraries, 1970 (first published, 1903).

Peterson, Martin Severin. *Joaquin Miller, Literary Frontiersman*. Palo Alto, California: Stanford University Press, 1937.

Petrik, Paula. *No Step Backward*. Helena, Montana: Montana Historical Society Press, 1987.

Pinzer, Maimie. *The Maimie Papers: Letters from an Ex-Prostitute*. New York: The Feminist Press at the City University of New York, 1997.

Powers, Ron. *Mark Twain—A Life*. New York: Free Press, 2005.

Pratt, Grace Roffey. "Charlie Bemis' Highest Prize." *Frontier Times,* Winter 1961, pp. 26–28, 38.

Pricco, Jeff David. "Homeless Strangers Among Us: The Chinese Community of Portland, Oregon 1860–1900." MA thesis. University of Oregon, 1978.

Quinn, John Philip. *Fools of Fortune or Gambling and Gamblers*. Chicago: The Anti-Gambling Associaton, 1892.

Raffel, Burton. *Politicians, Poets, & Con Men: Emotional History in Late Victorian America*. Hamden, CT: Archon, 1986.

Reynolds, C. N. "The Chinese Tongs." *The American Journal of Sociology* 40.5, March 1935, pp. 612–623.

Riley, Glenda. *The Female Frontier: A Comparative View of Women on the Prairie and the Plains*. Lawrence, Kansas: University Press of Kansas, 1988.

Rock, Francis J. *J. Ross Browne: A Biography*. Washington, D.C.: Catholic University of America, 1929.

Rohe, Randall E. "After the Gold Rush: Chinese Mining in the Far West, 1850–1890. *Montana: The Magazine of Western History*. Autumn 1982, pp. 2–19.

Rudolph, Frederick. "Chinamen in Yankeedom: Anti-Unionism in Massachusetts in 1870." *The American Historical Review* 53.1, October 1947, pp. 1–29.

Russell, Jo Anne. "A Necessary Evil: Prostitutes, Patriarchs & Profits in Boise City, 1863–1915." MA thesis. Boise State University, 1991.

Rutter, Michael. *Upstairs Girls: Prostitution in the American West*. Helena, Montana: Farcountry Press, 2005.

Safley, James Clifford. *The Country Newspaper and Its Operation*. New York/London: D. Appleton and Company, 1930.

Salyer, Lucy E. *Laws Harsh as Tigers: Chinese Immigrants and the Shaping of Modern Immigration Law.* Chapel Hill/London: University of North Carolina Press, 1995.

Sanchez-Eppler, Karen. "Copying and Conversion: An 1824 Friendship Album 'from a Chinese Youth.'" *American Quarterly* 59.2, June 2007, pp 301–332.

Sandmeyer, Elmer Clarence. *The Anti-Chinese Movement in California.* Urbana: University of Illinois Press, 1939.

Saxon, A. H., ed. *Selected Letters of P. T. Barnum.* New York: Columbia University Press, 1983.

Scharnhorst, Gary. *Bret Harte.* New York: Twayne Publishers, 1992.

Scharnhorst, Gary, ed. *Bret Harte: Opening the American Literary West.* Norman: University of Oklahoma Press, 2000.

Scharnhorst, Gary, ed. *Bret Harte's California: Letters to the Springfield Republican and Christian Register, 1866–67.* Albuquerque: University of New Mexico Press, 1990.

Scharnhorst, Gary, ed. *Selected Letters of Bret Harte.* Norman and London: University of Oklahoma Press, 1997.

Schwendinger, Robert J. *Ocean of Bitter Dreams: Maritime Relations Between China and the United States 1850–1915.* Tucson, Arizona: Westernlore Press, 1988.

Seagraves, Anne. *Soiled Doves.* Hayden, Idaho: Wesanne Publications,1994.

See, Lisa. *On Gold Mountain.* New York: St. Martin's Press, 1995.

Sensmore, G. B. *The Chinese in California: Description of Chinese Life in San Francisco. Their Habits, Morals and Manners.* San Francisco: Pettit & Russ, Printers and Publishers, 1880.

Shadduck, Louise. *Doctors with Buggies, Snowshoes, and Planes: One Hundred Years and More of Idaho Medicine.* Boise, Idaho: Tamarack Books, 1993.

Shenon, Philip J., and John C. Reed. "Down Idaho's River of No Return." *National Geographic* 70.1, July 1936, pp. 95–108, 117–135.

Shepard, Charles R. *The Ways of Ah Sin.* New York: Fleming H. Revell Company, 1923.

Siu, Paul C. P. *The Chinese Laundryman: A Study of Social Isolation.* (Edited by John Kuo Wei Tchen.) New York/London: New York University Press, 1987.

Soule, Frank, John H. Gibson and James Nisbet. *The Annals of San Francisco.* Berkeley, California: Berkeley Hills Books, 1999 (originally published 1855).

Speer, William. *The Oldest and the Newest Empire: China and the United States.* Hartford, Connecticut: S.S. Scranton and Company, 1870.

Starr, Kevin. *Americans and the California Dream 1850–1915.* New York/Oxford: Oxford University Press, 1973.

Steiner, Stan. *Fusang: The Chinese Who Built America.* New York: Harper & Row, 1979.

Stewart, Jr., George R. *Bret Harte, Argonaut and Exile.* Boston/New York: Houghton Mifflin, 1931.

Stockard, Janice E. *Daughters of the Canton Delta: Marriage Patterns and Economic*

Strategies in South China, 1860–1930. Stanford, California: Stanford University Press, 1989.

Storti, Craig. *Incident at Bitter Creek: The Story of the Rock Springs Chinese Massacre.* Ames: Iowa State University Press, 1991.

Stratton, David H. "The Snake River Massacre of Chinese Miners, 1887." *Chinese on the American Frontier.* Ed. Arif Dirlik with the assistance of Malcolm Yeung. Lanham, Maryland: Rowman & Littlefield Publishers, 2001.

Sung, Betty Lee. *Mountain of Gold: The Story of the Chinese in America.* New York: Macmillan, 1967.

Taylor, Bayard. *Eldorado: Adventures in the Path of Empire.* (Foreword by James D. Houston. Afterword by Roger Kahn. Annotations by Robert M. Senkewicz.) Berkeley, California: Heyday Books, 2000.

Taylor, Bayard. *India, China, and Japan in the Year 1853.* New York: G. P. Putnam's Sons, 1885

The Raid of the Dragons into Eagle-Land. San Francisco: Mission Mirror Job Printing Office, 1878.

Tong, Benson. *Unsubmissive Women—Chinese Prostitutes in 19th Century San Francisco.* Norman/London: University of Oklahoma Press,1994.

Townsend, L. T. *The Chinese Problem.* San Francisco: R and E Research Associates, 1970.

Trull, Fern Coble. "The History of the Chinese in Idaho from 1864 to 1910." MA thesis. University of Oregon, 1946.

Trumble, Alfred. *The "Heathen Chinee" at Home and Abroad or a Complete Panorama of the Chinese in America by an Old Californian.* New York: Richard K. Fox, Publisher, 1882.

Tsai, Shih-Shan Henry. *China and the Overseas Chinese in the United States, 1868–1911.* Fayetteville: University of Arkansas Press, 1983.

Tsai, Shih-Shan Henry. *The Chinese Experience in America.* Bloomington/Indianapolis: Indiana University Press, 1986.

Tung, William L. *The Chinese in America 1820–1973.* Dobbs Ferry, New York: Oceana Publications, Inc., 1974.

Twain, Mark. *Mark Twain in Eruption.* New York/London: Harper & Brothers Publishers, 1922.

Twain, Mark. *Roughing It.* New York: Signet Classic, 1962.

Tzu-kuei, Yen. "Rock Springs Incident." *Chinese Studies in History* 7. 3 (Spring 1974).

Walker, Franklin. *San Francisco's Literary Frontier.* New York: Alfred A. Knopf, 1939.

Wallace, Irving and Amy. *The Two: A Biography.* New York: Simon and Schuster, 1978.

Washburn, Josie. *The Underworld Seer: A Prostitute Reflects on Life in the Trade, 1871– 1909*. Lincoln/London: University of Nebraska Press,1997 (reprinted from 1909).

Wegars, Priscilla. "Charlie Bemis: Idaho's Most 'Significant Other.'" *Idaho Yesterdays* 44–3, Fall 2000, pp. 3–18.

Wegars, Priscilla. *Chinese at the Confluence: Lewiston's Beuk Aie Temple*. Lewiston, Idaho: Confluence Press in association with the Lewis-Clark Center for Arts & History, 2000.

Wegars, Priscilla., *Hidden Heritage: Historial Archaeology of the Overseas Chinese*. Amityville, New York: Baywood Publishing Company, 1993.

Wegars, Priscilla. *Uncovering a Chinese Legacy: Historical Archaeology at Centerville, Idaho*. (U.S. Department of the Interior/Bureau of Land Management) Idaho Cultural Resources Series—Number Five, 2008.

Wegars, Priscilla. *Polly Bemis: A Chinese American Pioneer*. Cambridge, Idaho: Backeddy Books, 2007.

Wegars, Priscilla. "Researching Polly Bemis." *PNLA Quarterly* 68.2, Winter 2004, pp. 4, 17–20.

Weisner, Stephen G. *Embattled Editor: The Life of Samuel Bowles*. Lanham, Maryland/New York/London: University Press of America, 1986.

Whitney, James A. *The Chinese and the Chinese Question*. New York: Tibbals Book Company, 1888.

Wiggins, Robert A. *Ambrose Bierce*. Minneapolis: University of Minnesota Press, 1964.

Wikoff, Melvin D. "Chinese in the Idaho County Gold Fields: 1864–1933." MA thesis. Texas A & I University, 1972.

Wild, Peter. *J. Ross Browne*. Boise, Idaho: Boise State University Western Writers Series, 2003.

Williams, Albert. *A Pioneer Pastorate and Times*. San Francisco: Bacon & Company, Printers, 1882.

Williams, Dave., ed. *The Chinese Other 1850–1925—An Anthology of Plays*. Lanham, Maryland: University Press of America, 1997.

Williams III, George. *Mark Twain: His Life in Virginia City, Nevada*. Dayton, Nevada: Tree By the River Publishing, 1986.

Williams, Stephen. "The Chinese in the California Mines." MA Thesis. Stanford, 1930.

Wilson, Carol Green. *Chinatown Quest: The Life Adventures of Donaldina Cameron*. Stanford, California: Stanford University Press,1931.

Wimberly, Rosemary L. *"She Should Be Made an Example Of . . .": Gender, Politics, and Criminal Abortion in Idaho, 1864–1973*. MA thesis. Boise State University, 1996.

Wollenberg, Charles, ed. *Ethnic Conflict in California History*. Los Angeles: Tinnon-Brown, Inc., 1970.

Wong, Karen C. *Chinese History in the Pacific Northwest.* (n.p.) 1972.

Wong, Marie Rose. *Sweet Cakes, Long Journey: The Chinatowns of Portland, Oregon.* Seattle/London: University of Washington Press, 2004.

Woolston, Howard B. *Prostitution in the United States Prior to the Entrance of the United States into the World War.* Montclair, New Jersey: Patterson Smith, 1969 (reprinted from 1921).

Wu, Cheng-Tsu. *"Chink"—A Documentary History of Anti-Chinese Prejudice in America.* New York: World Publishing Company, 1972.

Yang, John C. ed. *Asian Americans in Utah: A Living History.* Salt Lake City: Utah State Office of Asian Affairs/Asian American Advisory Council, 1999.

Yin, Xiao-huang. *Chinese American Literature since the 1850s* (foreword by Roger Daniels). Urbana/Chicago: University of Illinois Press, 2000.

Yu, Li-hua. "Chinese Immigrants in Idaho." Ph.d. dissertation, Bowling Green State University, 1991.

Yung, Judy. *Unbound Feet: A Social History of Chinese Women in San Francisco.* Berkeley/Los Angeles/London: University of California Press, 1995.

Yung, Judy and Gordon H. Chang and Him Mark Lai. *Chinese American Voices: From the Gold Rush to the Present.* Berkeley/Los Angeles/London: University of California Press, 2006.

Zhu, Liping. *A Chinaman's Chance: The Chinese on the Rocky Mountain Mining Frontier.* Niwot, Colorado: University Press of Colorado, 1997.